M000289991

THE
SURVIVAL
OF THE
RICHEST

*An Analysis of the Relationship between the Sciences
of Biology, Economics, Finance, and Survivalism*

DR. ANTHONY M. CRINITI IV

CRINITI PUBLISHING

Copyright © 2015 by Dr. Anthony M. Criniti IV
All rights reserved.
Published by Criniti Publishing, Philadelphia, PA
ISBN: 098845954X
ISBN 13: 9780988459540
Library of Congress Control Number: 2015953710
Criniti Publishing, Philadelphia, PA
All cover and interior illustrations and photographs
copyright © 2015
by Dr. Anthony M. Criniti IV
Front cover photo top left: Crematorium I in
Auschwitz-Birkenau, Poland
Photo by Dr. Anthony M. Criniti IV
Front cover photo top right: The Hiroshima Peace Memorial (also
called Genbaku Dome) was the only structure left standing in the area
where the first atomic bomb exploded in 1945 in Hiroshima, Japan.
Photo by Dr. Anthony M. Criniti IV
The text of this publication, or any of its parts, may not be reproduced
in any manner without the prior written permission of the author.
This publication is for informational purposes only. It is sold with
the understanding that the author and the publisher are not engaged
in providing financial, legal, or other professional services. If
financial, legal, or any other form of advice is needed, please
consult a financial adviser, an attorney, or another professional
advice-giving entity.

I dedicate this book to my future self, whether poorer or richer. I am sending a reminder to you to never forget the painful struggles required to become wealthy and to maintain that wealth. Also, you should never forget the great ethical responsibilities that come with great wealth. Failure to remember these lessons will come at the cost of losing touch with reality.

I also dedicate this book to the victims of the many atrocities mentioned in this work (and others not mentioned), including, but not limited to, the victims of various genocides, wars, and other human atrocities throughout history. The struggles of these people have led me to do a five-day water-only fast in their honor from June 7 to June 12, 2015. In addition, I have honored their memory and the memory of the struggles of all humanity by creating a "World Memorial Week" from June 7 to June 14. Please join me annually to pay respects to our fallen brothers and sisters of the world. This is one more necessary step for world peace. Their struggles remind us that one of the greatest forms of wealth of our species is found in the unity of all peoples.

Disclaimer: This book is specifically targeted at adults. However, it may not be suitable for all adults due to the many sensitive topics of survival discussed, including genocide, human atrocities, war, and the deep conclusions inherent in our understanding of survival's relationship to biology, economics, and finance. If you have the courage and the desire to continue reading, please take your time with the material, as it may be overwhelming at an accelerated pace. Additionally, if you should encounter any physical or psychological issues resulting from your deep reflections on the various topics, please feel free to seek professional medical guidance. Thank you.

Table of Contents

Table of Exhibits xiii

Preface..xv

Part 1: Understanding Survival.. 1

    Chapter 1: Introduction 3

    Chapter 2: Our Infatuation with Survival...................... 7

    Chapter 3: Survival Terminology 9

        An Overview... 9

        My Survival Definitions 13

    Chapter 4: Defining Life and Death........................... 21

        An Overview... 21

        My Definition of Life 28

        My Definition of Death.................................. 35

    Chapter 5: Survival Literature Review....................... 39

        An Overview... 39

The Explorers 40

The Birth of Survivalism 47

Chapter 6: Why Survive? 55

Chapter 7: Real Extreme-Survival Examples 61

Chapter 8: An Unlimited Supply of
      Survival Scenarios 69

The Various Struggles 69

Survival Scenario Examples 70

Self-Defense 74

Chapter 9: The Survival Categories 79

An Overview 79

Defining Civilization 80

Defining Wilderness 82

The Survival Categories Elaborated 83

Chapter 10: The Survival Environments 87

Chapter 11: The Irony of Great Survivors 93

Chapter 12: The Survival Essentials 99

An Overview 99

The Immediate Survival Essentials 105

The Essential Survival Tools 117

Chapter 13: Part 1 Summary 119

**Part 2: Understanding the Relationship
between Economics, Finance, and Survivalism 123**

Chapter 14: Survival: The Root of Economics
      and Finance 125

The Necessity of Survival 125

The Role of Wealth in Survival 127

Prosperity Overview 130

The Root of Prosperity 138
The Parent of Economics............................. 148
The Necessity of Prosperity......................... 151

Chapter 15: The Edge of Survival............................ 157

Chapter 16: The Three Major Wealth-Management
Possibilities... 161

Chapter 17: Survival Resurfacing 169

Chapter 18: The Greatest Options of the Wealthy..... 173

Chapter 19: The Survival of the Richest Individuals ... 177

Chapter 20: The Survival of the Richest Groups 197

Chapter 21: The Survival of the Richest Nations...... 201

Chapter 22: Maximizing Guns, Germs, Steel, and
Other Forms of Wealth 207

Chapter 23: Surviving an Economic Collapse 215

Chapter 24: The Survival of the Richest Planets....... 219

Chapter 25: The Survival of the Richest Universe.... 225

Chapter 26: Conquering Struggles with Wealth........ 227
The Role of the Struggle.............................. 227
The Role of the Fight................................... 228
The Role of Wealth in the Human-to-
Human Struggle 229
The Role of Wealth in Other
Various Struggles....................................... 233

Chapter 27: The Survival and the Prosperity by a
Third Party 239

Chapter 28: Part 2 Summary 245

Part 3: The Reunion Party: Biology, Economics, Finance, and Survivalism Come Together 247

Chapter 29: A Divided Family Reunited...................249

Chapter 30: The Survival of the Fittest 255
    An Overview..255
    Problems with Its Related Terminology 259

Chapter 31: Biology's First Predicament:
        Defining Nature 263
    Who Is Nature in Natural Selection?.............263
    An Imaginary Picture of Nature 268
    Reformed Nature: Nature Is Everything........270
    Who Is More Powerful: Humans or Nature?.....272

Chapter 32: Biology's Second Predicament:
        Defining Evolution 279
    A General Overview of Evolution 279
    The Forgotten Individual 283

Chapter 33: The Evolutionary Control Scale
        of Nature...299

Chapter 34: Natural Luck 307

Chapter 35: The Evolution of an Individual..............311
    An Overview..311
    External and Internal Natural Selection.........315
    The Three Major Processes of Unique
    Individual Evolution 318

Chapter 36: The Evolution of a Population...............325
    An Overview..325
    Negative and Positive Selection 328

The Evolutionary Selection Processes:
The Traditional Processes 331
    An Overview 331
    Traditional Natural Selection 338
    Traditional Artificial Selection 339
    Traditional Sexual Selection 339
The Evolutionary Selection Processes:
The Upgraded Processes 340
    Reformed Natural Selection 340
    Reformed Artificial Selection 348
    Reformed Sexual Selection 349
The Evolutionary Selection Processes:
The Other Processes 353
    Descendant Selection 353
    Miscellaneous External Reformed
    Natural Selection 355

Chapter 37: The Evolution of Evolution 357
    An Overview 357
The Evolution of Money:
Monetary Selection 362
The Evolution of the Nonliving:
Technological Selection 367

Chapter 38: Self-Selection 375

Chapter 39: Evolving to Survive and to Prosper 383

Chapter 40: The Wilderness Is Shrinking 395

Chapter 41: The Wealth Management of Other
    Living Things 399

Chapter 42: The Survival by a Third Party Applied
to All Nonhuman Life 403

Chapter 43: The Extinction of the Richest 411

Chapter 44: Part 3 Summary 415

Part 4: The Wake-Up Call 419

Chapter 45: An Overview: It's Time to Wake-Up 421

Chapter 46: What Are We Capable Of? 425
We Are Capable of Doing Great Evil 425
We Are Capable of Doing Great Good 435

Chapter 47: What Is at Stake? 439
Time Is Running Out 439
The Sixth Mass Extinction 444

Chapter 48: Who Are We? 447
The Ultimate Universal Survivors 447
The Ultimate Universal Managers 450

Chapter 49: Part 4 Summary 455

Part 5: Final Summary and Conclusions 457

Chapter 50: Final Summary 459

Chapter 51: Conclusions 465

Bibliography 469

Additional Survival Literature 475

Index 493

Table of Exhibits

Exhibit 12.1: The Survival Essentials 101

Exhibit 14.1: The Survival-Prosperity Sequence 132

Exhibit 14.2: The Five Major Scientific
Phases of Prosperity 136

Exhibit 14.3: The Survival-Prosperity Sequence
Incorporated into the Five Major Scientific
Phases of Prosperity 140

Exhibit 16.1: The Three Major Wealth-Management
Possibilities 163

Exhibit 31.1: The General Control Scale of Nature 276

Exhibit 32.1: The Evolution of an Individual Example 290

Exhibit 32.2: The Traditional Evolutionary Model 294

Exhibit 33.1: The Evolutionary Control Scale of Nature 302

Exhibit 35.1: External and Internal Nature 317

Exhibit 36.1: The Reformed Natural Selection Formulas
for Population Evolution 335

Exhibit 36.2: The Evolutionary Schematics for Life 343

Exhibit 36.3: The Reformed Natural Selection
Evolutionary Formulas 347

Exhibit 37.1: The Two Major Causes of the
Evolution of Evolution 361

Exhibit 39.1: The Modified Survival-Prosperity
Sequence for Evolution 387

Exhibit 39.2: The Five Major Evolutionary
Phases of Prosperity 391

Exhibit 39.3: The Modified Survival-Prosperity
Sequence for Evolution Incorporated into
the Five Major Evolutionary Phases
of Prosperity 392

Exhibit 46.1: Too Many Genocide Examples 428

Preface

This book was written as an advanced follow-up on a specific aspect of my first book, *The Necessity of Finance*, which taught that learning the science of economics is necessary for *economic entities* (that is, nations and their divisions) to survive, and it taught that learning the science of finance is necessary for *financial entities* (that is, individuals, groups, and organizations) to survive. Survival's role was clearly mentioned there, but it was not fully analyzed because of the wider goals of that book. In this book, we will further explore the relationship between survival and these two fields.

The analysis made of the concept of survival is also unavoidably linked with several other fields of scientific inquiry. Thus, my journey to write this book brought me to research a diverse range of topics, including wilderness survival, advanced martial arts, biology, and the darkest aspects of human atrocities. I continuously pushed the limits of my research to ensure that

I treated this subject with the respect that it deserves. The end result took a huge toll on my health: from sleepless nights to hair loss. This is why I caution anyone who reads this to be prepared to deal with possible emotional issues. If you do not have the stomach to read about the horrors of survival or the truth about the current human predicament, then I suggest that you do not read this book. The conclusions are not easy to accept, and acceptance may only come after breaking down the inner walls of safety that our minds put up to protect us. Yet these conclusions are inevitable and severe, and they must be faced with courage by all who are ready to deal with them.

The biological aspects of the book are actually a continuum of a subject deeply rooted in the birth of Charles Darwin's theory of natural selection in the nineteenth century. The title of this book is also a variant on the phrase "the survival of the fittest," which was created by Herbert Spencer, a key biologist of Darwin's time. This phrase, which described Darwin's theory and the concept it represents, has been misinterpreted since its creation. Its faulty misinterpretations became an underlying theme in many of the atrocities committed in the nineteenth and twentieth centuries. Wealth provided the support for negative variations of Darwin's theories, for example, social Darwinism and eugenics. Wealth also played a large role in various genocides and wars, including the deadliest wars in history, World Wars I and II. It may be because of this dark past between the concepts of evolution and wealth that the relationship has not been comprehensively analyzed until now.

To avoid having the title of this book meet the same fate of misinterpretation as Spencer's phrase, I would also like to be clear that the title of this book *does not* imply that the richest entities, whether people or nations, will survive just because they are rich. On the contrary, the richest people can also be the first to die under the right circumstances. **However, as will be demonstrated, a major point this title implies is that more wealth provides more options for the wealthiest entities to survive better; it does not necessarily mean that those entities will choose the best options.** Further, living economic and financial entities have three major wealth-management possibilities: 1) to minimize wealth and survive poorly, which comes with an increased risk of death; 2) to break even and merely survive day by day—a risky survival position; or 3) to maximize wealth and survive and prosper (this must be a continuous goal).

This book is divided into five parts. In part 1, we will explore the science of survival, which will be referred to as "survivalism." In this part, many aspects of survival are analyzed, and it includes a review of survival literature, survival definitions, survival examples, survival scenarios, and so forth. To my knowledge, this is the most comprehensive overview of survival that exists.

In part 2, economics and finance are woven into the analysis of survival. In this part, I trace the roots of prosperity, especially those of economics and finance, all the way back to survivalism. This part also explores the role of the struggle, the survival of the richest as applied to various entities, surviving an economic and/or financial collapse, and the important concepts of the survival and the prosperity by a third party.

In part 3, biology becomes a part of the analysis. Here, I present an overview of the concept of the survival of the fittest; give nature and evolution a more realistic definition; explain how evolution occurs in both an individual and a population; and subsequently, provide an upgraded version of the theory of natural selection (and other related evolutionary selection processes). I also introduce the important concepts of descendant selection, the evolution of evolution, reformed nature, self-selection, and other related concepts.

In part 4, I demonstrate how humans are capable of the best and worst imaginable outcomes; responsible for the birth of the sixth mass extinction; probably the solution to this extinction; potentially the ultimate universal survivors; and possibly the ultimate universal managers. Finally, I present a final summary of and the conclusions for the entire book in part 5.

This book is targeted mainly at a specific adult audience, particularly intermediate- to advanced-level biology, economics, finance, and survival students. Nevertheless, I also welcome the interested layperson to read this book and to reflect on its important conclusions. It is highly recommended that all readers read my earlier books, *The Necessity of Finance* and *The Most Important Lessons in Economics and Finance*, before proceeding to this book, as they will provide a better introduction to the various concepts covered in this work. This book builds on those books, so readers may be at a disadvantage, perhaps to the extent of not understanding key points, if they do not read those books first.

In part 3, I present my interpretations of some of the most important evolutionary selection processes in biology and derive other processes tied to wealth. Thus, you may want to read several beginner biology books before you read this book, particularly in regard to natural selection. This is instrumental to understanding the biological aspects analyzed here and the role wealth plays in the evolutionary process.

This book is designed to be student friendly, and it can be used as a required or supplemental text for colleges or universities. Finally, this book may also serve as a direct learning tool to help you create your own path to economic and financial independence. If you understand the relationship between survival and prosperity, then you may be more inclined to make better financial decisions.

This book integrates some of the hardest concepts of several of the most important sciences. It covers many topics in order to come to serious conclusions about the future of humanity. Certain aspects of this book could be viewed as a roadmap for where our species should be heading, particularly in reference to the Major Scientific Phases of Prosperity. We are more prepared to understand our role on this planet and possibly the universe when we thoroughly analyze what our species is capable of and what is truly at stake.

Economics and finance can be better understood from the perspective presented in this book. However, I want to be clear that this may not be easy for the average student. Some of the material may interest you, and some may not. The best way to approach it is with patience. I encourage you to take notes throughout your readings. Later, you can always review the book, in part or in whole, for maximum results.

I highly recommend reading this book slowly. If you move too fast, then you may not have time to reflect deeply enough on the underlying lessons, and/or you may become overwhelmed with information. In particular, I recommend that you read this book one chapter at a time and more than once to increase your understanding of the subjects presented.

Finally, I have attempted to write this book as objectively as possible, but from time to time, my opinions may appear. However, this should have a very limited effect on achieving the various major goals of the book, which are the following:

1. To provide the most comprehensive overview of the science of survival;
2. To reinforce the point from *The Necessity of Finance* that the goals of economics and finance are interrelated with the survival goals of economic and financial entities;
3. To clarify the proper order of prosperity, particularly that finance is the precursor to economics;
4. To show that being wealthier increases your probability of continuously surviving and prospering by providing you the greatest options to obtaining survival essentials;
5. To indicate that wealthier entities have the option to help other economic or financial entities (including nonhuman ones) survive and prosper, particularly through the concepts of the survival and the prosperity by a third party;
6. To demonstrate the inevitable relationship between biology, economics, finance, and survivalism;
7. To improve our understanding of nature and evolution;
8. To demonstrate that both individuals and populations of species evolve;
9. To summarize, reform, and add to existing evolutionary selection processes;

10. To confirm that the management of money, and the technology that it can buy, is an advanced, necessary stage in the process of evolution—that is, the evolution of evolution;
11. To illustrate the severity of and the potential solutions for the current human predicament;
12. To demonstrate that *the survival of the richest* is a more accurate concept than *the survival of the fittest*; and
13. To prove that all humanity should have the united goal of maximizing our wealth for our survival on this planet and beyond.

With so many goals for one book, we shouldn't waste any time. So please fasten your seatbelts, and enjoy the ride!

PART 1
Understanding Survival

CHAPTER 1

Introduction

It is absolutely fascinating that there is a widespread lack of basic knowledge of a subject that every one of our direct primitive ancestors mastered. No matter what part of the globe they ended up, from Africa to South America, we are the result of their drive to survive. Even the most skilled outdoor survivalists today will acknowledge the unique toughness that our ancient forbearers had and admit it is greater than that of the current population. Our ancestors survived all types of conditions including extreme desert heat, many exotic jungles, and even the most recent ice age. You name it, they survived it, and we are here as the proof!

But the situation has changed since then, and our ancestors' daily struggles are almost incomprehensible to many people today. Most of their problems have been figured out, only to leave us with new ones in exchange. But this comes at a cost of potentially forgetting their original solutions and their connection to our current problems. For example, very few people know or care to know how to hunt or build a fire, a skill set needed by the ancients. It can be argued that because we have easy access to modern conveniences, such as supermarkets and automatic heaters, learning about primitive survival skills is pointless.

The problem with this line of thought is that it creates a huge disconnect with the present-day perspective of where we came from, who we are, and where we should be going. For example, there are still many people who do not know that everything we eat was once alive or came from a living thing. To them, food was mysteriously born in some company's factory only to be sold later at the grocery store. They can't imagine that someone had to actually kill what they are eating, a notion that was common sense to primitive hunters. No wonder so much food is wasted every day across the developed world! *A lack of understanding of and respect for the subject of survivalism leads to unnecessary waste of necessary assets.*

This same phenomenon has occurred in economics and finance. Many people have long forgotten the connection between the management of wealth and survival, as well as their many related common-sense lessons. For example, a person may gamble away his paycheck while his children sit at home hungry because there is not enough money to buy food. Nations make these mistakes too! For example, in a time of great famine, a nation can hoard its agriculture instead of distributing some to its people, such as what occurred in the Ukrainian famine in the Soviet Union and in China's Great Leap Forward. Lessons learned from studying survival will spill over into a better understanding of economics and finance, as you will see in part 2.

In part 1, we will get our survival priorities straight as we examine survival from a human perspective (the survival of other living things will be considered in part 3). Here I will provide an analysis of various survival topics necessary to lay the foundation for the remainder of this book. This analysis scans the realm of survivalism and includes information from my academic research, as well as from my various personal survival-training experiences. To our academic analysis, I also add my experience of practicing martial arts, which I will hereafter refer to as *martial science*. I have practiced various forms of martial sciences over many years, including, but not limited to, boxing, Brazilian jiu-jitsu, karate, krav maga, mixed martial arts, muay thai, and wrestling. Also, I have personally trained with many professional fighters from various combat sports as well as worked directly with black belts of pure self-defense sciences. I mention this because these experiences have added to my knowledge by looking at survival from an often-neglected perspective.

Certain specific survival topics may have volumes written on them by survivalists—for example, making survival shelters or brain-tanning deerskin. Although this knowledge has survival value, it is not my intention to overload this book with information that will distract from its major goals. An exhaustive treatment of many highly specialized survival topics may be an impediment to the reader's learning experience. My major goal for part 1 is to provide the most comprehensive general overview of survivalism that exists. This is a very challenging task, however, considering the constraints of the small space I have allotted for this part. Thus, a limitation of the book is that many specialized survival topics may only be mentioned briefly or omitted altogether.

Hopefully, you will enjoy learning about survival. After all, how many topics are as important as learning about how to survive?

CHAPTER 2

Our Infatuation with Survival

Although survivalism was officially created in modern times, humans have been infatuated with this subject unofficially since our origins. Understandably, one could argue that the ancients may have had no choice but to want to know everything necessary to survive. To them, the alternative was quick death. But the desire to learn about survival has not vanished in our ascent from the wilderness into modern civilization; it has only taken on a different form. The desire to learn about wilderness survival skills has increased almost at the same speed as recent technological advancements. As you will see in the literature review, modern survivalism didn't officially start until around the World War II era. It then went into overdrive by the time of the Internet revolution.

In particular, the first season of the TV series *Survivor* demonstrated the mass appeal of this subject. *Survivor* was extremely successful and is still running strong as of the time of this publication. When other television networks realized its success, a number of competing shows were immediately created to capture viewers. Survival books also followed a similar path. The number of survival books published in the past twenty years or so is astounding compared to the relatively few survival-themed books published in the whole of the twentieth century.

I suspect a reason for this is that many people are gradually realizing the significance of this subject and how little they may know about it. This is frightening to many! Deep down inside, they are realizing that it is their duty to understand how to survive better just like our ancestors. It also may be a hidden instinct calling us back to the wild as depicted by Jack London in his famous book *The Call of the Wild*. Whatever the reason, it appears that modern people will progressively become more fascinated with survival, especially as the wilderness becomes smaller and more mysterious.

CHAPTER 3

Survival Terminology

An Overview

This chapter is essential to understanding survival and its applicability to economics, finance, and biology. The terms used here were derived after much research and careful consideration of the perspectives of various survival experts. I must note that although there is no shortage of survival books (especially in the past twenty years or so), ironically, I had much difficulty in obtaining a definition of "survival" or "survivalism" from many survivalists (a very similar problem to what I faced years back in economics and finance). Thus, this section includes an overview of the best survival terminology that I could find, gleaned from various survival literatures. I will conclude with my own definitions, which will be the ones used throughout this book.

There are only two survival definitions that are both commendable and very useful to our understanding of survival derived from all of my researched survival literature. In both of these two rare cases, the authors actually make clear that these are their definitions. John Wiseman's definition is this: "Survival is the art of staying alive" (Wiseman, 2009, 14). Peter Kummerfeldt's definition is that survival is "the ability and the desire to stay alive, all alone, under adverse conditions, until rescued" (Kummerfeldt, 2006, 1).

There are several other survival books that define survival more or less indirectly. The following is the closest that I could get from several experts on this subject. To emphasize, these statements are not their definitions. They are just statements in their books from which I can infer approximately what their definition of survival is. I will start chronologically.

First, starting in the early eighteenth century, Daniel Defoe indirectly defines self-preservation in his famous novel *Robinson Crusoe* yet does not mention the word *survival*. However, from this quote we can infer that it means the same thing: "…that it was Self-preservation in the highest Degree, to deliver my self from this Death of a Life, and was acting in my own Defence, as much as if they were actually assaulting me, and the like" (Defoe, 2008, 168).

Second, the introduction to the US Navy's first edition of *How to Survive on Land and Sea* helps form an idea of what survival is: "Knowledge acquired from this manual supplemented by field exercises offers the most practical method of giving sound individual instruction in a given period of time. Our fighting men must be prepared to enter battle zones with a maximum chance of survival. No matter where stranded they must have every aid to assist them to both live and fight again" (Aviation Training Division, 1943, vii).

Third, Larry Dean Olsen gets very close to a definition by focusing more on the qualities of the survivor: "A survivor accepts the situation as it is and improves it from that standpoint...A survivor also possesses a utopian attitude. This does not reflect an orientation toward comfort but an artistic ability to make even the most miserable existence seem like millennial splendor" (Olsen, 1997, 5).

Fourth, the US Army derived the acronym SURVIVAL, which is a foundation to its survival training: "Size up the situation; Undue haste makes waste; Remember where you are; Vanquish fear and panic; Improvise; Value living; Act like the natives; Learn basic skills" (US Department of the Army, 1970, 5).

Fifth, Tom Brown Jr. shows the link between survival and life and death when drinking possibly contaminated water: "Before you drink from any chosen source, then, ask yourself whether you'd be willing to stake your life on that water—because in a survival situation that's exactly what you'll do if you drink it" (Brown, 1983, 48).

Next, John McPherson implies a link between surviving, death, and prosperity: "I am far from being an expert on woodsmanship. I have, though, taught myself what I need to know to go naked into the wilderness and, not only survive, but before long to be living fairly comfortably (if I wasn't to freeze to death first)" (McPherson and McPherson, 2013, 59).

Finally, the following statements from Cody Lundin suggest a similarity to Kummerfeldt's survival definition above: "*Adopt a positive survival attitude.* Keep things in perspective and focus your attention firmly upon the goal of keeping you and your family alive and safe until rescued" (Lundin, 2007, 54).

Putting all this together, the statements of the above survival experts point to the conclusion that survival has to do with people keeping themselves alive. Although I think this is mostly true, something still seems to be missing. Thus, I think Wiseman's definition is a good starting place but needs some adjustments. Unlike Wiseman, I view survival as a science and not an art. If our life depends on making only one decision correctly, then we better be sure to make the best decision possible.

I would like to analyze Peter Kummerfeldt's definition of survival stated above before I conclude this chapter with my own survival definitions. Kummerfeldt's definition has the opposite problem of Wiseman's: it is too wordy. There are many good aspects to it though. First, I do agree that a person must not only be *able* to survive but must *want* to as well. This desire is a common theme found in survival books. It is represented by a phrase that every survival expert knows, although few attempt to define it: "the will to live." This phrase is a very important concept in survival, and it will later be demonstrated to be one of the most important survival essentials. Thus, this aspect of survival should be retained, but I think it is better placed in the goal of survival and not in the definition (as discussed below). I also agree with Kummerfeldt that survival has to do with staying alive under adverse conditions. This element becomes a part of my definition of a "struggle." The struggle, as you will see below, is an often neglected but inseparable part of survival.

I disagree with Kummerfeldt's survival definition in two out of its last three points though—that is, in reference to "all alone" and "until rescued." Although these parts of his definition may apply to *many* situations, they do not apply to *all* situations. First, survival situations are not always going to happen when you're alone. Actually, groups as large as nations strive to survive together, and they are far from alone. It is best to learn how to survive both individually and with others to optimize your chances of success when the unexpected happens.

Second, I don't believe that it is in someone's best interest to implement survival skills while investing all of her or his efforts in the hope of an unknown party possibly saving the day. To be clear, in many survival situations, it may be an ideal conclusion to be rescued. However, a safer proposition is to learn how to survive without being dependent on unknown external factors. *After all, who will save you if the hero never shows up? The only person who will always be available (even if badly injured) in any survival situation is the potential survivor.*

My Survival Definitions

The following are my personal definitions of survival and related concepts. They were derived after much reflection on the topic and are an attempt to be an improvement on existing definitions. They will be the official terminology of this book.

Survival is the management of the present struggle to stay alive for a living entity. Survivalism is the science of survival. Additionally, for the purposes of this book, survival and

self-preservation **mean the same thing.** Let's break these definitions down!

First, survival deals with management, which is the conducting of various activities for the purpose of meeting specific goals. In other words, management includes performing any necessary action to get the job done.

Second, pure survival, unlike prosperity, which I will analyze in part 2, pertains only to the present struggle. There is little to no preparation or planning involved in survival. You will need to manage the struggle in whatever condition you were in when it arrived. *Survivalism is a moment-to-moment science that can teach you how to stay alive if a given struggle occurs, especially if you were completely unprepared for it.* The planning and saving aspects are incorporated into the prosperity steps that I will present later.

Third, the word *struggle* has been paired with survival in every possible context that I have researched. In particular, biologists have a hard time mentioning one word in a single sentence without the other. There must be a reason inherent in the qualities of a struggle that causes this to occur. Survival expert Peter Kummerfeldt also tried to capture this idea by adding "adverse conditions" to his definition of survival. It is a good time to define the "struggle."

The struggle is the confrontation with a hardship of being alive. The word *struggle* can be used in a comprehensive manner and can include a range of hardships confronted from minor complications to large-scale conflict. There are also simple things that one can struggle with—for example, a math problem. That simple problem will most likely not have any impact on a person's state of being alive, even if she has the wrong answer. **However, in the context of survival, a struggle can only be a confrontation with a potentially deadly hardship.** It is inseparable from the realities of survival and, thus, inseparable from its definition.

In chapter 8, we will review various examples of struggles in survival. The elimination of all struggles is probably impossible. Besides, we shouldn't desire to do that anyway, as struggles have made us the leader of all of Earth's species. However, we should respect and manage them well and learn to appreciate them in order to make progress. In other words, we should manage struggles like a tool to make us stronger; yet, we should ensure that they do not eliminate us. More on this later!

The next major aspect of the definition of survival deals with staying alive. There must be a difference between just being alive and surviving, or else these terms would be redundant. You can be alive but not surviving. There are people who have no desire to live anymore and have given up all efforts at self-preservation. They may not have the courage to commit suicide, so they become the "walking dead." These people may be physically alive, but they are not surviving. They may hope for external factors to fulfill their wish to die.

For example, imagine a person who is walking across a highway slowly, one lane at a time, hoping that someone will run him over. He may not have the courage to buy a gun and directly commit suicide. He is putting zero effort into managing the struggle to stay alive. Instead, his choice is to allow random events to determine his fate. Yet miraculously, he may make it alive to the other side of the highway. He may still be alive, but he is not a survivor. Other forces may have been the key determinant of whether he lived or died. But a person must show at least a tiny effort at managing the present struggle to stay alive in order to be a survivor.

The final major aspect of the definition of survival is that survival involves a living entity. The entity must already be alive. A dead body can't benefit from survivalism. Neither can an old refrigerator. Nothing gets an admittance ticket to the theater of survival unless it is already alive. The only sticky part to this component of the definition involves groups. However, with a little analysis, we can see that an explanation is easier than it looks.

There are all types of groups of things. Survival deals with living groups. Some may argue that the living group as a single unit is not alive, as it is composed of many individual units. Yet, very few will deny that the individual units of a living group are alive. It is these units that make the whole alive. On the other hand, if you were presented with a group of thirty marbles placed on a table, would you consider this a living group? Probably not. It is definitely a group, of course, as its members are related parts of a whole. But since they are not alive (see the next chapter on defining life for more information), they can't be considered a living group, and hence, they do not have the ability or capability to survive. Some examples of living groups range from a chess club to a public corporation to a school of fish. *In short, the group is alive if its members are alive.*

Now that survival is defined, it is time to recognize its major goal. **The major goal of survival and survivalism is for a living entity to stay alive for the maximum desirable amount of time.** Let's break this statement down. Living entities are

16

already alive and generally strive to stay that way for a period of time. This part is very straight-forward, but the last part needs more explanation. Some major questions arise. For how long should we survive? Is survival a one-time event or a continuous process?

A new struggle may always appear and create a new survival situation. For example, our survival plan shouldn't stop if we survive a small flu epidemic because the flu may come back again next year. Survival is continuous because the present moment is continuous. The real last day to practice survival is always either the day chosen by the survivalist or the actual date of death, whichever comes sooner. It is the survivalist who decides how long he or she wants to live, whether it is one hour or one hundred years. If death comes unexpectedly before that date, then, of course, survival practice is over as well. The word "maximum" in the goal accounts for the many survival events that we might experience until our death.

Note that I used the word "desirable" in the goal of survival, instead of "probable." A person can desire to live for much less time than she probably would live under normal conditions for a person her age, health, sex, and so forth. In this case, there may be very little that she will need to learn about surviving. Alternatively, a person can desire to live for much longer than he probably would under normal conditions. In this case, he will need to learn as much as possible from survivalism to increase his probability of reaching his desirable age of death. We build into the goal the ambiguous, but necessary, concept of "the will to live" when we use the word "desirable." The "desire to stay alive" that was noted by Kummerfeldt in his definition now has a place to call home. In short, learning survivalism may help you to live longer.

On the other hand, if you don't want to live, then learning about survival is unnecessary as the maximum desirable amount of time to stay alive would be equal to zero. This would meet the goal of an unnamed science that is the direct opposite of survivalism; let's call it *suicidalism*, **or the science of the management of the present struggle to die for a living entity.** Thankfully, studying about *suicidalism* is beyond the scope of this book.

A few other terms are in order. First, **a survivor is an entity that has successfully managed a past struggle to stay alive.** The suicidal maniac mentioned earlier who crossed a highway while leaving his destiny to the flow of traffic was not a survivor when he made it unscathed to the other side. I think "lucky" is a more appropriate term for him. Instead, the honorary title of "survivor" should be reserved for those who displayed the will to live in the presence of a deadly struggle. Also, a person is not guaranteed to survive other present or future struggles just because he or she was a survivor of a past struggle. It is a lifetime commitment to continuously keep this title.

Second, **a survivalist is a scientist who studies survivalism.** A survivalist is not always also a survivor. Many expert survivalists have studied survivalism their entire lives. Ironically, they may never have encountered a serious struggle with death; thus, they may not have had an opportunity to successfully manage it. On the other hand, history is full of examples of survivors of major catastrophes who have never studied one aspect of survivalism. This is not a testimony for the uselessness of studying survivalism—never that! It is only a notation that it is possible, although unlikely, to be a survivor before becoming a survivalist. *Ultimately, well-prepared survivalists will have increased their probability of becoming survivors if the occasion presents itself.*

This is a good time to distinguish between two types of survivalism. In general, the term survivalism is often automatically used in practice to imply that the surviving living entity is a human. However, it is important for biologists and students of this book to recognize that much of what we learn about survival may also be applied to other living species. Therefore, I think it is more sensible to have two major categories of survivalism: human survivalism and comprehensive survivalism. **Human survivalism is the science of survival for all living humans. Comprehensive survivalism is the science of survival for all living entities (including humans).** Unless stated otherwise, it should be assumed that the use of survivalism in this book refers to human survivalism.

I will conclude this chapter with a note on prosperity. **Prosperity is the progressive state after successful survival that occurs through an accumulation of wealth.** The popular expression "survive and prosper" illustrates that this process is comprised of two separate steps that work together. The proper order is survival first and prosperity next. The relationship between the two terms is the main road that extends survivalism into the science of finance and then into the science of economics. This relationship also becomes the foundation for part 2 of this book. Thus, I prefer to reserve further analysis of this subject until later to avoid spoiling the fun!

CHAPTER 4

Defining Life and Death

An Overview

What does it mean to be alive? I tried very hard to avoid this question when I wrote this book because of the high risk that my analysis may digress into irrelevant territory. But my efforts were in vain. I quickly realized that if I avoided this discussion, then I risked having the reader not fully understand the most important component of survival's definition: "to stay alive." I also recognized that it would be very difficult to understand the further connections to biology, economics, and finance without a solid understanding of life. Thus, the following is my humble attempt to answer one of life's biggest questions. Please note that this definition is a work in progress. Yet, after much reflection, I feel that it is sufficient for the purposes of this book.

It is easier to define "alive" than to define "life" because you can simply pass the hard work from one word to another. **Alive is the adjective of life; thus, it is anything that has life.** Therefore, a person who is alive has life. That was easy! Yet this still leaves the bigger question: "What is life?" Before I answer this question, it is a good idea to start with an overview of others' thoughts on this topic. I've carefully chosen the input of a diverse group of various experts on the subject to ensure a well-rounded discussion.

To start, let's take a look at the following statements from two of the most well-known survival novelists, Daniel Defoe and Jack London. Defoe, speaking from the beginning of the eighteenth century, makes a connection between alive, self-preservation, and its opposite qualities after his character Robinson Crusoe has a close encounter with death: "...but it ended where it begun, in a meer common Flight of Joy, or as I may say, *being glad I was alive*, without the least Reflection upon the distinguishing Goodness of the Hand which had preserv'd me, and had singled me out to be preserv'd, when all the rest were destroy'd..." (Defoe, 2008, 77).

Jack London has such a beautiful way of describing the feeling of being alive: "There is an ecstasy that marks the summit of life, and beyond which life cannot rise. And such is the paradox of living, this ecstasy comes when one is most alive, and it comes as a complete forgetfulness that one is alive" (London, 1998, 28). London's works always seem to find a connection to struggling, survival, and life. This next quote conveys his thoughts on life: "On the sled, in the box, lay a third man whose toil was over—a man whom the Wild had conquered and beaten down until he would never move nor struggle again. It is not the way of the Wild to like movement. Life is an offense to it, for life is movement; and the Wild aims always to destroy movement" (London, 1998, 80). The next statements from London demonstrate how novelists sometimes contradict their earlier writings. Unlike his previous quote, the following conveys life when there is no movement: "…and old One Eye might have been dead. Yet all three animals were keyed to a tenseness of living that was almost painful, and scarcely ever would it come to them to be more alive than they were then in their seeming petrification" (London, 1998, 116).

I will now take a look at quotes on life from various nonfiction scholars. Cody Lundin, a survival expert who specializes in desert survival (particularly in Arizona), links life to water: "It is therefore no exaggeration to say that water is life itself" (Lundin, 2007, 134).

Arthur Koestler, one of the most brilliant thinkers of the twentieth century, recognizes the connection between repair, reproduction, and life: "The connection between the emergence of biological novelties and of mental novelties is provided by one of the basic attributes of living things: their capacity for *self-repair*. It is as fundamental to life as the capacity for reproduction, and in some lower organisms which multiply by fission or budding, the two are often indistinguishable" (Koestler, 1989, 173).

Stephen Corry, an anthropologist and the longtime director of Survival International, the global movement for the rights of tribal people, makes the connection between culture and life (this may add value to the concept of life as it applies to groups): "Real culture is not a dead mask. It is alive, but not like an organism which is born, grows old, and then dies: it is more like the weather, which is always there and never disappears and can show a thousand different aspects in the course of a day or a year" (Corry, 2011, 31).

The following quote from Edward Wilson adds much value to our analysis of life. He points out that our reasoning process and our emotions are what make human life unique: "But consider: human advance is determined not by reason alone but by emotions peculiar to our species, aided and tempered by reason. What makes us people and not computers is emotion" (Wilson, 2010, 348).

I think our analysis of life would not be complete without the thoughts of actual survivors of major encounters with death. We could analyze a survivor who confronted *many* deadly encounters to add even more validity to this discussion. Military veterans are the right place to look, and Chris Kyle is the right guy. Kyle, a US Navy SEAL who wrote a book titled after his nickname—*American Sniper*—recorded the most career sniper kills in US military history. I found two quotes from his book that help us to better understand the concept of life.

First, Kyle worked on a beautiful ranch in Texas *before* he joined the military. He made a connection between that place and feeling alive: "I want to tell you, this was a beautiful place, with gentle hills, a couple of creeks, and open land that made you feel alive every time you looked at it" (Kyle, 2013, 16). The next quote is from *after* he became seasoned in the military, and it stands in contrast to the first. The context of this quote has to do with the horrible things that he saw in war and how the troops often made jokes about death to keep their sanity. "You laugh because you have to have some emotion, you have to express yourself somehow" (Kyle, 2013, 274). This need for emotion seems highly related to Wilson's thoughts above.

Life is the basis of many sciences today, particularly biology. However, very few scholars have directly attempted to define life. Let's now take a look at some of the brave who did! For simplicity, I will revert to an old analysis by Herbert Spencer, one of the greatest thinkers of the nineteenth century. Unfortunately, although he was very famous in his time, he is often forgotten by modern academia. Spencer digs deep and produces profound conclusions for his era in his *The Principles of Biology*, a two-volume book in which he first coined the term "the survival of the fittest." In the first volume, he courageously spends much time struggling with his definition of life (one major chapter was devoted to the subject, but the discussion resurfaced in several later chapters). In the end, his final conclusion on this ancient inquiry only demonstrated to me the path not to take. As I will show you, Spencer also appears to be dissatisfied with his conclusions.

Spencer assists our analysis in chapter 4 of volume 1 of *The Principles of Biology*, titled "Proximate Definition of Life," by supplying definitions of life from key thinkers of his time. The following quotes from other scholars are derived directly from this chapter. First is this: "Schelling said that Life is the tendency to individuation" (Spencer, 2014, 60). In other words, life is the process in which an individual separates from its parents to become its own entity. As Spencer demonstrates, this definition becomes weak once you consider those processes of "inorganic objects" that also have a tendency to become individuals, such as in crystallization.

Second, Spencer quotes Richerand as saying, "Life is a collection of phenomena which succeed each other during a limited time in an organized body" (Spencer, 2014, 60). As Spencer points out, this definition becomes weak once you consider that the process of decay after death can be applied here as well. Third, Spencer records that life according to De Blainville "is the two-fold internal movement of composition and decomposition, at once general and continuous" (Spencer, 2014, 60). As Spencer points out again, this definition is too vague. On the one hand, it excludes too much, such as muscular and nervous functions. On the other hand, it includes too much because it allows inorganic objects into the definition, such as a galvanized battery.

Finally, Spencer considers this definition by G. H. Lewes: "Life is a series of definite and successive changes, both of structure and composition, which take place within an individual without destroying its identity" (Spencer, 2014, 61). Although there are many flaws with this definition, I will mention one major one that Spencer highlights. That is, many vital changes are not a series of changes. Instead, many changes happen at the same time, for example, in the various systems of the body.

It is time to review Spencer's definitions of life, which eventually are consolidated into one final version. First, he wrote, "Elsewhere, I have myself proposed to define Life as "the co-ordination of actions;" and I still incline towards this definition as one answering to the facts with tolerable precision" (Spencer, 2014, 60). This definition is too vague though and can include unlimited lifeless objects. On the next page, he also admits that: "But, like the others, this definition includes too much…" (Spencer, 2014, 61).

Therefore, he refines his definition once more: "Thus then, we conclude that Life is—*the* definite combination of heterogeneous changes, both simultaneous and successive" (Spencer, 2014, 70). This definition is obviously still weak. I will let Spencer critique his own work: "Nevertheless, answering though it does to so many requirements, this definition is essentially defective. It does not convey a complete idea of the thing contemplated" (Spencer, 2014, 71). Spencer's last definition that I will mention appears to be his final consolidated one: "...the broadest and most complete definition of Life will be—*The continuous adjustment of internal relations to external relations*" (Spencer, 2014, 80). This final attempt to define life by Spencer appears to me to be unsuccessful. He struggled so hard to derive an answer to this riddle. Yet, in the end, his most updated definition was still too abstract (as he admits on the page after the last quote).

In conclusion, despite the above individuals' attempts to define life, their solutions were inaccurate, too abstract, or both. This demonstrates why this subject generally has been directly avoided; the definer is liable to meet the same fate as those above. Nevertheless, I suspect that the reason Spencer did not come closer to a better definition is not because of his intelligence, which he surely had, but because of the era that he lived in. If he were to experience what we take for granted today, I am sure he would have done much better. Artificial intelligence, the Internet, mass machinery for almost every product conceivable, and robotics are some of the many examples of things that could have shown him the other side of the argument.

Actually, my conclusions on life's definition below take a clue from Spencer's approach: "Manifestly, that which is essential to

Life must be that which is common to Life of all orders. And manifestly, that which is common to all forms of Life, will most readily be seen on contrasting those forms of Life which have the least in common, or are the most unlike" (Spencer, 2014, 62). In contemporary layman's terms, he means that it is easier to understand what life is when you can analyze its most different forms. As you will see, that is exactly what I did.

My Definition of Life

Although it is easy to find fault with many of the quotes on life in the prior section, admittedly, my definition is built on an aggregate of all of their strengths. I want to acknowledge my appreciation of the insights of both those who were and were not mentioned earlier as they have helped shape my perception of life. Additionally, I realize that I am limited in the same way that Spencer was; that is, his definition was based on the information available in his time. Consequently, he was disadvantaged in being able to correctly form a conclusion. I have the advantage of humanity's accumulated knowledge over time by writing this book about one hundred and fifty years after Spencer's work. With that said, my definition, as close as it may be, may also suffer the same fate as Spencer's. One day, the definition may easily be shown to be inaccurate in light of key events that have not yet happened—for example, possible interactions with aliens or the future capability to turn the inorganic into the organic (e.g., living robots). If these events happen and prove me wrong, please excuse the limitations the present placed on us.

For the purposes of Planet Earth (and possibly elsewhere), **life is a reproduced, energy- and water-requiring entity that has the ability and/or the potential capability of feeling, self-repairing, and thinking.**

To form this definition, I took my clues from Spencer (as noted above) by comparing the most extreme forms of life and looking for the common denominator among them all. These commonalities that exist in all known species, from the smallest to the biggest to the strangest, must have some weight in defining life. If there is even *one species* that is missing one of the aspects in the definition, then we must automatically suspect that this aspect is not common to *all* life. Actually, let's carry this statement a few steps further: **If there is even *one individual* alive today (or who was alive in the past) who is missing one of the aspects in the definition, then we must automatically suspect that this aspect is not common to *all* life.** In other words, the definition of life must contain the qualities of every living thing since the beginning of life itself. These are some tough requirements but are absolutely necessary if we are to make any progress. Let's take this one step at a time!

First, every known species on the planet requires water. Even the most unusual forms of life, called *extremophiles*, which are living organisms who live in the most difficult conditions, still need water. Are other human survival essentials, such as oxygen and heat, also required for all life-forms? It is common to think that all life needs oxygen. But according to the prestigious The Encyclopedia of Earth website, "Anaerobic bacteria are microorganisms that thrive in the absence of oxygen; in fact numerous anaerobes cannot survive in the presence of oxygen" (Hogan,

2014). If this is true, surprisingly, oxygen must be ruled out as a requirement for *all* of life. Some extremophiles also live in places with excessive heat and others live in places without any heat. But water, even among all extremophiles, is something we all need. These facts contribute much weight to Cody Lundin's quote above on life. Maybe water is life itself!

Second, this would be a good opportunity to explain why the above definition doesn't include "food"; instead, it uses the word "energy." Food is an ambiguous term and its specific definition can alter whether or not most would agree that it is required. First, if food were defined as solids that living things eat, then that is not required for all of life. It is true that carnivores such as lions generally eat only meat. Additionally, herbivores such as deer and hippos generally eat only plants. Next, omnivores such as humans basically eat everything. However, some organisms, such as bed-bugs, eat only the liquid part of the body—that is, blood. Thus, solid foods are not a good universal requirement for all of life.

Next, there are organisms called *autotrophs* that make their own "food," generally from the sun and inorganic material. The most famous members of this group are plants, but we are also starting to discover that many extremophiles fall into this cate-gory. In summary, there are so many varieties of ways that living organisms can obtain their own energy that I am very hesitant to include the term "food" in the definition. Instead, it is simpler to state that all known life needs energy, somehow.

Third, reproductive systems of both sexual and asexual liv-ing entities are extremely diverse among species. The general rule of thumb is that smaller and more primitive species need to reproduce more in order for that species to survive. That is why some fish reproduce offspring in the millions and humans reproduce in the singles. Either way, the reproduction process ensures that life goes on, and it is a reason that we are here. However, that is where the confusion begins!

It is a common misconception, especially taught in biology, that all life has the ability to reproduce. Although in general this statement is true, it is not absolutely true. How then would we explain men born impotent, women born without eggs, and people born without part or all of their reproductive system? Unless helped by artificial means, if living organisms cannot reproduce, then they are the end of their small branch on the tree of life. They will have no offspring to pass their genes onto. In other words, if the whole of life wants to continue, it must find another way, use another form.

However, as shocking as this thought may be, it is more shocking when you hear it in the following way: *all* life, past and present, was reproduced from at least one other living organism (ignoring the possibility of a universal common ancestor that will be discussed in part 3). This truth demonstrates the connectedness that we all have to one another and the reason why I used the term "reproduced" in the definition of life and not something like "capable of reproducing." Life is like a members-only club that you must be born into—if you were not born a member, then you *can never* become a member. This distinguishing feature ensures, as you will see below, that even a lifeless creature that we may create to appear lifelike, like a robot, can never be alive unless it was born from some member of *Club Life*. **In short, we are alive not because we *all can reproduce life* but because we all *were reproduced from life*.**

Of the remaining three attributes in the above definition of life, the word "feeling" would probably generate the most resistance from critics. They may argue that we don't have absolute proof that a bacterium, a fly, or any other life-form can feel, especially considering the communication barrier between us. Yes, I agree, it is more difficult to prove this attribute because we do not have direct feedback from all species in question. However, indirectly, if we can demonstrate that a wide variety of species from various branches of life can feel at least one emotion then, with lack of proof of the contrary, we can infer that at least it is highly probable to be true.

For example, particularly in the animal kingdom, it is very easy to demonstrate that a crab, a dog, a fish, an insect, a reptile (and so on) can at least feel pain and have negative emotions. If you were to attack them, then they would react negatively and freeze, take flight, or fight. They may only do this because they don't like you and/or what you did, and subsequently they may feel negatively about you and/or the situation. This is unique to life and is common sense for many pet owners. I have realized from my own personal observations of animals how much we don't know about their emotions. They always seem ready to surprise you. For example, I once witnessed a goldfish that demonstrated spitefulness by purposely splashing water on the owner who did not feed her on time. If the owner pretended not to want to feed her, then the splashes would increase. Pet owners around the world could probably fill volumes with examples like this.

I admit this explanation is weak and would be especially difficult to prove when we venture outside the animal kingdom (plants, fungi, etc.), yet, I feel confident that feelings are something that all life has, and if I had the time and space, this point could be argued fully. But since it will take us beyond the scope of the book, I will have to be content with my argument in its current form.

The other two remaining attributes are easier to prove and may generally be agreed on by most biologists. First, all life must be able to think. However, thought does not always have to be of the type familiar to humans. Life-forms that don't have brains still have other unique ways to make decisions, such as with a more primitive nervous system. All living things (such as bacteria, fungi, or plants) must make big decisions at some point in their life cycles. For example, they need to decide on at least one of the following: where to grow; how tall to grow; when to have offspring; with whom to have offspring; how much to eat; what to drink; where to go; who their enemies are; who their friends are; and so forth. Although this is just a small list of many potential decisions, I think most biologists would agree that all living things have to make at least one of these choices during their lifetimes. How else can these decisions be explained unless we assume that the individual organisms are making them themselves? *To make a decision, whether it is right or wrong, you must somehow think about it first; or, in the case of muscle memory, you must have at least thought about it in the past.*

Finally, all life at all levels can repair itself somehow, from the snake that sheds its skin to the tree that repairs the hole from a lost branch. Countless examples of self-repair exist in the human body alone, ranging from the production of scar tissue to the regeneration of the liver. Life would destruct more quickly without the ability to repair itself. Repair, like reproduction, is Club Life's insurance plan that it will continue on.

Also, I added the words "ability" and "potential capability" to the definition of life to reflect the fact that living things may not be able to have all of the qualities of life at every moment. However, they should be capable of having all of those qualities at least at some period during their lifetime. These words help to eliminate some obstacles to the previous definition.

For example, some may argue that when you sleep you are not thinking and feeling, which may be an obstacle to my definition. The following is some commentary on this. First, your conscious may not be thinking but your subconscious is. Second, in regard to feeling, your body should be feeling comfortable or it will probably not allow you to sleep very long. Third, this is where the words "potential capability" comes in. The sleeping body, like the person in a coma, is still potentially capable of waking at some point in time and then thinking and feeling in the normal sense. *Death occurs when that option expires for that individual organism.*

You may be wondering why the concept of "action" was not included in the above definition of life. Are you dead when you can't move or are incapable of ever moving? One of the most common mistakes biology students make is to associate life with physical movement. Many nonliving things move, such as glaciers, mountains, and trucks. Contrarily, many living things don't move, such as trees and other plants. Those who are paralyzed may not be able to move any part of their bodies, yet they still can think and feel. This last example automatically promotes the strength of thoughts and feelings over physical action as a superior requirement for being alive. In short, these examples illustrate that physical movement cannot be a basis for defining life.

One of the biggest obstacles to my definition of life, and certainly one that broke down Spencer's definitions, appears when it is applied to robotics. However, to my knowledge, there is not a robot that can meet all of the criteria of the above definition at the same time. With that said, I suspect that the way technology is progressing, a time may come when that may no longer be true (as you will see in chapter 37). At the moment, *many* robots can think and require energy; *some* can repair and run on water; and *a few* can even replicate. It is the emotional part that is still the wild card.

As hard as it is to prove that all real living things feel—for example, a plant—it will be even harder to prove this on robots. Here is where Edward Wilson's quote from above may have truth to it. To rephrase it, out of all of the other requirements of life, perhaps emotions are what make all living organisms uniquely alive and not robots. However, even if we do learn how to equip robots with emotions, I have put a safeguard in the definition of life to ensure its long-lasting success. That is, as long as robots can never be reproduced as *our* offspring, they will never be allowed to be members of *our* ancient and honorary *Club Life*!

My Definition of Death

This section analyzes life from the opposite perspective to ensure that my earlier definition doesn't have any leaks in it. **In short, death is the absence of life in an entity that was once alive. In**

long form, for the purposes of Planet Earth (and possibly life elsewhere), death is defined as a formerly reproduced, energy- and water-requiring entity that no longer has the ability and the potential capability of feeling, self-repairing, and thinking.

It is a common mistake to think that something that is not alive is also dead. Some other miscellaneous nonliving objects called the *inorganic*, such as a rock or a piece of steel, are neither alive nor dead. To be dead, you must have been alive first. Further, both the *living* and the dead are called *organic*. However, the *nonliving* consists of both the dead and the inorganic. These distinctions can become very useful in our analysis in part 3.

Admittedly, this definition is open to criticism at the micro-level because some people might contend that the inorganic can also be considered dead. They might argue that after a certain point, when a body has decomposed into various chemicals, it is now similar to other miscellaneous nonliving material. If this is true, then this inorganic material can also be considered dead because it was alive at some earlier point (that is, before it was completely decomposed). If you combine this line of thinking with those scientific theories that postulates that life began with the inorganic, then you may form the following life-cycle model: 1) inorganic; 2) alive; 3) dead; 4) repeat life cycle, starting with the inorganic. But until all scientific evidence is in, I think it is much safer to take the perspective from the macro-level without getting caught in the above argument. Thus, in general, something can only be dead if it was once alive.

To reflect better on this definition of death, let's consider a piece of scrap lumber used for various construction projects. This piece of lumber was once alive; for example, it may have been a part of a pine or an oak tree. The tree once qualified as a life-form because it was reproduced from another tree; it needed energy (mostly from the sun) and water; it also was able to feel (even if not as humans feel); it could repair itself; and it was able to think. (For the last requirement, it needed to make at least one decision in its life—for example, knowing when to shed its leaves.) The tree immediately started to die after it was cut down.

Let's now take a look at the tree at the official moment of death. The dead tree, similar to the lumber product it later became, no longer met *any* of the requirements of life and, consequently, met *all* of the criteria for the definition of death. The tree was once an entity that was reproduced (from another living tree), and it used to require energy and water (but no longer does). Actually, now the dead body can become a supply of energy for other living entities. The dead tree also once had the ability and/or the potential capability of feeling, self-repairing, and thinking when it was alive (but again it no longer does). Yes, this tree is officially considered dead!

CHAPTER 5

Survival Literature Review

An Overview

As long as the written record has existed, various themes of survival have been discussed. Sumerian clay tablets, Egyptian hieroglyphics, the Bible, the Chinese classics, Greek and Roman literature, among many other ancient writings, are filled with various thoughts on survival. So where do we start our analysis with all of these data sources? I decided to start my research of survival literature with famous early explorers. I think we can learn much about the ordeals that they went through. Their stories highlight the wide variety of survival scenarios that could exist. Interestingly, they have used many of the various survival techniques taught in modern survivalism. Let's explore these explorers below!

The Explorers

Saint Brendan, from the sixth century, is one of the most famous early explorers. Ancient Latin texts depict Brendan as a man who sailed the ocean to a foreign land in a boat made of oxhide. If this is true, Brendan might have made it to America way before the Vikings and Columbus. In Brendan's book *Navigatio Sancti Brendani Abbatis* (or *The Voyage of Saint Brendan the Abbot*), he documents his travels at sea. Some scholars say that his voyage was not possible, and the book is not reliable. Interestingly, Tim Severin, a modern explorer and author, set out in May of 1976 from Ireland to prove that this voyage was possible under the conditions stated in the text.

Severin recreated Brendan's voyage to the best of his ability using the exact materials and the design of the original boat. He followed approximately the same path, and a little over a year later, sure enough, his little oxhide boat landed in Newfoundland, which increased the credibility of Brendan's story. Severin tells his tale of survival in his book *The Brendan Voyage*. His description of the voyage suggests what Brendan likely had to survive as well. Severin described the medieval conditions on his boat: "Historians say that medieval life was cramped, uncomfortable, and sometimes dangerous. They are right" (Severin, 2000, 83). Severin used many of the sea survival skills taught in the various survival literatures mentioned in this book including bird fishing, collecting rainwater, and using mirrors as rescue signals. One encounter with his boat and a modern large factory ship depicts the new issues of survival created in the modern era: "How ironic, I thought to myself, that our greatest danger should be from Man, not from Nature, a risk that Saint Brendan never had to face" (Severin, 2000, 10).

Marco Polo is generally regarded as the most famous traveler and explorer in history. He survived about thirty years of wild adventures in his travels from Venice, Italy, to various parts of China. His book is what made him famous though. It is what inspired almost every famous explorer after him, including all that will be mentioned later. He wrote *The Travels of Marco Polo*, also known as *Il Milione*, in 1298 in a prison in Genoa, Italy, with the help of an inmate named Rusticello. It is a very interesting account of where Polo went and the people who lived in each place he visited. Unfortunately, as important as this book is to geography and history, it contributed very little to survival literature. I think Morris Rossabi, the general editor of an illustrated edition of *The Travels of Marco Polo*, said it best: "But Marco does not offer an adventure story. Nor does he wish to write about himself and his own travels or successes. The book is remarkably impersonal" (Polo, 2012, xvi). The survival lessons that could have been related by Polo are especially disappointing considering the many difficult terrains that he must have learned how to successfully navigate. Nevertheless, as we shall see, Polo paved the way for useful survival knowledge from the many explorers whom he inspired.

Christopher Columbus is known as the famous explorer who officially discovered America (although he thought he was in Asia). The stories of survival from Columbus's four voyages to America from 1492 to 1504 have been dramatized in many biographies and movies. However, his journals reveal as close to his true story as possible. Columbus, inspired by

Marco Polo's book, had many close calls with death during his adventures at sea, especially with the natives and his fellow seamen. Columbus's son, Hernando Colon, describes one of these events in which his father may have been experiencing a nervous breakdown: "He was afflicted by a serious illness, something between an infectious fever and a lethargy, which suddenly blinded him, dulled his other senses and took away his memory" (Columbus, 1969, 185).

Another one of Columbus's survival encounters was out at sea in the middle of eight days of intense heat. Fortunately, most of those days were cloudy, or as Columbus put it, "If these days had been as sunny as the first I do not think any of us would have survived" (Columbus, 1969, 207). In a letter written during his fourth and last long voyage from Spain to the Americas, Columbus recounts his long struggle: "As for myself I had won little profit in twenty years of toilful and dangerous service, for today in Castile I have no roof to shelter me. When I want a meal or a bed I must go to an inn or tavern, and more often than not I have not the money to pay the bill" (Columbus, 1969, 286–287).

In a continuation of Columbus's dream to reach Asia from Europe, Ferdinand Magellan, another great explorer, and his five vessels set sail from Spain in 1519 to accomplish the unimaginable. Magellan's crew was the first to successfully sail from Europe to Asia going west. Unfortunately, he did not make it back home to appreciate the conclusion of the journey. Out of five ships and about 260 men, one ship called *Victoria* returned in 1522. The eighteen survivors were the first people in human history to circumnavigate the globe and survive one of the most famous maritime adventures on record.

Laurence Bergreen, a modern expert on Magellan's life, best describes Magellan's survival abilities: "He overcame natural hazards ranging from storms to scurvy, and human hazards in the form of mutinies. In the end, the only peril he could not survive was the greatest of all: himself" (Bergreen, 2003, 284). Bergreen also paints a great picture of the life of a sailor in Magellan's fleet. "Most sailors were in their teens or twenties. Anyone who had reached his thirties was considered a veteran scalawag; by the time he had survived to that age, he had seen what life at sea held: brutality, loneliness, and disease; he had experienced flashes of camaraderie and heroism, as well as persistent dishonesty and callousness" (Bergreen, 2003, 112–113). Ironically, the second major hero of the Magellan story, and ultimately one of the best survivors, was not like the sailors just described—or a sailor at all. Antonio Pigafetta, one of the eighteen final survivors, was the man responsible for giving a narrative of the entire voyage. He left a legacy for survival literature.

"Antonio Pigafetta, who, joining the expedition as a volunteer, was in *Trinidad* when she sailed in 1519 and in the *Victoria* when she berthed in 1522, brought to his task of recording a capacity for keen observation, sympathetic interpretation, and expressive communication of experience which enabled him to produce one of the most remarkable documents in the history of geographical and ethnological discovery" (Pigafetta, 1994, 5). Although he appears to be the underdog in survival, Pigafetta constantly survived many ordeals (although not always intentionally) including falling off the boat and almost drowning; getting shot in the head with a poisonous arrow; and of course, not getting scurvy. The amazing consistency in his survival decisions allowed Pigafetta and the ship *Victoria* to successfully circumnavigate the world.

The next explorer that we will review is Captain James Cook: a legend in maritime exploration; a survivalist who was way ahead of his time; and a first-class survivor. Almost everything that modern survival shows do now, he had done over two hundred years ago when a dependable, professional rescue team was not an option. Cook survived many potentially deadly encounters with the sea, various hostile native tribes, and a tough, prolonged life at sea—all of which were described in his thorough journals.

To demonstrate how difficult sea life was in his era, the first few pages of the journal he kept on his first famous voyage in 1768 casually mentioned death as if it were as common as eating. The first fatality mentioned was in his entry for September 14, 1768. In the same paragraph, he discussed the weather, a dead man's body found entangled with rope, and how deep the water was in which the ship was moored (Cook, 2003, 16). On December 2, 1768, he dispassionately mentioned the second fatality, that of Peter Flower. Notice how death must have been so commonplace for a sailor that he digressed to another topic *in the same sentence*. "At 9 weigh'd and came to sea and turn'd down the Bay. Peter Flower seaman fell over board and before any assistance could be given him was drown'd, in his room we got a Portuguse" (Cook, 2003, 23).

Cook was also a pioneer in ship hygiene and keeping his crew safe from diseases. He was truly unique for his time because he knew how to survive, *and* he knew how to help his men survive. In particular, he was a pioneer survival expert for the biggest killer of all sailors of his era: scurvy. Unlike the survivors of the Magellan voyages, Cook knew what was keeping the scurvy victims alive. There are many examples in his journals of him feeding his sailors sauerkraut, malt, celery, and so forth, to combat the disease. He may not have known why it worked (the real reason is that scurvy victims lack vitamin C), but he knew it worked. He also noted putting lime in the water to purify it when the men had fevers.

Captain Cook's ability to help his crew survive is demonstrated by the lower death rate in his last two voyages when he used his experience and determination to combat poor hygiene, scurvy, and other issues. Cook discusses the unprecedented survival record of his crew: "Every innovation whatever tho ever so much to their advantage is sure to meet with the highest disapprobation from Seamen, Portable Soup and Sour Krout were at first both condemned by them as stuff not fit for human being[s] to eat. Few men have introduced into their Ships more novelties in the way of victuals and drink than I have done; indeed few men have had the same oppertunity or been driven to the same necessity. It has however in a great measure been owing to such little innovations that I have always kept my people generally speaking free from that dreadful distemper the Scurvy" (Cook, 2003, 595).

The last great explorers that we will review in our analysis are Meriwether Lewis and William Clark. They were commissioned by President Thomas Jefferson primarily to discover the most efficient water route from the east coast to the west coast in the United States. Essentially, this goal was a continuation of the missions of all the previous explorers mentioned starting from Columbus—that is, to find the Great Northwest Passage (experience taught us later that it only truly exists in Northern Canada). Lewis and Clark were extraordinary survivalists who practiced what they preached. Their trip of 1804–1806, documented by their detailed journals, demonstrated that they were what I call *universal survivors*. That is, no matter what the struggle, they found a way to overcome it.

Lewis and Clark and their small crew journeyed in almost every type of environment, both by boat and by land, to the continent's western coast and back. Some of the things they survived included the following: encounters with some hostile native tribes; various encounters with grizzly bears (one of which took ten rifle shots to kill); Clark was once almost bitten by a rattlesnake; the crew was almost crushed by a large tree that fell where they were sleeping; Lewis and his friend slipped and almost fell off a cliff (Lewis creatively used a survival technique in which he used a knife to dig a foot hole into the cliff so they could climb to safety); Lewis amazingly survived an attack by a grizzly bear without the use of his rifle; the crew survived an inadequate supply of water by melting snow in order to quench their thirst; Lewis survived a fall down the side of a steep mountain; the crew survived a violent robbery attempt (which led Lewis to shoot one of the robbers through the belly); and Lewis survived being shot accidently by his friend, Pierre Cruzatte.

One of the most important survival observations to make of Lewis and Clark is that they were completely self-sufficient. They knew how to do almost anything it took to survive. They made their own bullets, candles, fire, shelter, soap, and even knew how to remove a bullet and dress a wound (for example, when Lewis was shot by Cruzatte). They also knew how to barter well, which saved them in certain circumstances. In particular, I noticed that at the end of their journey when they were almost out of supplies and didn't have any products to barter, they started to barter their own services. They pretended to be physicians, and the tribes they encountered helped them in exchange for their medicinal services. Although some of their prescriptions were dangerous, such as the use of mercury and bloodletting, this can be forgiven, as these were the accepted practices of even the best doctors of their day. Otherwise, although not officially medical doctors, they appeared to be able to truly help their patients to get well from various illnesses.

After Clark cured two patients, he had this to say about the services they provided to help them survive their return trip: "those two cures has raised my reputation and given those na- tivs an exolted oppinion of my skill as a phi[si]cian. I have al- ready received maney applications. in our present situation I think it pardonable to continue this deception for they will not give us any provisions without compensation in merchendize, and our stock is now reduced to a mear handfull" (Lewis and Clark, 1997, 372–373). Some examples of their many medical services include Lewis's prescription of opium for pain relief to Sacajawea, a native female member of his party; Clark's use of first aid on a patient with a broken arm; their use of a poultice of onions on a swelling baby; and their use of a sweating technique made from a fire in a hole in the ground that cured a sick patient.

The Birth of Survivalism

It can be argued that the true birth of modern survivalism literature began with novels. *Robinson Crusoe* was the first great English *novel*, published in 1719 by Daniel Defoe. This book was also an excellent survival story, supposedly inspired by a true event. The character Crusoe was stranded alone on an island in the Caribbean where he learned to be self-sufficient. This publication was so successful that it inspired an onslaught of other survival novels through the present day. For example, *The Swiss Family Robinson*, a novel by Johann Wyss that was first published in 1812, took island survival up a notch. This book included a whole family that was stranded instead of just one person.

Not only did *Robinson Crusoe* inspire other survival novels, it also inspired other *survivors*, in particular, the members of the Donner Party almost 130 years later. The following illustrates how the characters of this novel resonated in the consciousness of the survivors of one of the most extraordinary survival stories: "With thoughts of Robinson Crusoe the emigrants named him Thursday, thinking this to be the day of the week, although it was really Friday" (Stewart, 1992, 61).

The standard for survival novels exponentially increased by the time Jack London came on the scene around the turn of the twentieth century. London was the highest paid and the most famous American writer of his time. What was the general theme of his books? You guessed it right: survival, particularly wilderness survival. He didn't just write meaningless stories though. His novels, leveraging his many personal survival experiences, attempted to reconnect humanity to its deep past. Some of his famous books that should be studied by any survivalist include *The Call of the Wild* (1903) and *White Fang* (1906). He also wrote a famous short story called *To Build a Fire* (1908) that eventually was made into a movie in 1969 with Orson Welles as the narrator.

Besides reading survival novels in the earlier era of survivalism, you could have read nonfiction works based on the real stories of many different types of survivors (the most popular ones generally being about explorers or war heroes). For example, you could have read Vilhjalmur Stefansson's book based on his exploration of the Arctic in *My Life with the Eskimo* (1913). Alternatively, you could have read about one of the greatest modern warriors, an Apache Indian named Geronimo, whose life story was originally published in 1906 as *Geronimo's Story of His Life*. Geronimo has become a symbol to many of the essence of survival. He knew how to survive off the land so well that the United States and Mexico couldn't capture him for many years when he became an outlaw. It took other Apaches to finally apprehend this great war chief.

Two survival stories have become a must read for survivalists. First is the story of the Donner Party in *Ordeal by Hunger: The Story of the Donner Party* by George Stewart (originally published in 1936). This story dealt with a group of eighty-seven people who set out for California in 1846 via wagon train. The members of the Donner Party attempted a new route to their destination, but that decision left them trapped in the snowy Sierras. As their food supply diminished, many resorted to cannibalism to help them survive.

The second must-read story for survivalists is *Alive* (originally published in 1974) by Piers Paul Read. This book is the official story of a Uruguayan rugby team whose plane crashed in the snowy peaks of the Andes Mountains in 1972. Out of forty-five passengers, there were only sixteen survivors. Similar to the Donner Party's story, cannibalism became a major theme of this amazing survival experience that lasted seventy-two days. We will talk more about these two survival stories in chapter 7.

A movement to become closer to the outdoors started to sprout in the beginning part of the twentieth century (probably as a result of the works of Jack London). That is, literature on camping increased in popularity. In particular, a thick book by Horace Kephart called *Camping and Woodcraft* was introduced in 1906 for campers and outdoor enthusiasts.

The scouting movement was another major step in the direction of creating survivalism. Lord Robert Baden-Powell, a famous British general, is credited for starting the scouting movement in Great Britain in 1907. In 1908, he published the famous scouting book called *Scouting for Boys*. Not long after this, in 1910, the Boy Scouts of America organization was founded in the United States, and then the first edition of its famous work *The Boy Scouts Handbook* was published in 1911. Scouting enthusiasm was catching on! In 1912, the Girl Scouts was founded by Juliette Gordon Low in Savannah, Georgia. Two more popular outdoor books need to be mentioned: *Woodcraft* (1919) by Elmer Harry Kreps and *Camp-Lore and Woodcraft* (1920) by Daniel Beard, one of the founders of the Boy Scouts of America. As you can see, camping and woodcraft books were becoming popular as they planted the seeds for future survival books.

From the previous paragraph, you may have noticed that publications from the early to almost the middle of the twentieth century generally did not use the word "survival" in their titles. The concept of survivalism of that time floated around the themes of "camping," "outdoors," and "woodcraft." However, that began to change at the end of World War II. The true roots of official modern survivalism can be argued to have sprung from military necessity. In World War II, the militaries of the various combating nations faced a unique problem that had occurred for the first time in warfare. That is, they encountered a risk of accidentally being stranded in *any* environment on Earth because their soldiers were traveling above, around, or through every continent.

For millennia, wars had generally been fought in a specific place where the terrain was familiar to the warriors. However, World War II was fought in the air, on land, and at sea in almost all environments. New knowledge was necessary to survive a variety of unique scenarios. This comprehensive survival knowledge that was required for the modern soldier led to a landmark book called *How to Survive on Land and Sea*, published by the US Naval Institute in 1943. This book was later revised and published in several more editions, and it is still recognized as a major reference book on the subject. This publication also set the trend for other departments of the US military. For example, the US Department of the Army published the first edition of *Survival (Army Field Manual: FM 21-76)* in 1957. Later, the US Department of the Air Force published *United States Air Force Search and Rescue Survival Training: AF Regulation 64-4.*

The next step in the survival movement was to make a survival book targeted at civilians and not just military personnel. Larry Dean Olsen spearheaded the civilian wilderness-survival movement from the western part of the United States with his landmark 1967 book *Outdoor Survival Skills*. Olsen's book became very popular and inspired many other pioneer survivalists to teach wilderness survival courses and to write about the subject. In 1978, Tom Brown Jr. helped pioneer the wilderness-survival movement by starting the Tracker School in New Jersey. Brown, specializing in tracking techniques, wrote his best-selling book *The Tracker* in 1978. However, his *Tom Brown's Field Guide to Wilderness Survival*, published in 1983, is still considered one of the best books on the subject.

In the mid-1980s, several survival authors helped take survivalism up another notch. First, John 'Lofty' Wiseman's *SAS Survival Handbook* was published in 1986. Wiseman served many years in the British Special Air Service (SAS), one of the world's elite military special forces, and wrote his book based on the techniques taught there. While Wiseman was enlarging the survivalist movement from Europe, Mors Kochanski wrote a book with a similar theme as Olsen's but for northern Canada. Kochanski's *Bushcraft: Outdoor Skills and Wilderness Survival* was published in 1987. He is generally considered the pioneer of the northern bushcraft wilderness survival movement.

Bushcraft is another ambiguous term derived from survivalism that became a popular movement. You may get a different definition of it depending on whom you ask. This confusion has led to various branches of bushcraft in different locations, which appear to be very similar but not united. For example, you have a line of bushcraft in the United States and Canada that can be traced back to Olsen first and then to Kochanski later, as noted above. However, in the UK, British bushcraft expert Ray Mears, founder of the School of Wilderness Bushcraft in 1983, appears to have a unique approach to bushcraft. According to Mears, "Bushcraft is the term I employ to describe a deeper knowledge of the wild and of nature. It is a huge tree that branches out in many directions to botany, zoology, craft work, outdoors leadership and countless other divisions. At its root, though, is reliance upon oneself and on nature. In the study of bushcraft we step beyond survival and learn the subtlety that makes outdoor life both certain and enjoyable" (Mears, 2003, 9).

John and Geri McPherson produced a book in 1993 called *Primitive Wilderness Living & Survival Skills: Naked into the Wilderness*. This book is a very good resource for unique aspects of wilderness survival, particularly brain tanning of buckskin. The book was also unique because of the many photos in it of the authors showing the reader how to perform certain survival skills. The McPhersons became very popular, thus enlarging the survivalism movement. Actually, one of their students was Les Stroud, also known on television as the *Survivorman* (more on him in a moment).

We can now advance into an analysis of survivalism in the new millennium. Once the show *Survivor* was aired, survivalism rocket launched into a new era. The amount of survival literature and reality TV programs since then has disproportionately increased compared to before *Survivor*. The following is a brief list of some of the major players in the modern survival reality-television movement.

First, Ray Mears (mentioned earlier) has been a leader in survival television for many years and is famous for a variety of wilderness shows. Second, Bear Grylls, who once served in the British SAS, starred for several seasons in the *Man vs. Wild* series. Grylls has become a legend in modern survivalism and even has his name on various survival products. Third, Les Stroud, a Canadian survival expert, became famous from the television series *Survivorman*. Stroud's shows are unique because he films them alone in various wilderness locations without any production crew.

Finally, Cody Lundin is an internationally recognized professional survival instructor who was a co-host for the show *Dual Survival*. Lundin has produced two major books that I highly recommend for all survival students: *98.6 Degrees: The Art of Keeping Your Ass Alive* (2003) and *When All Hell Breaks Loose: Stuff You Need to Survive When Disaster Strikes* (2007). He has a unique approach to survivalism. Particularly, he also applies survivalism to urban areas and not just the traditional wilderness.

To conclude, I would also like to mention a book by survival expert and instructor Peter Kummerfeldt called *Surviving a Wilderness Emergency: Practical Advice on What to Do When You Find Yourself in Trouble in the Backcountry* (2006). Kummerfeldt's short book includes an admirable amount of wilderness survival information. In addition, his bibliography is an exceptional supplemental resource for learning more about various survival topics. Further, many of the publications listed in the "Additional Survival Literature" section in the back of this book were derived from the excellent survival bibliographies of Kummerfeldt's book and the US Naval Institute's *How to Survive on Land and Sea* (from the first and fourth editions). To my knowledge, the information presented in this chapter, and other related information found throughout this book, serves as the most comprehensive overview of survivalism (in all its forms) currently available.

CHAPTER 6

Why Survive?

A book like this would not be complete without a chapter on why we should want to survive. However, I am well aware that it could easily take us off course. This extensive required analysis becomes a limitation. Hence, the following serves as an ultracondensed version of my reflections on the subject.

I believe that an individual's desire to stay alive, also known as the "will to live," is highly related to his or her "will to meaning." My research on various survivors and my personal survival experiences collaborate with many of the conclusions of one of the best experts on this subject, Viktor Frankl, a psychologist and a survivor of four Nazi concentration camps over a period of about three years. In Frankl's *Man's Search for Meaning*, he reveals his conclusions as a survivor and a scientist on the "why" question. In general, he concludes that the answer to the riddle of why people survive is for personal reasons that vary over time. "These tasks, and therefore the meaning of life, differ from man to man, and from moment to moment. Thus it is impossible to define the meaning of life in a general way" (Frankl, 2006, 77).

Originally from Vienna, Austria, Frankl started his education in psychology the traditional way learning about the works of Sigmund Freud. However, his unique survival experiences gave him new insights into the subject that led to his creation of a new branch of psychology called "logotherapy" (*logos* is the ancient Greek word for *meaning*). "According to logotherapy, this striving to find a meaning in one's life is the primary motivational force in man" (Frankl, 2006, 99). In other words, we desire to stay alive because of the motivation of our own personal purpose. Those people who have a purpose, a reason to live, increase their probability of staying alive longer. Let's take a look at what Frankl derives as the three major sources for meaning, and thus, the three major reasons why people want to live.

"According to logotherapy, we can discover this meaning in life in three different ways: (1) by creating a work or doing a deed; (2) by experiencing something or encountering someone; and (3) by the attitude we take toward unavoidable suffering" (Frankl, 2006, 111). The following is my interpretation of this statement. First, people want to live because they love their work. For example, one of the reasons that helped Frankl to survive the Holocaust was to ensure the completion of his book: "Certainly, my deep desire to write this manuscript anew helped me to survive the rigors of the camps I was in" (Frankl, 2006, 104).

Second, Frankl's logotherapy states that people live for something or someone else, generally, those they love, such as family and friends. Fernando "Nando" Parrado, the hero in the story of the Uruguayan rugby team whose plane crashed into the Andes Mountains, is a great example. Piers Paul Read, who wrote the book on the story, gave Parrado's reason for wanting to survive: "Parrado's mind was less on his Father in heaven than his father on earth. He knew how his father was suffering; he knew what need he had of his son. He was walking through the snow not so much to save himself as to save this man he loved so much" (Read, 2005, 281).

Finally, Frankl's logotherapy states that people live to demonstrate their courage while suffering during a struggle. This is one of the more difficult meanings to comprehend. It was a reflection of Frankl's attempt to explain people who survived or attempted to survive the horrors of the concentration camps who may not have had either of the other two motivating reasons. Frankl can explain this one better: "But let me make it perfectly clear that in no way is suffering *necessary* to find meaning. I only insist that meaning is possible even in spite of suffering—provided, certainly, that the suffering is unavoidable" (Frankl, 2006, 113).

I would like to add some other points to this analysis. First, procreation should not be viewed as the major reason why someone should survive. As the prior chapter on defining life demonstrated, we cannot be alive only to reproduce because not all of living things are capable of reproducing. Surely these individuals who are incapable of reproducing must also have a purpose. Thus, although we all are a direct consequence of reproduction, it is an incomplete reason for someone to live because he or she wants to have offspring. The more comprehensive question is this: Why would someone want to reproduce? Most would agree that the answer might be found in logotherapy's second way to discover the meaning in life: to eventually experience love through one's offspring.

Further, Frankl gives a good illustration of how reproduction becomes a poor example of a meaning for life. He discusses a rabbi who lost his first wife and six children in the concentration camp of Auschwitz only to find out his second wife was sterile. How do you explain a man who wants to live but lost all of his off-spring and is not in a position to have any more? Frankl's struggle to help the rabbi find a meaning for his life led him to the following conclusions: "I observed that procreation is not the only meaning of life, for then life in itself would become meaningless, and something which in itself is meaningless cannot be rendered meaningful merely by its perpetuation" (Frankl, 2006, 119).

Three other insufficient reasons to survive are also commonly cited: money, pleasure, and power. As Frankl puts it, these are "various masks and guises under which the existential vacuum appears" (Frankl, 2006, 107). In order to keep this simple, I will only comment on money, which can buy both pleasure and power. Although having money (and other wealth) explains *how* someone should survive, as this book strives to demonstrate (among other goals), it is not a major reason in itself *why* someone should survive. Money is a tool used to buy goods and services. Thus, to say that you want to stay alive just to make purchases only stalls for time to answer the larger question: Why? History has provided plenty of examples of wealthy people without any reasons to live other than obtaining more money who became frustrated with their existence. Suicide is the most common ending to this scenario.

The best way to reflect on this problem is through the following question: *If you were to attain all of the money, pleasure, and power in this world, what reasons would you have left for living?* If you would still feel compelled to survive under this hypothetical scenario, then your reasons for living *must* be more complex. **The answer to this question also consolidates the whole argument into the most important reasons to survive: you love your work; you love something or someone; and/or you love the struggle.**

In summary, my analysis of the purpose of our lives and, hence, the reasons why we should want to survive, have led me to the same conclusions as the psychologist and Holocaust survivor Victor Frankl: they are different for all of us at different points in our lives. These reasons are held deep within us, even deeper than the desires for great amounts of money, pleasure, and power. If we don't know our purpose yet, then we must search for it in order to avoid the potential fate of existential frustration. It is only after extensive soul searching that each one of us can answer our own "why" question. Thus, the real question of this chapter translates to: **Why do *you* want to survive?**

CHAPTER 7

Real Extreme-Survival Examples

Life is a nonstop daily supply of unique survival examples. Thus, in order to keep this chapter concise, we will only review some of the major popular survival examples found in literature. First, we will start with a brief overview of the explorers already discussed in chapter 5. As was demonstrated, these early explorers were continuously face-to-face with death. If you have ever sailed on an old-fashioned ship run only by sails, you would know the feeling of how fragile life is. Those ships were at the extreme mercy of the shipbuilder, waves, wind, and the knowledge of their captains (among other things). If any of those ingredients were not conducive, then everyone on board was in grave danger.

In addition, many areas of early technology, especially medicine, were not as advanced as our current technology. Therefore, many risks that were substantial then are minimal or nonexistent when voyaging in open waters now. Some examples include attacks by large fish or marine mammals; cockroach and rodent infestations on the ship; getting lost at sea; mutiny; pirate attacks; risk of scurvy and various infections; being stranded at sea or in a desolate location (for example, an island); and so forth. These are all examples of extra things that early explorers had to worry about surviving in addition to the already tough environment of their era.

In contrast, a modern navigator can sail on a giant steel-hulled ship with a current map of the whole world and a GPS device. Modern search-and-rescue teams can locate and help passengers in an emergency usually in less than forty-eight hours, regardless of their location. All of this security is present while passengers cruise anywhere at any time with cell phones, the Internet, and a seemingly endless supply of luxury goods and services on board. Let's face it: the survival methods of the past are different from those today. This can be demonstrated by two of the most consistently referenced survival examples in survival literature: the Donner Party and the Uruguayan rugby team (both briefly noted in chapter 5).

I think most survivalists would agree that extreme emergency survival knowledge is like insurance; it is something that everyone should have yet should hope never to have to use. Although a person may be an extremely intelligent survivalist, it doesn't necessarily mean that he has survived an extreme-survival situation. The famous survivalist Les Stroud wrote, "Therein lies one of the greatest problems I and other survival instructors have always faced. We rarely get the opportunity to really do the one thing we are best at: getting caught and subsequently tested in a true survival situation" (Stroud, 2010, 1–2).

The following two true-life stories are so compelling because they demonstrate what happens when people encounter the harsh wilderness unexpectedly and unprepared. In both cases, the survivors resorted to one of the most extreme methods of survival: cannibalism. Cannibalism, although subject to various ethical debates, contributed to the success of the survivors.

First, let's take a look at the story of the Donner Party, told best by George Stewart in his book *Ordeal by Hunger: The Story of the Donner Party* (originally published in 1936). This story demonstrates how a group's survival can be threatened by the poor decisions of its leaders. In the days of the wagon train, a group of eighty-seven people set out for California. The leaders chose a new trail that was supposedly the most direct route, called the Hastings Cutoff. This decision resulted in the group getting lost in one of the continent's deadliest places at the worst time of the year.

The members of the Donner Party spent the winter of 1846 to 1847 stuck in the Sierras. Stewart describes the conclusion: "To the number of dead may also be added Sutter's two Indian vaqueros, Luis and Salvador. The totals are therefore: dead, forty-two; survived, forty-seven. In addition, many emigrants and men of the relief parties had lost toes from frost-bite and were otherwise injured. The oxen and dogs had all perished, and the horses and mules, too, with the possible exception of three..." (Stewart, 1992, 271). Stewart also cautions the reader not to think that the Donner ordeal was typical of those heading west in that era just because it was spectacular. He even wrote, "In short, the disaster was the most spectacular in the record of western migration" (Stewart, 1992, 271).

The various members of this story confronted conflict after conflict, some successfully and some unsuccessfully. The story illustrates how a terrible major decision may be hard to undo, no matter how many good minor decisions are made. In their struggles, some members of the Donner Party fought harder than others to live. In the end, the strong desire to live, regardless of the reason (although having a good reason is essential for the will to live), seemed to be one of the most important characteristics of the survivors: "For though despair is often close at hand, it never triumphs, and through all the story runs, a sustaining bond, the primal force which humanity shares with all earthly creatures, the sheer will to live" (Stewart, 1992, 298).

Next, let's take a look at another classic survival story, which was depicted best in the book *Alive* (1974) by Piers Paul Read. This book is the official story of the Uruguayan rugby team whose plane crashed in the snowy peaks of the high Andes in 1972. The sixteen survivors of this seventy-two day ordeal should be the defining image of the phrase "will to survive." Although they were not trained in the methods of wilderness survival, it is amazing how many creative techniques they discovered independently to resolve their many problems. This group was absolutely determined and resourceful!

Everything that they were stranded with became a potential survival tool, which included the remaining part of the plane that served as their shelter. They rationed all food and melted the snow on top of the plane for their water supply. They made snow shoes out of the seat cushions when they needed to walk to search for the remaining parts of the plane. And of course, they found a final lifeline when their available food became scarce:

dead human bodies preserved by the cold. This was a tough, yet crucial, decision for most of them: "They all believed that virtue lay in survival and that eating their dead friends would in no way endanger their souls, but it was one thing to decide and another to act" (Read, 2005, 81).

Alvaro Mangino, a survivor, later gives a good recap of his experience: "There might be people who have had much more difficult experiences...I can't even imagine how hard it must be to be a survivor of the World War II concentration camps, or from the war...The only thing I know is that words cannot even begin to explain what we had to go through up there" (Read, 2005, 9: at the back of the book). The world discovered the truth in this statement when two representatives from the group, Fernando Parrado and Roberto Canessa, found civilization after many intense days searching for help in the Andes Mountains. When the two heroes finally made contact with the authorities, a rescue team was sent for the remaining survivors.

Both of these survival stories were absolutely amazing. The main theme from both though is that the survivors were generally fueled by this phenomenon called "the will to live." No matter what the crisis, an answer was supplied. The survivors were relentless in their drive to survive, motivated by unique personal reasons. They wanted to and needed to survive.

Despite the similarities, considering the timing of the events, the Donner Party had a much different struggle than did the Uruguayan rugby team. The members of the Donner Party did not have helicopters or modern technology that could have saved them. In fact, several of their party members did make it back to notify potential rescuers. In modern times, this would have ended their ordeal with a quick rescue. But they lived in pioneer days, with small settlements and few resources. They didn't have GPS, helicopters, or even automobiles. Thus, the struggle was harder for them, as their best chance of survival included more reliance on themselves and less on a rescue team. Ironically, several of the Donner Party's rescue teams had to be rescued. This is a major reason why I disagree with the phrase "until rescued" in Kummerfeldt's definition of survival. As stated earlier, who will save you if the hero never shows up?

If the Donner event had happened in 1972 and not in 1846, the ending to their story might have been much less severe. The wealth of technology might have saved some or all of them much faster. Contrarily, if the Uruguayan rugby team's event happened in 1846 and not 1972 (ignoring the part about the plane not being invented yet), sad to say, without helicopters and other modern technology, their outcome might have been the worst-case scenario. **Wealth surely has played a role in two of the most popular real-life survival stories on record.** We will see later in part 2 that this is no coincidence!

Additionally, Les Stroud reflects on some of the most famous survival stories in his book *Will to Live*, which include Yossi Ghinsberg's survival alone in the Amazon jungle in 1982; Fernando Parrado and the Uruguayan rugby team who survived a plane crash in the Andes in 1972 (discussed above); the Robertson family's survival at sea in 1971; Chris McCandless's attempt to survive alone in Alaska in 1992 (the subject of the movie *Into the Wild*); the Stolpa family's survival in northern Nevada in 1992 when they were stuck in the wilderness; the Karluk ship trapped in the Arctic in 1913; and Douglas Mawson's survival of three unbearable months in Antarctica in 1912. As the title of Stroud's book demonstrates, the "will to live" becomes one of the most important characteristics of the survivors of these great ordeals, which is consistent with the conclusions of the earlier survival examples noted in this chapter. The desire to live is again demonstrated to be a powerful force in the survival process, and hence, a reason it deserves to be included as a part of the goal of survival.

CHAPTER 8

An Unlimited Supply of Survival Scenarios

The Various Struggles

As the title of this chapter suggests, an individual or a group can survive an almost unlimited supply of potential scenarios. Any one of the many forces of nature, alone or in combination with others, can represent the major hardship that must be confronted within an individual's struggle to stay alive. **Remember, a survival situation exists whenever a struggle includes any chance of death**. Some examples of various struggles that we may have to manage to stay alive include, but are not limited to, accidental personal injury (such as falling down a manhole); aging; alcohol or drug abuse; alien invasion; android rebellion; animal attack; being stranded in the wilderness; broken heart; burglary; car accident; child abuse; dehydration; depression;

disease (mental or physical); near drowning; earthquakes; economic issues; electrocution; electromagnetic pulse (EMP); embarrassment; extreme loneliness; financial issues; fire; gangrene; genocide; global warming; heart attack; heat-related illnesses (lack of or overabundance of heat); inadequate sleep; lack of shelter; landslide; life imprisonment; loss of all reasons to live; low self-esteem; malnutrition; maritime disasters; meteorite strike; plane crash; poisoning; predation; rape; sexual frustration; shock; starvation; stroke; suffocation; suicide attempt; terrorist attack; torture; violence; volcanic eruption; war; and weather-related issues. Had enough yet?

Survival Scenario Examples

This chapter is partially an extension of the analysis of the survival examples presented in chapter 7. However, here we will take a look at more survivors of different survival scenarios. To start, I would like to point out that wilderness-survival scenarios are not a recent phenomenon. People have been struggling with the wild since the origins of humanity.

Throughout prehistory, ancient humans had daily encounters with animal predators, getting lost, sickness, weather, and so forth. They lived in harmony with the wilderness while study-ing its deadly capabilities because civilization was not fully con-structed yet. Many early explorers of the past millennium had similar problems that I already noted in my previous analysis. For example, sea navigators like Columbus, Magellan, and Cook had many potentially deadly encounters with the wild ocean.

Another example is Meriwether Lewis, who had to survive extreme thirst, falling off cliffs, and fights with grizzly bears (among many other things).

This struggle with the wilderness still happens in modernity, which is often reflected in the daily newspaper. Here are two examples of amazing wilderness survival success stories as told in the first edition of the US Navy's *How to Survive on Land and Sea* book. First, "The record for survival at sea was set by a Chinese seaman who drifted 133 days in the Atlantic. He subsisted on fish and rain water, and was able to walk ashore when rescued" (Aviation Training Division, 1943, 134). The next story is equally compelling. "Three members of a torpedoed merchantman survived 83 days on a raft catching 25 or 26 birds during that time" (Aviation Training Division, 1943, 141). These stories may sound unbelievable, but they are not impossible. If you *know how to survive* potential disasters like these, then you exponentially increase your chances of *actually surviving* them.

In more recent times, there is a similar fascinating survival story about Jose Salvador Albarengo. According to the February 3, 2014 article from Reuters, "A fisherman thought to be from El Salvador who washed ashore on the Marshall Islands said he survived more than a year adrift in the Pacific Ocean, drinking turtle blood and catching fish and birds with his bare hands" (Ong and O'Boyle, 2014). Imagine being lost in the terrifying Pacific Ocean for over a year in a twenty-two-foot fiberglass boat with no food and water! His knowledge and will to survive triumphed and saved his life.

This next survival scenario is very different. How does one survive being imprisoned in a concentration camp, particularly in Nazi Germany? This is certainly a much different experience than being lost in the high Andes Mountains, as noted in chapter 7 by Alvaro Mangino, a survivor of the Uruguayan rugby team. However, they have one thing in common: the goal of survival. One of the best and most direct resources for understanding this unique type of scenario is Viktor E. Frankl, a psychologist and a survivor of four Nazi concentration camps, including the notorious Auschwitz-Birkenau camp. Frankl explains the daily struggle in these camps: "It is easy for the outsider to get the wrong conception of camp life, a conception mingled with sentiment and pity. Little does he know of the hard fight for existence which raged among the prisoners. This was an unrelenting struggle for daily bread and for life itself, for one's own sake or for that of a good friend" (Frankl, 2006, 4).

In these camps, life could end quickly, starting from the moment of arrival. As soon as the potential prisoners came off the train and arrived at the gates of the camp, the flick of an SS officer's finger determined the life or death of each person in line. If you looked healthy and the officer pointed to the right, then, unlike the majority, your life was temporarily spared. This decision was generally made because you appeared useful. Although you had made it through the first round, to continue to stay alive, the same appearance had to constantly be maintained. As a colleague warned Frankl on his second day in the Auschwitz camp, "If you want to stay alive, there is only one way: look fit for work" (Frankl, 2006, 19).

Next, we will look at a war-survival scenario from the perspective of a soldier, Chris Kyle, the legendary US Navy SEAL who recorded the most career sniper kills in US military history. It is very difficult for many to grasp how someone can kill other people in war. However, in a war situation, soldiers are given two options: kill or be killed. If they don't shoot the enemies, then they lower their odds of getting out alive. Kyle explains war from a veteran's perspective: "The first time you shoot someone, you get a little nervous. You think, can I really shoot this guy? Is it really okay? But after you kill your enemy, you see it's okay. You say, *Great*. You do it again. And again. You do it so the enemy won't kill you or your countrymen. You do it until there's no one left for you to kill. That's what war is" (Kyle, 2013, 6).

Geronimo, one of the greatest warriors on record, can provide us with additional insight into war survival. He was one of the most difficult American Indian warriors for the United States to capture throughout the Indian Wars. Geronimo can be considered a universal survivor because he appears to have been able to survive almost anything. Ultimately, he survived the slaughter of his family; many wars with the Mexicans and the Americans; imprisonment on reservations; and as a businessman later in life by selling personal photographs and autographs.

We must understand Geronimo to understand how to survive like Geronimo. In particular, what events shaped him? The deadly struggle had a continuous presence in his life starting from his youth when he was trained to be an Apache warrior. However, a Mexican ambush was Geronimo's first major struggle and the one that made him into a great warrior. His discovery of his dead mother, wife, and three children left him without any reason to live—that is, until he discovered the motivation of revenge. In a battle with the Mexicans, Geronimo's will to live was in full bloom: "In all the battle I thought of my murdered mother, wife, and babies—of my father's grave and my vow of vengeance, and I fought with fury" (Geronimo, 1996, 82).

Geronimo was wounded eight times in various places throughout his many battles with the Mexicans. In addition, like Kyle, he was no rookie when it came to killing the enemy: "I have killed many Mexicans; I do not know how many, for frequently I did not count them. Some of them were not worth counting" (Geronimo, 1996, 110). Geronimo's success as a survivor in war and in other aspects of his life are more evidence that the will to live can allow one to overcome even the worst struggles. Despite his many obstacles, Geronimo still survived until his eighties.

Self-Defense

Self-defense is a potential solution to the many struggles that you may encounter, particularly when being attacked by a human or another animal. I have decided to include this section as separate from the chapter because my own personal experiences may add more value to this analysis. I have practiced various forms of martial sciences over many years including, but not limited to, boxing, Brazilian jiu-jitsu, karate, krav maga, muay thai, and wrestling. Further, I have also personally trained with many professional fighters from various combat sports, including world champions, and I have worked directly with black-belt masters of pure self-defense sciences. With that said, I think that self-defense is an often neglected part of survivalism. Much of survivalism today basically approaches the subject from a wilderness perspective. However, as this book demonstrates, survivalism is more comprehensive than that.

Self-defense can be used in a range of situations from dealing with being mugged by a petty thief to overcoming an enemy on the battlefield. There is a reason why self-defense is taught and has been taught to the soldiers of the best militaries throughout history: to help keep them alive in a direct combat situation. Martial science, or the science of war, may be considered the big picture of self-defense systems and combat sports, which are often labeled as martial arts. In war, military leaders must reflect on various military considerations, for example, strategy and individual combat concerns. Every great military leader and master martial scientist should know how, when, and where to fight a battle. More importantly, they should know how to avoid it completely.

The best, most experienced teachers of any of the forms of martial science know that the best fights are the ones that are avoided. Fighting should always be an option of last resort as violence begets only more violence. The conflict may then continue into perpetuity. Many later escalations can be avoided, and many lives can be saved if a peaceful solution can be found. Unfortunately though, peace is not always an option, especially when a violent struggle is hand delivered to you.

David Kahn is one of America's leading experts (and from my own personal experience training with him, also a great instructor) in krav maga, a world-renowned hand-to-hand defense system used by the Israeli military. Interestingly and appropriately, the Hebrew word *krav* means "struggle." In his book *Krav Maga*, Kahn explains well why self-defense can be helpful in survival: "You may be your own first and last line of defense in an increasingly violent world. The best law-enforcement and security agencies in the world cannot be everywhere at all times. The attacks of September 11, 2001, and terrorism's global scourge confirm the vulnerability we all face as ordinary citizens. Whether the threat comes from a mugger, rapist, or terrorist, your life is at stake. You must be prepared to do whatever it takes to survive. There are no rules on the street" (Kahn, 2004, 3–4).

Unfortunately, I know too well from personal experience of the threats Kahn refers to in the above statements. I grew up in a rough neighborhood in the city of Philadelphia, Pennsylvania, during a time when crime plagued the streets and graffiti was the closest many young people came to experiencing art. This environment was very similar to the one in the movie *Rocky* starring Sylvester Stallone. You may have been the nicest kid on the block, but that wasn't enough to stop you from getting jumped every day while waiting for the school bus. This was the type of environment where you could lose your life for wearing an expensive pair of shoes. Robbery was a common occurrence for many people while corruption, drugs, gangs, and violence ruled the streets.

In the past several decades though, Philadelphia (and other similar cities, like New York) have been revitalized. It is now easier to find more beautiful, expensive homes and neighbor-hoods than graffiti. Those days of old may be gone, and the major threats may have changed forms (for example, terrorism is now ranked high). However, despite all the positive changes, even a great city like modern Philadelphia still has basic criminals. Particularly in urban environments, there will always be a good supply of people ready to hurt you for any reason, especially to deprive you of your wealth.

What else can you do if someone backs you into a corner and puts her or his hands around your throat? Your only option is to fight. You may not have asked for this violent struggle, but the struggle doesn't care what you want. It is here regardless. In this case, self-defense may save your life.

CHAPTER 9

The Survival Categories

An Overview

Survival situations can be categorized in many ways. For example, Peter Kummerfeldt has organized many of the wilderness survival scenarios into five major categories. "As I see it, there are five broad categories that encompass most situations where you may have to survive until rescued or until the weather conditions improve and you can rescue yourself. The categories are: becoming lost; being caught out after dark; becoming stranded; becoming ill or injured and unable to proceed; inclement weather that makes continuing on dangerous" (Kummerfeldt, 2006, 27). Kummerfeldt's breakdown is an excellent way to organize wilderness-related survival scenarios. However, as you can see from the previous chapter's sample list of potential struggles, it is not broad enough to be comprehensive.

To resolve this problem, I have created a wide-ranging categorization of survival scenarios. **That is, there are three major survival categories of survival scenarios: civilization survival, wilderness survival, and miscellaneous-location survival.** We will need to go over some terms first in order to better understand these categories. The next section may digress a little, but it will certainly be helpful when we return to this discussion in part 3.

Defining Civilization

"Civilization" is a term that has held many meanings over the past few centuries, including racist ones. However, a deep investigation of survivalism illuminates the true meaning. **Civilization is a place where a human society resides, survives, and is the dominant life-form.** The main thing that civilization and the wilderness have in common is that they represent a place. This could be as small as a backyard or as large as a modern nation. Someone who is "civilized" is simply a person from a civilization. The key word in this definition is "human." The term and its meaning become useless to us without our species incorporated into it.

Are all humans civilized—that is, from a civilization? Generally speaking, yes, all humans are civilized. Only in rare exceptions can we make a case for a human not being civilized. For example, if someone were raised by a pack of wolves or apes in the wild, as some children's movies depict, then we can say that this person is not civilized because he is not from a civilization. Instead, he will be considered wild because he is from the wilderness (more on that in a moment). However, he can still become civilized if he can relocate and become a member of a civilization.

A particular, unique example challenges the above definition, but with some reflection, the definition still holds strong. Can a civilization be in motion? In general, civilizations are permanent settlements; however, there can also be nomadic civilizations. For example, many nomadic people in Mongolia live in many places during the course of a year. Their lifestyle has existed for centuries. Their location generally becomes a civilization wherever they reside, whether it is for a brief moment or a year, as long as it meets all of the other criteria noted in the above definition.

Next, it is important to note that humans must be the dominant life-form in a civilization. If another species is in control over that space, then humans cannot be the primary decision maker. They will have to appease the wishes of the dominant species first. This is an often-overlooked aspect of civilization nowadays, as we generally don't have to worry about grizzly bears, lions, snakes, tigers, or wolves killing us. Although it was not always that way, we are now mainly in control of most of living nature. *Thus, we can take this analysis one step further and say that the first civilization began when humans were able to truly become the dominant life force in their environment.*

There are all different degrees of civilization. Some civilizations are very remote and disconnected from other civilizations, for example, the tribes in the Andaman Islands in the middle of the Indian Ocean. They were, and are generally still considered to be, disconnected from the rest of the world. They are civilized, however, because they are a human society that has been living in, surviving in, and dominating their environment together for possibly tens of thousands of years.

On the other hand, many civilizations today are not remote and are globally connected, particularly through telecommunication systems. These include all of modern nations as recognized by the United Nations. Additionally, sometimes a civilization of a particular nation breaks down for various reasons (for example, war). When this happens, it may not be able to survive collectively anymore. Its civilization may be considered to be in a transition period until a new, more concrete one evolves.

I think it is a good time to add Robinson Crusoe to our discussion. Is a civilization present if a person, such as Crusoe, gets trapped on an island and masters how to survive there? How about if you add another person to the picture, as in Crusoe's friend Friday? A limitation to the above definition of civilization is that there may be a debate about what the magic number is that constitutes a human society, thus (assuming all other requirements are met) creating a civilization. The number of humans needed to form a society is a gray area that I will leave for the anthropologists.

Defining Wilderness

The wilderness is a place where a human society does not reside, does not survive, and/or is not the dominant life-form.

In short, the wilderness is wherever civilization is not present. In theory at least, the wilderness plus civilization equals all possible locations. Anything that is considered "wild" is from the wilderness. The above definition is consistent with all of the various usages of wilderness in all of the sciences mentioned in this book. That is, the term can now be equally applied whether we are talking about Jack London's *Call of the Wild*, *Tom Brown's Field Guide to Wilderness Survival*, or the term "wild" as applied by biologists. For example, the following statement from the famous biologist Edward Wilson is indirectly in sync with the above definition: "To biophilia can be added the idea of wilderness, all the land and communities of plants and animals still unsullied by human occupation" (Wilson, 2010, 350).

The Survival Categories Elaborated

Now that we have defined civilization and wilderness, we are in a better position to understand **the three major survival categories of survival scenarios: civilization survival, wilderness survival, and miscellaneous-location survival**. Civilization survival includes survival scenarios that can occur within civilization. Please note that civilization usually refers to urban survival, but this is not always so. There are other areas in a civilization as well, such as the suburbs, the country, and even remote villages or tribal areas (such as those mentioned in the Andaman Islands example above). In general, your odds of survival are better when you are closer to an urban part of civilization. This is because there you may have better access to people, specialized services, and supplies to better manage your struggles.

The drawback to being in urban civilization is that many of the self-defense struggles discussed in chapter 8 generally happen there. Some examples include burglary, child abuse, genocide, predation, rape, terrorist attacks, torture, violence, and war. Various accidents also occur in civilization, such as automobile accidents and falls. Additionally, many health-related struggles generally occur in civilization including aging, alcohol or drug abuse, broken hearts, dehydration, depression, diseases (mental or physical), heart attacks, heat-related illnesses (lack of or over-abundance of heat), inadequate sleep, loss of all reasons to live, malnutrition, poisonings, and so forth.

Wilderness survival includes survival scenarios that happen within a wilderness. This survival category is mainly what many modern survivalists focus on. Most wilderness survival experts agree that a person needs to be able to find a way to survive starting from *nothing* in order to master the wilderness. When I say nothing, I mean absolutely nothing! The phrase used to describe this survival test is going *naked into the wilderness* (hence the reason why John and Geri McPherson included it in the title of their book). But most people who were stuck in wilderness-survival situations never came close to mastering the wild, even if they had all of their clothes. Peter Kummerfeldt's categorization of wilderness-survival scenarios (mentioned at the beginning of this chapter) is a great way to organize their potential struggles.

The first two survival categories of survival scenarios are meant to be for straight-forward situations. However, the final survival category, miscellaneous-location survival, was created to address a major issue with the above definitions of civilization and wilderness: many potential circumstances can be considered both wilderness and civilization, depending on the perspective taken. If you use any definitions of these terms rigidly, including the ones provided above, eventually there will be problems for several reasons.

First, the boundaries of civilization are always changing, for example, during human migration or war. A place that is civilized today may not be civilized tomorrow and vice versa. Second, it is difficult to account for the wild areas within civilization. For example, giant city parks like Fairmount Park in Philadelphia and Central Park in New York City are sort of a hybrid between civilization and wilderness. Generally speaking, people may live near the parks but not in the parks (at least without having permission).

National parks are another example of the fine line between wilderness and civilization. We have park rangers who live and survive there. If necessary, we can also bring out an army with weapons to prove that we are the dominating force. But humans allow those areas to be a home for other species with as little interference from us as possible. Those parks are obviously wild. Yet, at the same time, they are a part of our nation's big picture of civilization as well.

Thus, the big question is this: Where do we draw the boundaries of wilderness within civilization? Also, what about the air and ground space in civilization? Wildlife may be living above, below, or around us within parts of our civilization, even without our approval—for example, sewer rats and cockroaches.

All of these questions can be better addressed by relaxing the above definitions of civilization and wilderness and by allowing them to have general and not absolute boundaries. Thus, we can restate the definition of civilization as the following: **Civilization is, generally, a place where a human society resides, survives, and is the dominant life-form**. Although it works well in academic models, it may be a serious error to think that we can set the limits of these terms in an absolute sense.

In summary, the above three major survival categories should account for all possible survival scenarios. Additionally, some struggles can happen in more than one category, such as surviving a heart attack or a violent encounter.

CHAPTER 10

The Survival Environments

As noted in the previous chapter, there are three major survival categories in which one can survive. The focus of this chapter is to explore the various environments that could occur within each category. Humanity has been able to master almost every environment from the top to the bottom of the world. Let's take a look at some of these now!

First, we need to understand some human limitations. As John Wiseman puts it, "Man is a tropical animal and can only survive as we are born in the tropics. The moment we leave this area we have to provide our bodies with this tropical environment, hence the need for clothes" (Wiseman, 2009, 19). That is, in general, when the weather is warmer, we survive better without the dependency on many thermal related resources. In warmer weather, we need little, if any, clothing, and we have no need for external sources of heat other than the sun. Thus, I think it is safe to say that generally speaking, survival is environmentally easiest for humans (and most living things) at the equator.

More planning and resources are required as we move away from the equator toward the colder north and south poles. Thus, generally speaking, survival becomes environmentally harder in colder weather areas. It is no surprise that you will find most of life in the regions bordering the equator and only very few species in the coldest parts of the globe. The extreme cold kills many plants and animals, which affects the whole food chain. It is indeed hard to obtain food with few things on the menu!

We must take our clues from the Inuit, possibly the best Arctic survivors, to learn how to survive in colder environments. They have been surviving freezing conditions in the Arctic areas for centuries. Their houses include tents and the famous igloo made from ice blocks. They know how to find a food supply, including seals and whales, in the most extreme living conditions on this planet. They are also able to use every part of the body from their caught food to meet their various lifestyle needs, such as for clothing and shelter.

Heat is certainly helpful for survival. That is, until you encounter a place like Death Valley, California, or the middle of an Arizona desert. The excessive heat of the desert environment presents unique challenges for life. It is indeed very difficult to survive there, especially because having plenty of water is always a major concern. Care must be taken to avoid losing too much sweat from the heat, or heat stroke may sneak up quickly.

Survival environments include, but are not limited to, being adrift at sea, caves, concrete jungles (this term works for many urban survival areas), deserts, forests, islands, jungles, mountains, plains, polar regions, rain forests, swamps, and valleys. Within these environments, severe weather can add difficulty to the survival scenario. Some examples of severe weather-related disasters that may affect one's chances at survival include, but are not limited to, avalanches, blizzards, cyclones, droughts, earthquakes, floods, hailstorms, heat waves, hurricanes, lightning strikes, monsoons, thunderstorms, tidal waves, tornadoes, and tsunamis. As you can see, the many potential combinations of environmental components may result in many different survival scenarios.

Also note that there can be various environments within different survival categories. For example, there could be a desert in both the wilderness and civilization. There are plenty of examples of cities that are built into the desert, including the first cities the civilized world had seen. The floor of such cities can be the same as the desert floor or it can be a concrete jungle within the desert, such as the cities in Arizona and Nevada.

One important thing to learn from this chapter is that there are different strategies to survive depending on what survival environment you are in (and also your own personal circumstances). As survival expert John Wiseman puts it, "We are all used to surviving on our home ground – though we may not think of our lives in that way – but the true survivor must learn how to survive when taken from familiar surroundings or when those surroundings are drastically changed by man or nature" (Wiseman, 2009, 14). This is one point anyone will quickly learn from watching the various survival shows on television, in particular, the popular series *Dual Survival*.

In *Dual Survival,* two survival experts must deal with various survival environments as a team. Each one of the experts has certain environments in which he survives best, according to his survival specialization. For example, Cody Lundin is an excellent well-rounded survivalist; however, he specializes in desert survival (particularly in the desert areas of Arizona). His intense knowledge helped his team in various circumstances. Yet, in one episode in season two, he was forced into an environment that conflicted with his survival specialization and capabilities. In this episode, he was adrift at sea on a raft and became extremely seasick. He had to rely almost exclusively on his partner, Dave Canterbury, (who had much experience on boats) until he made it to dry land.

On the other hand, Cody's teammate Dave is an expert in mountain and swamp survival. Generally speaking, it was in these environments that his survival skills appeared the most useful to the group. However, Dave mostly relied on Cody's knowledge to help them survive successfully when the two were paired together for an episode in Arizona. This show continuously demonstrated that even the best survivalists, like Cody and Dave, have trouble surviving in unfamiliar conditions.

Additionally, urban survival may not be easy for those who live exclusively in the wilderness (and vice versa). For example, a person who survives best in the wilderness may not last a day if he were moved to the toughest inner-city neighborhood of Philadelphia. Contrarily, a person who survives best in the toughest inner-city neighborhood of Philadelphia may not last a day if she were moved to the wilderness. I have often witnessed people from very secluded areas having a very difficult time surviving in the city. On the other hand, I have met very tough city folks who are deathly afraid of anything that comes from the outdoors, even bugs and mice. This paradox confirms what Wiseman was saying above. **In other words, an environment that one person may call home, another may call a deadly struggle!**

Larry Dean Olsen, one of the pioneers of the modern survivalism revolution, concurs: "What becomes a survival situation to one person may not concern another" (Olsen, 1997, 4). That is a major reason why Mexican and American troops found it so difficult to catch Geronimo. He was a master of *his environment*, unlike his more powerful and larger enemies. It took other Apaches with similar knowledge of his environment to catch him.

This same rationale can be applied to whole countries. A nation's mastery of its environment gives them a survival edge over an invader. The British learned this lesson fighting Americans during the Revolutionary War. Many of the Americans during that timeframe were born and raised on North American soil. Over the years, they learned how to master their terrain with the help of local American Indians. This knowledge gave them a crucial edge. A few decades ago, the Soviets learned this lesson in Afghanistan fighting a people who had mastered survival in their difficult mountainous environment. The Soviets eventually moved out of Afghanistan after many years of occupation.

France and the United States have also learned this lesson each spending time fighting in Vietnam Wars. In addition to having an iron will to live, the Vietnamese were masters at surviving their difficult jungle and swamp terrain environment. This edge helped them defeat much larger opponents. Contrarily, if the locations had been reversed in all of the above examples, the conclusions to those conflicts might have been very different (for example, if the Vietnamese had been fighting on French or US soil). However, as you will see in part 2, the will to live and a mastery of one's environment are not enough to make one nation superior over another. Undoubtedly, the right wealth and excellent, comprehensive wealth management are the missing ingredients.

CHAPTER 11

The Irony of Great Survivors

I decided to include this chapter because my research unveiled a very strange pattern that is consistent with some of the conclusions from the last chapter. The ironic discovery was that several great survivors, who varied in survival specializations and time periods, had died in the most unexpected ways. *The conclusions demonstrate that the probability of survival varies from person to person and situation to situation.* Just because someone is a survival expert in one environment does not mean that he will survive in another. Also, just because someone has survived a particular environment many times in the past does not guarantee that she will always survive in that same environment. Survival must be a continuous effort because every situation is unique.

First, let's take a look at some of our early explorers. To avoid redundancy, you may want to review chapter 5 for more information about their survival encounters. Ferdinand Magellan discovered the Strait of Magellan, and his crew (what was left of it) became the first people to circumnavigate the globe. Magellan survived almost every struggle he encountered, ranging from mutiny to navigating difficult waterways. Also, Magellan often demonstrated his ability to deal with various natives that he encountered during his travels. Yet, as stated by his biographer Laurence Bergreen, there was one thing he couldn't survive: himself. His support for a local chief in the Philippines, helping the chief to conquer his rival, led to Magellan's murder on the island of Mactan. In short, this was a very unusually bad decision for such a generally great survivor, one that cost him his life. He certainly had no reason to fight someone else's battles, especially when the survival of his crew and the accomplishment of their original goals were at stake.

Ironically, Captain James Cook, another one of the greatest explorers, made a similar mistake a little over 250 years later. This man had survived almost every kind of oceanic climate that you could think of. He was the first person on record to discover Antarctica, among many other places. He treated scurvy with solutions that were unique for his time. He avoided conflicts with Russian sailors around the Bering Sea. He avoided countless skirmishes with the many natives of his various voyages (actually befriending many).

However, on one rare case, he dropped his guard and let his ego get the best of him. He could have easily avoided escalating an incident with the Hawaiians. Instead, he attempted to kidnap one of their main chiefs and threatened their people with musketry. This mistake resulted in his stabbing and, ultimately, his death. As with Magellan, his death might have come from the mistaken belief that European firepower would ultimately protect him against primitive weaponry. He might have become convinced that he was almost invincible based on his incredible skill of dodging death. Indeed, it should never be forgotten that survival is a lifetime commitment, regardless of your past record!

Meriwether Lewis is another example of a legendary survivor whose death was inconsistent with his survival record. Considering the unbelievable struggles that Lewis had overcome in so many situations (ranging from being shot to fighting grizzly bears one on one), it was very ironic that he allegedly died at his own hand just a few years after his famous expedition. That is, most experts agree that he committed suicide in a remote cabin by shooting himself. A particular passage in his journals a few years before he died really makes his death even more unexpected. "This day I completed my thirty first year, and conceived that I had in all human probability now existed about half the period which I am to remain in this Sublunary world" (Lewis and Clark, 1997, 206). This gives the perception that he had planned to live much longer, not that he would shortly take his own life. It is sad to see a man with so much more potential just give up the fight!

Geronimo, a legendary survivalist, who has been discussed many times in this book, also died in a way that contradicted his overall success. Although Geronimo had fought and been wounded in many battles during his lifetime and had survived various gunshot and stab wounds, he died from something completely unrelated to combat. That is, he fell off his buggy drunk and then lay out in the cold and rain the whole night. He was discovered the next day and then taken to the hospital, where he died. How could this man, who was like the real-life version of a nineteenth-century Rambo, die in that manner?

A man similar to Geronimo can be found in modern times. Chris Kyle was a US Navy SEAL who survived many deployments to various war zones in the Middle East. Unfortunately, Kyle passed away in an unexpected tragedy in 2013, ironically, when he was fatally shot on a Texas gun range while trying to help a fellow veteran. How does a man who appeared unassailable in war get killed as a civilian in a generally peaceful environment? In this case, Kyle can possibly help to explain the irony of his death and others mentioned in this chapter. He gives us a hint in his book, which was released shortly before his died: "I always seemed more vulnerable at home. After every deployment, something would happen to me, usually during training. I broke a toe, a finger, all sorts of little injuries. Overseas, on deployment, in the war, I seemed invincible" (Kyle, 2013, 95).

Although I am convinced that volumes could be written about this subject, only two more different examples will be given to avoid going beyond the scope of this book. First, Haing Ngor survived the Khmer Rouge in Cambodia for four years. He later went on to play the lead role in the famous movie representing this tragedy called *The Killing Fields*. Tragically, Ngor was shot and killed in 1996, supposedly by a random street gang in Los Angeles, California. Ngor had escaped death countless times, surviving one of the world's worst genocides, in which so many people had been killed. Ironically, he died a victim of random violence in a generally peaceful environment.

Finally, the last example is about a hero named Raoul Wallenberg. During World War II, he was a Swedish representative in Budapest who helped Jews escape the concentration camps in Auschwitz. His campaign may have saved as many as a hundred thousand Jewish lives through his many tactics, which included issuing fake passports. According to genocide specialist Adam Jones, "In the grimmest of ironies, Wallenberg the rescuer survived the Nazis, only to disappear into the custody of Soviet forces occupying Hungary. For reasons unknown, he appears to have spent years in detention before finally dying in the camps sometime in the 1950s" (Jones, 2011, 403).

CHAPTER 12

The Survival Essentials

An Overview

We must now learn what we need to survive in any survival scenario and in any environment, civilized or wild. This chapter is crucial to our understanding of part 2 because what I will cover here can be translated into wealth. **That is, all of human life's survival essentials can be considered our most basic forms of wealth.** Once that connection is understood, then it will be easier to understand the connection between survival and economics and finance in part 2 (and ultimately biology in part 3).

While most survivalists generally agree on what many of the essentials of life are, they don't always agree on their ranking. In addition, the lack of clarity of the types of essentials often results in an overall poor organization of these items. For example, there is clearly a difference between needing water and clothes. They both are necessary, but what is their relationship to each other? To solve this problem, I have arranged the survival essentials into the following two major categories: ***immediate survival essentials*** and ***essential survival tools***. Please see Exhibit 12.1 for a detailed breakdown of the survival essentials. Also note that the categories apply specifically to human life. The survival essentials of other living organisms may vary from species to species.

Exhibit 12.1

The Survival Essentials

I. The Immediate Survival Essentials

1. The Primary Physical Immediate Survival Essentials
(The most important requirements for our body in order for us to stay alive. *They are ranked based on approximately how much time it would take for the average human to die without each one.* Please note that this is a general ranking, and it can vary for each person and each unique survival situation.)

1) Quality air and proper blood circulation (It is easier for us to consider these two essentials a tie because their ranking is debatable.)
2) Thermal balance of the body
3) Relief of immediate life-threatening bodily injuries
4) Quality water
5) Conservation of energy
6) A means to relieve bodily waste products, such as by defecation and urination
7) Quality food
8) Quality sleep

2. The Secondary Physical Immediate Survival Essentials
(This debatable list is in alphabetical order, and it is not exhaustive.)

1) Beauty
2) Companionship
3) Fitness

4) Good health
5) Sanitation
6) Sexual activity

3. **The Primary Mental Immediate Survival Essentials**
(The most important requirements for our mind in order
for us to stay alive. *They are ranked based on approximately how much time it would take for the average human to die without each one.* Please note that this is a
general ranking, and it can vary for each person and each
unique survival situation.)

1) <u>**A purpose to live**</u> **(The most important survival essential: a will to live can only be present when there
is a reason to live.)**
2) <u>**A will to live**</u> **(The second most important survival
essential: having a reason(s) to live may not always
ignite the will to live.)**
3) A positive attitude (a good psychological state)
4) Survival knowledge
5) Ingenuity
6) Mental preparation

4. **The Secondary Mental Immediate Survival Essentials**
(This debatable list is in alphabetical order, and it is not
exhaustive.)

1) Awareness
2) Being able to divide a large struggle into small manageable tasks
3) Being analytical yet able to see the big picture
4) Discipline
5) Displaying apathy (under certain struggles)

6) Humor
7) Motivation
8) Proper emotional usage (for example, hope or love)
9) Remaining calm in the presence of the struggle
10) Spirituality (relative to the person)
11) The ability to endure physical and mental suffering

II. **The Essential Survival Tools** (These are some examples of essential survival tools, also known as "the survival kit." The list is in alphabetical order, and it is not exhaustive.)

1. An ax
2. A bag
3. A bed
4. A blanket
5. Books
6. Clothing
7. A communication means (sometimes called signaling)
8. A container
9. A cooking pot
10. Cord
11. Disinfectant
12. Kitchenware
13. A knife
14. Lighting sources
15. A means to start and maintain a fire
16. A medical kit
17. Money
18. Music
19. Navigational equipment
20. Security

21. Shelter
22. A transportation means
23. A wash kit
24. Weaponry
25. Other miscellaneous personal items that can increase the potential survivor's odds of staying alive during a survival situation

To further organize the immediate survival essentials category, it will be divided into physical and mental essentials and then again into primary and secondary essentials. The physical essentials are survival requirements for the body, and the mental essentials are survival requirements for the mind. Primary essentials are the most important essentials. Many of these were derived from the analysis of the requirements of life as applied to all living things. You may want to review chapter 4 to see the connection to these essentials. Secondary essentials are ranked lower in their importance than primary essentials but are still crucial to survival. However, some of these essentials may be significantly more applicable in very specific scenarios, such as apathy in the case of surviving war or concentration camps.

This new organization of survival essentials is far from perfect. Nevertheless, it is a major improvement over what currently exists, as it provides more clarity of structure. Additionally, some of these essentials may be debatable, and the list may be considered incomplete. Yet these limitations should not deter the book from meeting its goals. Let's now take a look at the first major category of survival essentials!

The Immediate Survival Essentials

A brief overview of all immediate survival essentials will be provided before any further analysis. Let's start with our *primary physical immediate survival essentials*, the most important requirements for our body in order for us to stay alive! Without these, we would die in a short time, hence the use of the word *immediate*. I will rank these in accordance with approximately how much time it would take for the average human to die without each one. We could die the fastest without the first essential and the slowest without the last essential. Please note that this is a general ranking, and it might vary for each person and each unique survival situation. The primary physical immediate survival essentials are these: 1) quality air and proper blood circulation (it is easier for us to consider these two essentials a tie because their ranking is debatable); 2) thermal balance of the body; 3) relief of immediate life-threatening bodily injuries; 4) quality water; 5) conservation of energy; 6) a means to relieve bodily waste products, such as by defecation and urination; 7) quality food; and 8) quality sleep.

Next, we will look at our *secondary physical immediate survival essentials*. As these essentials may be too debatable for our current purposes, a ranking for them will not be provided. They may include, but are not limited to, beauty, companionship, fitness, good health, sanitation, and sexual activity.

Our *primary mental immediate survival essentials* are the most important requirements for our mind in order for us to stay alive! Without these, we may not live very long. I will rank these in accordance with approximately how much time it would take for the average human to die without each one. We could die the fastest without the first essential and the slowest without the last essential. Please note that this is a general ranking, and it might vary for each person and each unique survival situation. The primary mental immediate survival essentials are these: 1) a purpose to live; 2) a will to live; 3) a positive attitude (a good psychological state); 4) survival knowledge; 5) ingenuity; and 6) mental preparation.

Next, we will look at our *secondary mental immediate survival essentials*. As these essentials may be too debatable for our current purposes, a ranking for them will not be provided. They may include, but are not limited to, awareness; being able to divide a large struggle into small manageable tasks; being analytical yet able to see the big picture; discipline; displaying apathy (under certain struggles); humor; motivation; proper emotional usage (for example, hope or love); remaining calm in the presence of the struggle; spirituality (relative to the person); and the ability to endure physical and mental suffering.

Now that we have listed the immediate survival essentials, it is time to analyze them further. First, the ranking of our primary physical immediate survival essentials differ from survivalist to survivalist. The difference in priorities can be found even as far back as the novel *Robinson Crusoe* in the early eighteenth century: "I consulted several Things in my Situation which I found would be proper for me, 1st. Health, and fresh Water I just now mention'd, 2dly. Shelter from the Heat of the Sun, 3dly. Security from ravenous Creatures, whether Men or Beasts, 4thly. a View to the Sea..." (Defoe, 2008, 51).

Tom Brown Jr. does an excellent job in categorizing survival essentials in his book. He ranks four necessities of survival starting from the most important: shelter, water, fire, and food. "That leaves shelter as the most critical necessity in a survival situation. And with good reason. A person stranded in a harsh environment without adequate protection may not live more than a few hours" (Brown, 1983, 23).

According to John Wiseman, "The main elements of survival are Food, Fire, Shelter, Water, Navigation and Medicine. To put these in order of priority we use the acronym **PLAN**. No matter where you are in the world this will never change be it the Arctic, desert, jungle, sea or seashore" (Wiseman, 2009, 15). His acronym PLAN breaks down as follows (the main essentials are in parenthesis): 1) P – Protection (shelter and fire); 2) L – Location (emergency signals); 3) A – Acquisition (water and food); and 4) N – Navigation (Wiseman, 2009, 15).

Cody Lundin also helped shape the above order of essentials. He wrote, "The first and most obvious survival skill is keeping yourself alive in the face of a life-threatening emergency. Regulating core body temperature, keeping it at 98.6 degrees F (37 degrees C), is a prime concern" (Lundin, 2007, 12). Lundin also lists a pyramid of needs in the following order: 1) positive attitude; 2) clothing, oxygen, sleep, and water; 3) food, shelter, and sanitation; 4) lighting and first aid; 5) communications; 6) cooking; and 7) transportation (Lundin, 2007, 65).

Peter Kummerfeldt also stresses that life-threatening emergencies should be at the top of the survival essentials list: "Survival begins with being able to cope with the injuries sustained in the accident and then satisfying the other basic survival needs – protection, hydration, warmth, etc. If you can't stop the blood squirting out of your arm, the need for shelters, fire and signaling are immaterial!" (Kummerfeldt, 2006, 51).

The first edition of the US Naval Institute's legendary survival book also offers us some insight on the topic: "Water is the most important single factor in determining survival. Without it, the presence or absence of food is of little importance. You can survive many days without food if you have water" (Aviation Training Division, 1943, 40). Further, it states, "The ability to provide yourself with adequate shelter will increase your chances of surviving and greatly reduce your physical hardships. *Shelter and sleep are as necessary to a stranded man as food and water. You will tire as quickly from loss of sleep as you will from lack of food*" (Aviation Training Division, 1943, 122). As shown below, the order of a person's survival priorities was only slightly changed by the time of the book's fourth edition many years later. This later edition states, "Although there is no one predetermined set of priorities that applies to every situation, the following order applies to many: (1) Render first aid (2) Prepare signaling devices (3) Procure water (4) Find or build a shelter (5) Procure food (6) Prepare to travel, if necessary" (Craighead and Craighead, 1984, 13).

Their comments are very similar to those of the US Army *Survival* field manual: "A knowledge of field skills, including woodcraft, firemaking, food and water sources, shelter devices, and navigational techniques is necessary for survival" (US Department of the Army, 1970, 4). Further, it states, "The Greek philosopher Miletus was obviously thinking of survival when he declared, "The first of things is water." He couldn't have been more correct. Without water your chances of living are nil, and all the food in the area means nothing" (US Department of the Army, 1970, 47).

Stephen Corry, an anthropologist and the longtime director of Survival International, states, "We need few things to live: water and food; some shelter; and the sense of purpose and fulfilment from relationships" (Corry, 2011, 45). Les Stroud uses four major essentials, called *elements of survival*, to judge various survival situations listed in his book *Will to Live*: knowledge, luck, kit, and the will to live. Also, Dr. Ron Hood, a popular survivalist who owned survival.com (one of the first survival websites), gives some additional insight into survival priorities in his famous survival videos *Survival Basics I & II: The Adventure*. In the second chapter of the first volume, "Shelter is Important," Hood discusses the survival priority based on what he calls "the rule of threes." That is, in a survival situation, you have about three minutes to survive without air; about three hours to survive without shelter; about three days to survive without water; and about three weeks to survive without food (*Survival Basics I & II: The Adventure*, 2004).

Finally, Ray Mears's list of bushcraft essentials includes the outfit, cutting tools, water, fire, shelter, and cordage (this last one is often underappreciated). Mears also put together a list of essentials that should be in one's outfit for wilderness travel. It includes something to carry your outfit in; something to sleep under; something to sleep in; something to sleep on; navigational equipment; something to cook over; something to cook in; something to carry water; a mug; eating utensils; food; medical kit; illumination at night; wash kit; odds and ends to make life comfortable – 'possibles'; and clothing (Mears, 2003, 11).

My categorization of the survival essentials was derived from reflecting on the essentials mentioned in various sources in addition to some of my own contributions. For example, very few people have mentioned the importance of blood circulation in survival. However, I have discovered the priority of this essential the hard way—from my training in Brazilian jiu-jitsu where neck chokes are commonly used to force your opponent to submit. In this combat sport, it is not uncommon to witness a person (or to experience it personally) going to sleep in seconds from what is called a *circulatory choke*. If the choke were to continue in a real-life combat situation, the person can die in minutes or less due to the lack of blood flow to the brain. Due to the interrelation between the brain, heart, and lungs, it may be hard to determine at death what was more important: breathing or blood circulation. Simply, if the brain shuts down, the body will follow. For the purposes of this book though, it is easier to rank them as equally important.

Thermal balance was listed in the primary physical immediate survival essentials instead of clothing and shelter because it is the more crucial universal aspect of human survival. Clothing and shelter are listed by many survivalists as important, which they certainly are in the majority of situations. However, the real problem is regulating our core body temperature at the average normal human body temperature of 98.6 degrees (hence the title of Cody Lundin's first book, noted in chapter 5). Peter Kummerfeldt properly titles this concept "thermal balance," and that term is used here. It is important to remember that clothing and shelter are just a few of the ways that we can achieve this balance. In a tropical setting, humans can sleep without clothes or shelter as their own body heat may be sufficient (as in the ways of the ancient Australians).

It is worth noting that high quality air, food, sleep, and water should be striven for as the quality of those essentials will make a big difference to one's survival compared to those of inferior quality. For example, you can end up very ill quickly if you drink water that includes a harmful microorganism—such as a parasite. This same problem would happen if you were hungry and ate a deadly poisonous mushroom by accident. That is why the selection process as well as the use of heat to prepare food and water can be lifesaving.

Conservation of energy was listed as a primary physical immediate survival essential because it follows the same rationale as the need for food. Food gives us energy. However, if you use little energy and eat nothing, it may result in a more favorable circumstance then using too much energy and eating something. The whole situation must be looked at in terms of two ways to maintain your energy: conserving it and obtaining more. A survivor of the Stalinist terror of the Gulag demonstrated the significance of energy conservation: "He learned crucial survival skills, especially the fine art of faking work by "creat[ing] the illusion of activity" and thereby marshaling his energy" (Jones, 2011, 201).

Next, for the sake of brevity, we will analyze only some of our secondary physical immediate survival essentials. First, beauty may also be viewed as a survival essential because it can equip a person with a sexually desirable trait that may make others want to help keep her alive (this falls under the topic of sexual selection that we will discuss in part 3). Second, companionship is also an important essential. The survivors from the Uruguayan rugby team had to deal with the aftereffects of isolation. Read observes, "They had noticed from the very first two symptoms among them—first the compulsion to talk and second a dread of being left alone" (Read, 2005, 344). *Survivorman's* Les Stroud would understand this subject best because he does all his survival footage alone. Commenting on the nature of group survival, particularly in regard to the Uruguayan rugby team, Stroud says, "This certainly caused some tension between the remaining survivors, but if I had my choice, I'd take the tension of group survival over the loneliness of solo survival any day" (Stroud, 2010, 55).

Third, many may consider sex to be something that they can't live without, which is the reason that it was put on this list. However, the reason that sexual activity was not listed as a primary physical essential is because, contrary to common thinking, it is not necessary for the very immediate survival of an individual. It is instead necessary for the survival of humanity. It is also important to note that many of the survivors mentioned in this book have observed that sex was barely contemplated when the struggle included starvation; instead, food became the obsession. For example, as noted by Frankl of the people in the concentration camp, "Undernourishment, besides being the cause of the general preoccupation with food, probably also explains the fact that the sexual urge was generally absent" (Frankl, 2006, 32). Our bodies need energy to make their systems run properly before they can spend it on reproductive matters. In short, we will keep sex on the list to appease the critics. However, this matter is very subjective.

Let's now turn to an analysis of our primary mental immediate survival essentials. These essentials work in cooperation with acquiring the primary physical immediate survival essentials. Viktor Frankl lists a purpose to live as crucial: "There is nothing in the world, I venture to say, that would so effectively help one to survive even the worst conditions as the knowledge that there is a meaning in one's life" (Frankl, 2006, 103–104).

Tom Brown Jr. lists attitude as the most important survival essential. He even makes it the subject of his first chapter before he gets into the other essentials noted above. Brown wrote, "It is truly said that the most important survival tool is the mind. But to keep the mind functioning smoothly, you must establish and maintain a positive attitude" (Brown, 1983, 13). Bear Grylls has a similar message: "**The message is that attitude is king and the greatest resource we have is inside of us all.** Pack the right skills, and the right attitudes, and you don't need much else" (Grylls, 2012, 63).

This theme is continued with Cody Lundin: "Perhaps the greatest survival skill of all is the ability to maintain harmony in the feelings in the face of seeming chaos" (Lundin, 2007, 430). Attitude is also the key to survival as a US Navy SEAL. Chris Kyle says, "Getting through BUD/S and being a SEAL is more about mental toughness than anything else. Being stubborn and refusing to give in is the key to success. Somehow I'd stumbled onto the winning formula" (Kyle, 2013, 29).

The will to live was consistently mentioned by many survivalists to be essential. According to John Wiseman, *"You can have all the knowledge and kit in the world but without the will to live you can still perish"* (Wiseman, 2009, 10). The US Army *Survival* field manual provides some great insight into this topic: "The experiences of hundreds of servicemen isolated during World War II and Korean combat prove that survival is largely a matter of mental outlook, with the will to survive the deciding factor. Whether with a group or alone, you will experience emotional problems resulting from fear, despair, loneliness, and boredom. In addition to these mental hazards, injury and pain, fatigue, hunger, or thirst, tax your will to live. If you are not prepared mentally to overcome all obstacles and accept the worst, the chances of coming out alive are greatly reduced" (US Department of the Army, 1970, 4).

Putting a purpose to live as the first priority was a decision reached after much research and personal reflection. My conclusions are consistent with Viktor Frankl's, which I discussed in chapter 6. To understand this better, let's reflect on the following hypothetical example. Imagine if the most peaceful animal in the world (select any animal of your choice) were to be backed into a corner by someone who appeared like he was going to attack her. Now imagine if he did the same thing with two of her children present. Most people would probably agree that by threatening to attack a creature's children would provoke a more severe reaction from the prey than attacking just the parent alone. Her children may be the reason that she wants to live. She may care more about them than about her own life.

Having a purpose to live might create and strengthen the will to live. In turn, this might create the ideal psychological state. Reflect on this: Why would anyone desire to live if he can't find at least one reason? The difficulty you may have in answering this tough question is why I ranked having a purpose to live higher than a will to live. *Simply, someone who wants to live must have a reason for it, regardless of what it is. In contrast, someone with a reason to live might still not want to live.* Maybe the reason is just not good enough! There are countless examples of people who have given up on life when there were many reasons for them not to. In short, having a purpose to live makes an individual better prepared to deal with any struggle; consequently, the desire to live may then occur.

Learning about survival is absolutely unnecessary without having a purpose and a desire to live. Simply, what good is finding food, shelter, water, or anything else if someone doesn't want to be alive anymore? **Thus, obtaining any of the survival essentials is irrelevant if a person doesn't have a reason or the will to live. These two items are unquestionably the most important survival essentials.**

Knowledge of how to manage each struggle is crucial to overcoming it. Without the proper knowledge, a person can die helplessly when a simple solution may have been present. For example, a person who is lost in the woods only a few miles from civilization can figure out how to get home if she knows basic navigational techniques, perhaps orienting herself by the sun. If not, a mountain can be made out of a molehill, and the problem can escalate into death.

Next, for the sake of brevity, we will look at only some of our secondary mental immediate survival essentials. Humor was mentioned because it is an often neglected method of diffusing many survival situations. Frankl mentioned this as a technique used by many of the prisoners in the concentration camps. Interestingly, Stephen Corry mentions humor as a method used by many tribal societies to avoid conflict: "The use of self-deprecating laughter to diffuse tension, particularly following an exchange that is critical or could lead to an argument, is a common technique that small-scale societies use to avoid internal discord – which is one of their main concerns" (Corry, 2011, 201).

Apathy, or a lack of emotions, is another essential from this list worth noting, although it may only be valid in certain circumstances. It held much value as noted by Frankl in his depiction of the concentration camps during World War II: "Apathy, the main symptom of the second phase, was a necessary mechanism of self-defense. Reality dimmed, and all efforts and all emotions were centered on one task: preserving one's own life and that of the other fellow" (Frankl, 2006, 28). Ironically, apathy may help the body to avoid feeling any more mental pain, which may be highly useful after experiencing excessive levels of degradation and after witnessing too much death.

Finally, many survivors that I studied found relief in spirituality. A belief in a higher power enabled them to be very successful against their struggles. This was evident when the Uruguayan rugby team survivors went to mass after being rescued: "In all the weeks that they had waited for this day, never for a moment had they lost their faith in Him; never had they doubted His love or His approval of their desperate and ugly struggle to survive" (Read, 2005, 363).

The Essential Survival Tools

We will now look at our *essential survival tools*, which are sometimes referred to by survivalists as *the survival kit*. The following is a small sample of the major essential survival tools needed in a survival situation. These various tools are meant to help someone attain the immediate survival essentials needed to survive. Note that every survival situation and every environment may call for a unique set of tools. This section is highly subjective but is provided for a better general understanding. Some examples of essential survival tools include, but are not limited to, an ax; a bag; a bed; a blanket; books; clothing; a communication means (sometimes called signaling); a container; a cooking pot; cord; disinfectant; kitchenware; a knife; lighting sources; a means to start and maintain a fire; a medical kit; money; music; navigational equipment; security; shelter; a transportation means; a wash kit; weaponry; and other miscellaneous personal items that can increase the potential survivor's odds of staying alive during a survival situation.

Finally, we will conclude this chapter with a short analysis of the essential survival tools. Every survivalist studied has unique preferences for what to include in a survival kit, which may be linked to his specialized survival environment. I will mention just a few examples. First, for Ray Mears, "The knife is your number one tool, with which you can make almost anything you need, cut up food or craft beautiful objects" (Mears, 2003, 26). John Wiseman agrees, "A knife is your most important survival tool" (Wiseman, 2009, 12).

Mors Kochanski prefers the ax, which may be very useful where he lives in the northern wilderness of Canada. He wrote, *"The axe is the most important of the basic bush tools. Outside of fire, little else can contribute more to living comfortably in the wilderness than knowing how to properly use a well-chosen axe"* (Kochanski, 1987, 71). Some of the other tools highly ranked by many survivalists have already been listed above, such as clothing and shelter. These two items are very important; however, similar to other essential survival tools, their usefulness depends on the situation.

CHAPTER 13

Part 1 Summary

In part 1, we discussed so much about survival and its related science of survivalism. We started with an analysis of survival terminology including terms like *survival, survivalism, survivor,* and so forth. We also analyzed the qualities of life and death and their definitions. Chapter 5 included an analysis of survival literature before and after the modern survivalism movement began around the mid-twentieth century. Modern survivalism can be linked to the unique survival issues than many militaries faced during World War II. The publication of *How to Survive on Land and Sea* by the US Naval Institute became a foundation for countless survival books that appeared later.

The question "Why survive?" was also addressed in chapter 6. This chapter was analyzed from the perspective of a great contributor to this field of inquiry, Viktor Frankl. In short, people want to survive because of a personal reason that they may have, whether that reason is love for their work, something or someone, or the struggle itself. These three reasons appear to be the most common, but others may also exist.

I also provided many different survival examples. From these examples, we can conclude that survival depends on the person and the situation. Someone can be an expert in one area of survival (or many areas) but may not be able to survive in others. Hence, learning survivalism is a continuous process that the true survivalist should approach from a comprehensive perspective. Someone's odds of survival should increase if she can master additional areas of survivalism. As we saw in chapters 8 through 10, an almost unlimited supply of survival struggles and scenarios could arise in many conditions and places. Thus, the *ultimate universal survivor* would have to be able to survive any struggle in any scenario in any environment, civilized or wild. You will see in parts 3, 4, and 5 that the human species is in the best position to accomplish this feat.

Finally, we analyzed the various survival essentials. I created a new organized model with two major categories of survival essentials: immediate survival essentials and essential survival tools. The immediate survival essentials are broken into physical and mental as well as primary and secondary subcategories. The primary immediate survival essentials, both physical and mental, are the most important essentials of any survival scenario. Without them, death is inevitable! Further, a purpose to live and a will to live are the most important survival essentials. Collectively, all survival essentials should be considered our most important forms of wealth to be managed, which leads us directly to the next part of this book.

In part 2, we will explore the relationship that survivalism has with economics and finance. As we shall see, the three sciences and their goals are deeply interrelated.

PART 2
Understanding the Relationship
between Economics, Finance, and Survivalism

CHAPTER 14

Survival: The Root of Economics and Finance

The Necessity of Survival

In my first book, *The Necessity of Finance*, I posed a serious question: "**Understanding finance is about maximizing one's chance of survival. What is more important than learning how to survive?**" (Criniti, 2013, 58). This question persistently lingered in my mind with such great strength that it became one of the driving forces for me to write this book. Some more questions eventually surfaced. For starters, if studying finance and survival are necessary, then how exactly are they connected? Which one of them is more important? Part 2 is a reflection of my many inquiries into this subject. I realized that if I truly wanted to better understand the necessity of economics and finance, then first I must understand their relationship to the necessity of survivalism.

In part 1, I demonstrated that staying alive is a major part of the definition and goal of survival. Further, studying survival should be a requirement for any living thing that has a reason and a desire to keep living. The first thing that any living organism must learn from the moment it becomes a member of Club Life is how to survive. If it doesn't learn how to survive, especially in its local environment, then it may die quickly.

So to provide a clear answer to the above question, originally left rhetorical several years ago: **absolutely nothing is more important than learning how to survive**. How could there be? Well, there is actually one exception. In chapter 12, I mentioned that if someone does not have a purpose and a desire to live, then learning about survival is absolutely unnecessary. Thus, for those people, survival is not important at all. However, the paradox is that the survival goal becomes absolutely necessary for everyone with a purpose and a will to live. Even his personal purpose for living cannot be more important than learning survival because he may never fulfill it if he dies.

For example, a mother may never be able to realize her purposes in life—to stay alive for her children and her work—if she doesn't survive. In this case, if she doesn't know how to survive, then her children will become parentless, and her work will become unfulfilled. Survival must always be the priority! All of the various survival essentials listed in chapter 12 serve the united purpose of helping you to survive. Survival itself becomes the ultimate necessity, which all other essentials must bow down to. *Simply put, at the most basic level, everything must subordinate to the goal of survival.*

If you don't agree with what has been said in this chapter so far, then I don't encourage you to read this book any further, as many of its major points derive from this conclusion. If you do agree with the necessity of survival and its science of survivalism, then it is time to build off this foundation!

The Role of Wealth in Survival

In order to understand survivalism's relationship to finance, we must first review what wealth is. Net wealth has many definitions. However, a basic one that is commonly agreed on (and the definition that will be used in this book) is that it is the net worth of various entities: financial entities (individuals, groups, or organizations), economic entities (nations or their divisions), or other prosperous entities introduced later. Net worth is simply the sum of the various components of wealth on a balance sheet—that is, the entity's total assets (everything it owns) minus its total liabilities (everything it owes). A positive result is good, and a negative result is bad. (A negative result translates to insolvency.)

It is common practice in the financial industry to include a variety of things that we own in the "assets" section of any balance sheet. In this section, items may include, but are not limited to, accounts receivables, bonds, cash, collectibles, goodwill, real estate, stocks, and even intellectual property (any product of the human intellect protected by law). The ownership of these items generally carries with them certain legal rights. Thus, these various components of wealth are not only recognized in economics and finance but also in other subjects, for example, law.

If you also agree that commonly accepted economic and financial assets are a part of wealth, such as the examples noted above, then it should be easier for you to also view the survival essentials listed in chapter 12 as wealth. Certainly at a basic level, most economists and financialists would agree that most (or all) of those essentials are wealth. Those items could be listed in monetary terms on a regular balance sheet as long as they can hold value, which shouldn't be a problem, especially in a survival emergency. Everything tangible in the list of essentials would probably avoid the most criticism—for example, shelter, which many people already consider to be an investment called *real estate*. Further, most people would agree that other tangibles, such as clothing, food, and water, are also valuable assets.

Some survival essentials may encounter more criticism though when they are described as wealth. This would be especially true for those that deal with internal wealth, for example, a purpose to live. Oddly, some may argue that these essentials don't hold any value. I take a different stance. **If something is undoubtedly a survival essential, it should be one of the most valuable assets, regardless of whether or not it is commonly accepted as one**. Simply, at a comprehensive level, it is better to include all of an entity's assets into its wealth, even debatable ones, to maximize its understanding of its economic or financial health.

Some elements of the mind are already widely accepted as wealth, for example, different types of intellectual property. Knowledge is agreed to be very valuable in the real world. This fact is generally accepted by as many industries as the intellectual property lawyers have penetrated. Some examples of very valuable forms of intellectual property include copyrights, patents, and trademarks. In this regard, few disagree that wealth can also be found internally. The disagreement begins on the aspects of mental capabilities that should not be included as wealth. The most complete perspective on wealth though should include anything valuable, both internal and external.

I think even the toughest critics may agree that the majority of survival essentials are also considered forms of wealth compared to an average balance sheet's total asset column. *If it can be accepted that the survival essentials are wealth, then it should not be hard to understand that survivalism shares the same common denominator that links economics with finance—that is, wealth management. Managing these survival essentials is necessary to manage the present struggle to stay alive.* Let's review the definition of finance to better understand this connection.

In *The Necessity of Finance, finance* was defined as "**the science of management of wealth for an individual, a group, or an organization**" (Criniti, 2013, 10). On the other hand, *economics* was viewed for the first time as a separate science by defining it as "**the science of management of wealth for a nation or a division of a nation**" (Criniti, 2013, 15). The major goal of finance is to continuously maximize wealth for financial entities while the major goal of economics is to continuously maximize wealth for economic entities. The obvious correlation between the two sciences is that they both deal with managing wealth. However, the main difference pertains to whose wealth is being managed. As concluded above, survival also involves management of wealth, particularly our survival essentials. **Thus, in short, economics, finance, and survivalism all have to do with managing wealth.** With this general relationship built between the three sciences, it is important to demonstrate now the detailed linkage by resurfacing the concept of prosperity.

Prosperity Overview

Prosperity is a term that has been misunderstood by many for ages, even by many economists. If managing wealth is the main road shared by these three sciences—economics, finance, and survivalism—then prosperity is the bridge that connects them. In casual conversation, prosperity is generally lumped together with survival such as with the common expression "survive and prosper" (or sometimes stated as "survive and thrive"). Beyond the notion that prosperity has some connection with survival, the rest of its term is generally ambiguous. To understand its usage better, let's first look at some examples of what it is not!

First, the Donner Party and the Uruguayan rugby team in the moments of their struggles would not be considered prosperous. If anything, they were using all of their energy and resources available to survive. Some of the survivors would later become prosperous, but few people would disagree that prosperity would not have been the proper term to describe them during their historic moments of struggle. Second, a soldier in the middle of a war is not prosperous as he is fighting the enemy just to stay alive. Lastly, a starving family without any money for food would not be considered prosperous. If anything, it is a small group operating in survival mode.

In chapter 3, prosperity was mentioned briefly. It is time to recall the highlights of that section. **As stated previously,**

prosperity is the progressive state after successful survival that occurs through an accumulation of wealth. In other words, prosperity is an extension of survival; it is a better way to survive. This step happens after an entity passes the stage of survival and starts *accumulating* wealth in addition to what is absolutely required at the moment. This extra accumulation of wealth is the key feature that pulls someone out of survival mode.

Many degrees of prosperity are possible for an entity. At the lowest level, a survivor is just past the edge of survival with very few assets to account for beyond the fact that it is still alive. It may even dip back and forth between the survival and prosperity stage on a regular basis, which may occur so much that it is often difficult to distinguish which state it is in. However, the difference between survival and prosperity progressively becomes more apparent at the higher levels of prosperity.

To organize prosperity better, I present the following schematics for your convenience. In short, survival is the first step before prosperity begins, as it is a qualifying preliminary test for an entity. The actual process of prosperity then includes four more steps. This pattern will now be called the *Survival-Prosperity Sequence* (see Exhibit 14.1). Please keep in mind that this is a general framework that may vary depending on one's survival situation. **The steps of prosperity, in order, are as follows: 1) accumulate a short-term emergency reserve of survival essentials; 2) accumulate a long-term emergency reserve of survival essentials; 3) accumulate luxury items; and 4) expand and/or merge with other entities to create a larger, united entity.**

Exhibit 14.1

The Survival-Prosperity Sequence

These steps are listed in chronological order, but the order may vary in some circumstances. They occur in each Major Scientific Phase of Prosperity for each newly created entity.

The Survival-Prosperity Sequence = The Survival Test + The Four Steps of Prosperity

1. The Survival Test: The preliminary test before a new Major Scientific Phase of Prosperity begins. It is focused only on managing the present struggle to stay alive.
2. Prosperity Step 1: Accumulate a short-term emergency reserve of survival essentials. Each Major Scientific Phase of Prosperity begins here.
3. Prosperity Step 2: Accumulate a long-term emergency reserve of survival essentials.
4. Prosperity Step 3: Accumulate luxury items (there are two major types).
   a. Accumulate *luxurious survival essentials*: any survival essentials that are made beyond what is necessary.
   b. Accumulate *luxurious nonessentials*: any assets that are entirely unnecessary for survival.
5. Prosperity Step 4: Expand and/or merge with other entities to create a larger, united entity. Each Major Scientific Phase of Prosperity ends after this step. However, the last step is

omitted in the final Major Scientific Phase of Prosperity. This new entity must survive before being promoted to the next Major Scientific Phase of Prosperity. The steps of prosperity would begin again, and the sequence would continue.

First, an entity should accumulate a short-term emergency reserve of survival essentials immediately after survival (generally enough to last for up until twelve months). This will ensure that it has all of the basics covered to deal with whatever struggles that may arise over the next year. This is especially applicable in places with a very cold winter. Winter is a time when access to essentials is usually the most difficult to obtain, thus, preparation can be a life saver. Bears, beavers, and squirrels are examples of other animals that prepare well for the tough months to come. We can learn much from them!

The next step in prosperity for an entity is to accumulate a long-term emergency reserve of survival essentials (generally enough to last for at least one year to as many years as possible). The entity should ensure that it strengthens its shelter and increases its storage of clothing, food, tools, and everything else that will keep it surviving better for many years. This step requires extreme planning and saving. As you can tell so far, the first two steps of prosperity are starting to sound very familiar—like economics and finance. We are talking about setting up an emergency reserve for the short- and long-terms while mentioning key buzzwords like "planning" and "saving." If you made this observation, you will soon discover that you are correct.

The third step in prosperity includes accumulating what is commonly called "luxury items." Lack of these items will probably have no effect on our ability to stay alive now or in the future (although many who have become dependent on them may disagree). However, luxury items are assets that may help to increase the quality of life. This category of assets can be broken into two parts. First, *luxurious survival essentials* are any survival essentials that are made beyond what is necessary. For example, a large, four-story stone mansion with two separate garages and a swimming pool is a luxury. A simple, small brick house might have been sufficient.

The second category of luxury items is *luxurious nonessentials*, which refer to any assets that are entirely unnecessary for survival. That is, even the basic level of that asset (without the bells and whistles) is not essential to survival. You can usually find many examples of these items cluttered throughout a hoarder's house. Thus, in this case, these nonessentials are actually an impediment to survival because someone may get hurt by accidentally tripping over them.

Finally, the last step in prosperity occurs when an entity expands and/or merges with other entities to create a larger, united entity. *This new entity must then survive before being promoted to the next Major Scientific Phase of Prosperity (discussed below). The Four Steps of Prosperity would then begin again and the sequence would continue.*

Now that we have analyzed prosperity from a micro-level by listing its individual steps, we are now going to look at it from a macro-level. Prosperity can be segregated into five major phases with each phase having its own science (see Exhibit 14.2). **These Five Major Scientific Phases of Prosperity are listed in chronological order as follows: finance (starting first with personal finance and then with group finance), economics, planetonomics (pertains to the planet, but in our case it will be called Earthonomics), and universonomics.** All of these phases share a common denominator—that is, managing wealth to maximize it; however, they are different in their foci. The focus shifts to a larger entity as prosperity advances in each phase.

Exhibit 14.2

The Five Major Scientific Phases of Prosperity

These phases are listed in chronological order, but the order may vary in some circumstances. Each science's respective entity needs to advance through the Survival-Prosperity Sequence before being promoted to a higher phase. The entity begins each phase with Prosperity Step 1 after passing the Survival Test.

1. *Phase 1: Personal Finance*: The science of management of wealth for an individual (called a financial entity).
2. *Phase 2: Group Finance*: The science of management of wealth for a group or an organization (also called a financial entity).
3. *Phase 3: Economics*: The science of management of wealth for a nation or its divisions (called an economic entity). Humanity is currently in Phase 3 and may be approaching Phase 4 soon.
4. *Phase 4: Planetonomics*: The science of management of wealth for a planet. For our planet, the science is specifically called *Earthonomics*.
5. *Phase 5: Universonomics*: The science of management of wealth for the universe.

The following is a brief overview of the Five Major Scientific Phases of Prosperity. Please note that these concepts will be expanded further in various parts of this text. In the first and second phases, *finance* **is the science of management of wealth for financial entities,** as noted above. In the third phase, *economics* **is the science of management of wealth for economic entities,** which generally occurs with a larger population increase. The fourth phase is relevant to a new science that was created in my second book: *The Most Important Lessons in Economics and Finance.* That is, **Earthonomics is the science of management of wealth for our planet.** All nations would need to be operating together in unison to make this occur. This is a phase that we have not reached yet but are hopefully getting closer to. It is worth noting that Earthonomics is a form of planetonomics: the science of management of wealth for a planet. Hopefully, the points made in parts 3 and 4 will demonstrate its possibilities.

Finally, the fifth phase may sound more like science fiction. The term used to describe this phase and its respective science is new to this book. That is, *universonomics* may be the phase that we will enter within the next few hundred years. *Universonomics* **is the science of management of wealth for the universe.** If many humans' dreams are fulfilled, the whole universe may one day be colonized and managed in the same way that a nation is today. This is the ultimate phase of prosperity, as we will be able to have access to the widest range of places and resources (and hence wealth) to manage. Please note that there may be many additional phases that could be included between Phases 4 and 5 (for example, the management of wealth for various solar systems, galaxies, and so forth). However, it is unnecessary to make these distinctions at this time. I know this may sound a bit far-fetched, so please don't fall off your seat—we haven't even made it to part 3 yet! With prosperity thus clarified, it is time to revisit the connection between survivalism and finance.

The Root of Prosperity

To recall, the Survival-Prosperity Sequence must repeat itself in every Major Scientific Phase of Prosperity for each newly formed entity (see Exhibit 14.3). Additionally, each of these phases of prosperity begins right after the survival step, which is equivalent to an initial test applied to each entity. If each entity can survive, and hence pass the initial test, then it will be allowed to enter the next Major Scientific Phase of Prosperity to climb its steps of prosperity. With this information, we can now make some conclusions!

The first conclusion that we can make is that personal finance is an extension of survival as it is the first Major Scientific Phase of Prosperity that begins immediately after the very first Survival Test. In other words, survival must be the true root of finance. Second, if the prior statement is true, then survival must be the root of all other Major Scientific Phases of Prosperity, including group finance and economics. Finally, if all of these phases are in chronological order, then all earlier phases are also precursors to the later phases. This may seem obvious, but it has startling conclusions that should be acknowledged. For example, this means that unofficially, finance must have come before economics (even though economics was obviously created first in an official academic sense). The enormous implications of this statement may turn both fields on their heads. This is also the first time that I have mentioned this conclusion in any of my books, so it needs more elaboration to be understood. I will demonstrate this more in the next section, but first I would like to explain the first two conclusions above in more depth.

Exhibit 14.3

The Survival-Prosperity Sequence
Incorporated into the Five Major Scientific Phases of Prosperity

As mentioned in part 1, survivalism is the science of the management of the present struggle to stay alive for a living entity. It was noted earlier in this chapter that the survival essentials, especially those mentioned in chapter 12, are a form of wealth that must be managed properly in order to meet the goals of survival. We can now put these statements together to see the big picture clearly. **The extended definition of survivalism is the science of the management of the *present struggle* to stay alive (through the management of wealth) for a living entity.** The parentheses in the extended definition indicate what was added. Wealth has now found a home in survivalism!

What we did to survivalism, we can now do to finance. **The extended definition of finance is the science of (the management of *all struggles* to stay alive through) the management of wealth for a (living) financial entity.** We can now do the same with economics. **The extended definition of economics is the science of (the management of *all struggles* to stay alive through) the management of wealth for a (living) economic entity.** Again, the parentheses in these extended definitions enclose what was added to the original definitions. By answering the question "how" in the original definition of survivalism and "why" in the original definitions of finance and economics, as shown in the parentheses in the above statements, we can see that all three sciences have almost the same comprehensive definitions. Thus, the connection between them all is becoming more obvious.

Let's take a closer look at the changes made in the extended definitions above. First, for the extended definition of survival, all that was added was the statement "through the management of wealth." Everything else was kept in place. There is not much more to elaborate on here, as the general logic behind this was demonstrated earlier in this chapter. However, the majority of part 2 will demonstrate specifically how managing wealth properly can lead to not only meeting survival goals but also the goals of the various Major Scientific Phases of Prosperity.

Next, there have been some additions to (but no deletions of) the original definitions when forming the extended definitions of finance and economics. First, "the management of all struggles to stay alive through" was added to answer the question of why we are managing wealth. This slight change puts these definitions on the same playing field as survivalism. This point was never directly stated in the definitions in my earlier books, and, to my knowledge, this point may never have been directly stated in any economics or finance book for that matter. However, in this book, the full rationale must be stated in order to make the connection to survival.

In short, the real reason that wealth is managed for economic and financial entities is to ensure that they stay alive. It is not done for fun, although it can be, or for any other reasons. Additionally, although luxury can be a consequence of excellent wealth management, it is not the major reason for it. The main reason that wealth is managed is to protect us from death, both now and later. More on this in a moment!

Also, the word "living" was added to the extended definitions of finance and economics to note that wealth is being managed for living financial or economic entities. This point is best illustrated with Principle 163 from my second book: "*You can't take your wealth with you when you die*" (Criniti, 2014, 196). Living entities are the ones who manage their wealth, which is best understood by examining the process of estate planning. The deceased's assets are collected by the appropriate living beneficiaries, whether they are individuals or governments. The beneficiaries' duty is to determine the appropriate distribution of the deceased's assets. The dead does not need his wealth anymore as he is now in a state indifferent to surviving and prospering.

Next, one major change was made from the extended definition of survivalism to those of prosperity. The phrase "the present struggle" in the definition of survivalism was changed to "all struggles" in the definitions of finance and economics. In general, to survive, a living entity confronts one deadly hardship at a time. In other words, survival is situational. If you look at the examples of various struggles presented in chapter 8, you will see that they are generally isolated events. It would be rare that a few, let alone many, of those struggles would happen at exactly the same moment. However, sometimes several struggles may happen almost simultaneously in one survival scenario, such as an earthquake, a fire, and a lack of shelter, respectively. In this scenario, you would have to survive each one of them in chronological order.

The above example illustrates a major issue: your attention is always limited to 100 percent in any single moment. Thus, your chances of survival drop when there are more struggles that you must confront alone in any present moment, especially without the right technology. Prosperity acknowledges and embraces this human limitation. Ideally, wealth should be managed to protect an entity from all likely struggles in all phases of life, regardless of whether they happen now or in fifty years. Of course, the sciences of prosperity have not fully reached their ultimate aim yet, as many struggles still need to be better managed—for example, cancer. However, we progressively reduce or eliminate our struggles as our technology increases. This additional technology translates to more accumulated wealth that needs to be managed.

Wealth accumulation can lead to successfully managing multiple struggles even if they happen at the same time. Let's use the above survival scenario to demonstrate! A person can use technology to prepare, monitor, and alert for potential earthquakes. If one occurs and a person doesn't evacuate, then she may be protected in a structurally engineered building that can withstand even the strongest ground movements. If a fire begins while she is in the building, then she can be alerted by a smoke detector and possibly saved by a sprinkler system. If damage is done to her home, even total destruction, then her insurance may be able to pay her enough money so that she can find temporary shelter while rebuilding her new home (assuming she has the right policy and is paying her premiums). In this case, as in others, proper wealth management may have saved someone's life from these three different struggles, regardless of whether they occurred simultaneously. *In short, prosperity originates from survival, but it is more comprehensive because it requires managing wealth to combat any potential struggle at any time.* Additionally, sometimes in this book, the words *survive better* may be substituted for the word *prosperity*. This phrase is used as a matter of convenience, and it should not be an impediment to the existing framework presented here.

The extended definitions and logic are basically the same for the last two Major Scientific Phases of Prosperity. The only thing that is different than our previous definitions is that the living entity has changed. **The extended definition of planetonomics is the science of (the management of *all struggles* to stay alive through) the management of wealth for a (living) planetary entity.** For now, this only includes Earth, as in Earthonomics, but one day this science may include other individual planets as well. **Finally, the extended definition of universonomics is the science of (the management of *all struggles* to stay alive through) the management of wealth for a (living) universal entity.**

Let's now compare the major goal of survival to those of prosperity. To recall from chapter 3, the major goal of survival and survivalism is for a living entity to stay alive for the maximum desirable amount of time. Also, to recall from earlier in this chapter, the major goal of finance is to continuously maximize wealth for financial entities. We can now extend finance's goal the same way we extended its definition to compare it to survival. **The extended major goal of finance is to continuously maximize wealth for financial entities (in order to maximize both their desirable existence and their quality of life).** The words in parentheses indicate what has been added to reflect the answer to "why" wealth is being maximized. Make no mistake—the above answer is revolutionary in this field! The reason for wealth maximization has been inadequately addressed by modern academia. Let's break down this extended goal a little further.

To start, in survival mode, one usually has minimal quantities of survival essentials, if any at all. A survival candidate has little time to spend on accumulating wealth beyond the bare minimum needed for that survival situation. The accumulation generally begins when conditions become more favorable. To be clear, survival does not have to do with accumulating wealth beyond the basic survival essentials that the struggle demands.

Like survival, finance has to do with staying alive for the maximum desirable amount of time, but the difference is in the approach. As noted above, generally speaking, survival emphasizes staying alive for one struggle at a time. Although the ultimate aim is longevity beyond the struggle and possibly to an old age, it is the current crisis that demands the entity's undivided attention. On the other hand, all Major Scientific Phases of Prosperity, including finance, approach maximizing one's desirable existence from a comprehensive perspective. That is, *all* struggles must be planned for, both those that might occur *now* and those that might occur in the *future*.

Finally, one of the biggest differences in the extended major goal of finance and the other phases of prosperity is that they aim at maximizing the quality of life. There is no time for obtaining luxuries in a real survival situation. A survivor knows that she needs to use whatever she has to help her to stay alive. In addition, she generally must work fast in the use of her survival essentials. The struggle does not wait for someone to be prepared; it comes on its own terms and when it is ready. A potential survivor must have good reaction time and be prepared to be handicapped without some or all of the conveniences that she may be accustomed to. **Luxury has no place in pure survival.**

On the other hand, prosperity does have plenty of room for luxury, as that is its third step (generally after the short- and long-term emergency reserves are adequately met). By maximizing wealth properly, a person is able to do more than just merely exist for a long period of time. In theory, one can live to one hundred years old or more in survival mode. However, this may be a tough, risky existence with little or no comfort. Instead, many people would prefer to have luxuries to help make their lives more enjoyable and safer.

The extended major goal of economics will be briefly discussed. That is, **the extended major goal of economics is to continuously maximize wealth for economic entities (in order to maximize both their desirable existence and their quality of life).** There is very little room in this extended definition for tyrannical dictators, like the many examples throughout history. In their cases, they were barely in the realm of economics. The real truth is that an elite ruling minority is only concerned with managing its own wealth, usually at the nation's expense. On the contrary, nations are most successful when all of their citizens are rewarded for the nations' success. This extended goal of economics demonstrates prosperity's focus on the short- and long-term living situation of its various entities. In short, intelligent economic managers should consider the effects of their decisions on the quality of life of the people for whom they are responsible, both now and later. This important, but often forgotten, detail is how nations can live longer!

The extended goals and logic are basically the same for the last two Major Scientific Phases of Prosperity. The only thing that is different than what has already been covered is that the living entity has changed. **The extended goal of planetonomics is to continuously maximize wealth for planetary entities (in order to maximize both their desirable existence and their quality of life).** For now, this goal is mainly concerned with our planet, as in Earthonomics, but one day this may include other individual planets as well. Finally, **the extended major goal of universonomics is to continuously maximize wealth for the universe (in order to maximize both its desirable existence and its quality of life).** Now, that is far out!

To summarize this section, none of the major goals of the Major Scientific Phases of Prosperity can be met without first addressing the major goal of survival. However, without focusing on prosperity, one would be in a continuous state of deep struggle to stay alive. In short, survival is the root from which prosperity grows. Once allowed to mature though, the tree of prosperity can provide the best solutions for staying alive both in the present and in the future!

The Parent of Economics

Prosperity should be thankful for the knowledge earned through survivalism. If our ancestors had never mastered how to survive, then you would not be reading this book, and I would not be writing it. They did survive though, and they eventually entered the first and second Major Scientific Phases of Prosperity. Humans learned well how to hunt and gather food and how to do small-scale agriculture. However, it was the implementation of full-scale agriculture that led to an extraordinary amount of excess wealth, which enabled society to feed and support many more people. The inevitable result of this was a population increase. It increased to the point where populations eventually grew to the size of a small nation. This leads to a major conclusion: individuals were managing their wealth long before the nation was even dreamed of. Not only were they managing it, but they were managing it successfully. ***That is, individuals had to have been in an advanced prosperous state in order to create the population size that was necessary to form a nation.***

To envision this point more clearly, I want you to think of Robinson Crusoe stranded alone on his island. In the book, he became a successful survivor and learned how to do everything on his own. Now let's pretend that his pal Friday was a female instead and that their individual prosperity led them to produce a family with ten children (in the tradition of early farmers). Let's also assume that Friday's original tribe was eventually found and that they decided to join Crusoe's island family. If the island were big enough, then the family's farming efforts, in addition to hunting and gathering, might have been sufficient for them to accumulate more wealth and advance further into prosperity. If all of their descendants were to prosper for many centuries in the same way, then eventually their population might grow extremely large.

It may be in everyone's best interest to create some form of a nation to maintain order if a large enough population level is reached. Although not all families and tribes have progressed equally and in the same manner, the general pattern is the same. Small numbers must become large numbers if they increase. Similarly, if individuals increase in number, assuming they stay united, they must eventually become some form of a nation. **This demonstrates that individual entities must be successful at maximizing their wealth before nations can be created to manage theirs.** As a large related family can only form from the initial pairing of two individuals, the logic is not much different from compounding a large family into a nation. Thus, it should be clear that finance must be the precursor to economics.

The above statement should not be taken lightly as it is a revolutionary conclusion. In *The Necessity of Finance*, I provided a brief history of economics and finance as taught in an academic sense. Officially, economics can be argued to have started in 1776, when Adam Smith published his famous book called *The Wealth of Nations*. However, many modern finance textbooks officially recognize finance to have begun in 1952 when Harry Markowitz first produced an article called "Portfolio Selection." Thus, officially, economics is generally considered to come before finance. But the order of events promulgated by academia does not always align with the order of events in reality.

It took my first book to show the world that finance is not a subscience of economics but is instead a completely separate science. This point deeply contradicts how finance is taught and even how its related Nobel Prize is delivered. Many financial pioneers have been awarded Nobel Prizes in economics only because there are none in finance. It is this book that now takes *The Necessity of Finance's* conclusions one step further: finance is the main trunk from which sprung the branch of economics.

I think economics owes finance a deep apology for the many years that finance was placed in its shadow. Hopefully, these conclusions may even penetrate the consciousness of those who award the Nobel Prize in Economics who may finally give finance the credit it deserves. This is not meant to undercut the importance of economics. No, never that! Economics and finance have a special synergy, and together they can change the world for the better. However, the above conclusions are meant to put finance in its proper position. **It's time to set the record straight: originally, finance came before economics.**

Actually, to take this analysis one step further, all Major Scientific Phases of Prosperity owe much to both survivalism and finance. Even if we make it to Phase 5 (that is, managing wealth on a universal level) one day, the individual will still be owed thanks for his earlier contributions to this highest level of prosperity!

The Necessity of Prosperity

We learned in the first part of this chapter that nothing is more important than learning survival. All of our actions, goals, and reasons to live must first serve the necessity of survival. If we cannot keep ourselves alive, then we cannot do anything else in this life. That means that if we don't survive then we can't help our family and friends or even spend time with them; we can't get that better job; we can't build that bigger house; we can't help out that charity; and we can't make this world a better place. Simply, we can't do anything unless we first stay alive.

A new question begs to be answered, considering this chapter's other conclusions, which might even change the answer to our original question. Where does this new knowledge position the necessity of prosperity now that a direct link has been made to survival? In other words, what is more important than prosperity? This is a more difficult question than that of survival's necessity. You see, a person can technically live to an old age entirely within the survival step. His goals may be no more than enjoying the company of his family and friends in the present moment without any concern for what struggles lie ahead. This person may not care about what happens next week or even tomorrow, and hence, never accumulate even a short-term emergency reserve. If he is lucky enough, his future struggles may not be too much to handle, and he may be allowed to live.

It is a much safer proposition to plan ahead to obtain prosperity while also considering the dangers of living life on the edge of survival. By planning and saving, an entity may be able to maximize wealth to protect itself against the risks of future struggles. Survival has to do with managing struggles to stay alive in the present. On the other hand, prosperity has to do with living a quality life now and in the future. It might not be as important as survival in the present, but it certainly could be as important, or even more important, in the future.

For example, let's pretend that five years from now, an isolated tribe detached from civilization was going to have to face the worst drought ever. If that tribe operates strictly in survival mode, then when the drought comes, it might be unprepared. Lack of preparation will have decreased its chances of surviving until the drought is over. However, if the tribe members plan ahead starting now, maybe by farming and storing five years of harvest, supplies, and water, they will be more prepared to endure the drought. The result equates to a significantly increased chance of staying alive. In this case and plenty of others, finance will have done more to save people's lives than even survivalism. It could have provided all of the required survival essentials in their deepest time of need.

Even the best survivalist with the biggest will to live may be unable to survive in the absence of proper preparation for the worst-case survival scenario. As you can see, prosperity is also about life and death, and we should not forget that it is an extension of survival. In the long-term, its sciences can also prove to be just as, or more, valuable than survivalism. **In short, if prosperity can keep us alive better than survivalism, at least from a future standpoint, then prosperity should be considered more important.**

This point is easier to illustrate when we look at personal finance, which is the first Major Scientific Phase of Prosperity and the only phase that deals exclusively with the smallest living entity: the individual. Few, if any, individuals in the world would prefer to live the rest of their lives just surviving day by day, enduring one deadly struggle after another. What fun is life without some enjoyment and peace of mind? Even if you do not care for the third step in prosperity, luxuries, you would probably agree that you should at least learn finance to protect your future survival needs by preparing both short- and long-term emergency reserves. If you can agree with this, then you must understand that what you agreed to includes the first two steps of prosperity. Hence, you are also agreeing to the necessity of prosperity, specifically as it applies to finance.

Further, it is also important to point out that without finance, aside from survivalism, no other science in its official academic form would have been created. This is a bold statement, but with some reflection, you will see it has much merit. Without proper wealth management, humans would have never reached prosperity! Without prosperity, we would not have any surplus survival essentials to supply to the specialists in exchange for their labor! Further, without specialists, we would not have any specialized scientists or their sciences!

That's right—without proper wealth management by our individual ancestors, there would be no accomplishments from Copernicus, Kepler, Galileo, Newton, Darwin, Einstein, and so forth. Thus, there would also be no biology, chemistry, health sciences, physics, and so forth. Without surplus wealth to supply the specialist, or any time to think about anything other than surviving, our civilization itself would have never occurred. In fact, record keeping itself was invented to attempt to manage the wealth of earlier civilizations. Without the advancements in writing created by these early attempts, we would have no written history. Without finance, we never would have invented the "nations" that connect us to our long-lost human family members.

Of course, all prosperity credit cannot go solely to finance. It is economics in conjunction with finance that has magnified progress exponentially. The nations that managed their wealth best over time made the most long-term progress, particularly in the past two hundred years. It is these sciences that have led to every invention that you can think of including, but not limited to, the sewing machine, the railroad, the telephone, the movie, the automobile, the airplane, the radio, the rocket, the Internet, and countless more. Look around you. Everything in your room was invented from proper wealth management. *Good inventions take time to create, the kind of time mainly available in prosperity.*

Arts and entertainment also would have never surpassed a very basic level without the aid of finance and economics. Some examples include, but are not limited to, primitive tribal arts;

Egyptian, Chinese, Greek, and Roman arts; Renaissance art; bodybuilding art; modern art; movies; novels; plays; sports; and the countless games that we can play on our cell phones. That's right—without proper wealth management by the individual, artistic accomplishments from Da Vinci, Michelangelo, Monet, Picasso, and many more artists would never exist. Without proper wealth management, the works of famous movie stars and singers would never exist. Imagine a world without the music that we know today—no alternative, band, blues, country, folk, gospel, jazz, Motown, opera, pop, rap, reggae, rock, salsa, samba, tango, and so forth! From Mozart to Michael Jackson, the music of popular musicians would never exist without prosperity—and this would make our world a less exciting place to live. *Without humanity's proper wealth management, all of the people who became famous artists and entertainers would have never had the time to become great because they would have been forced to focus on just surviving.*

If everything in the above statements holds true, then prosperity, particularly finance and economics, account for the creation of *most*, and possibly *all*, inventions, arts, entertainments, and sciences. The biggest question is now this: How could the necessity of prosperity have been overlooked for so long? Principle 136 in *The Most Important Lessons in Economics and Finance* is: "*The history of money explains almost everything in history*" (Criniti, 2014, 168). As money is only one part of wealth, its history is not the complete story. We can now take this one step further: **Simply, without economics and finance, history would have never occurred**. Of course, I don't mean the official academic economics and finance taught in universities. I am referring to the essence of these sciences in primitive form, that which is concerned with the wealth management of its respective entities. Additionally, "history" describes the period from the first time humans starting recording events—before that is "prehistory." Further, with our knowledge of survival, now we also can add the following: **Without our ancient ancestors' mastery of survival, history and human prehistory would have never occurred.**

To conclude, prosperity, particularly finance and finance's child, economics, and prosperity's parent, survivalism, were as absolutely necessary to stay alive in the past, as they are in the present, and as they certainly will be in the future. In the next few chapters, we will explore this point further.

CHAPTER 15

The Edge of Survival

My experiences and research have taught me that you can never fully understand survival unless you are close enough to its edge to observe it. It is a dangerous place to stand, indeed, but if you truly want to understand the conclusions of this book, then you must go there. If you are ready, I would like you to take a virtual journey with me to the edge of survival to strengthen your comprehension of the significance of survival and prosperity. OK, let's go!

To begin, let me share with you a little story. Ironically, after I wrote the initial part of this chapter, something happened to me. I took a break, and then I went to the gym to practice Brazilian jiu jitsu. I was training with a friend who happens to be a first-class professional mixed-martial-arts fighter. We wrestled several rounds, and then he made a comment to me in the middle of our final round. He said, "Hey man, what's the matter with you today? You're just surviving! You gotta move and make something happen."

After all of the time that I have spent reflecting on this subject, in the middle of fatigue, I still replied, "Yeah, but it's better than dying!" Just a few moments later, he forced me to submit with a circulatory choke called a "guillotine." If this had been a real self-defense situation, my fate would have followed this pattern: sleep, coma, and then death. This example demonstrates that if we want to find the best way to stay alive for the long-term, then survival alone is just not enough.

I chose to share this story with you because we can take a glance at what the edge of survival is like if we can pause the moment above. I admit that I had had a long week, and I was extremely tired and overheated that day. Nevertheless, under normal conditions, with my training background, I usually would never have submitted to my friend with this move. Yet I still made some mistakes. First, my friend was right: I was just surviving. I rationalized that surviving was not so bad after all, especially against a professional fighter in excellent condition. Besides, I was tired, and the round was almost over. Thus, my first issue was the wrong mental outlook. I can describe my overall emotion with one word: "content." I was content with just staying alive.

Second, by being content with my position, I had little motivation to do anything else that would increase my chances of winning, which translates in a real survival scenario to eliminating the struggle and increasing my chances of staying alive. This problem led me to being more reactive than proactive. I mounted a defense to whatever offense he gave me. But playing too much defense in that situation resulted in a reduction of one of my primary physical immediate survival essentials: conserving energy. Particularly, I was wasting too much energy trying to undo the damage of his offense when that same energy could have been spent trying to force him to submit and end the match.

In a match, as in a real one-on-one struggle, you may not have time to take in energy. For example, you can't say to the person who is trying to choke you to death, "Excuse me, Mister Bad Gal or Guy, do you mind if I go and get some water first… on second thought…maybe a ham and cheese sandwich too. I just need some more energy before you continue to try to kill me." Although you can try that line out, I don't recommend it! If we can't take in energy in these kinds of struggles, then we must cherish energy conservation. The energy that we already have becomes a great source of our wealth.

My downward spiral of problems was in the following order: 1) I had the wrong attitude—that is, content with living on the edge of survival; 2) I lacked motivation; 3) I became reactive; and 4) I wasted energy. Finally, when fatigue set in, all of my essential survival knowledge started withering away. A lack of overall energy taxes your mental ability to make good decisions, even when you are well versed in that particular survival situation. Thus, poor wealth management eventually triumphed.

Please recall that the strongest will to live by itself is not enough to survive. In the story above, my will to live was there the whole time. Although I never gave up and continuously wanted to win, I became too content with my present position—that is, until it was too late. In jiu-jitsu, you must tap your opponent at the right time, or you risk serious injury. Unfortunately, that is what I had to do—tap out.

Although the above story only represents one struggle out of countless others that we can potentially encounter, we must not overlook its implications. Many parallels can be made here to other deadly struggles. For starters, my response to my friend was only partially correct. Surviving is better than dying because at least we still have a chance to stay alive. When you're dead, you lose that option!

However, survival by itself is not sufficient—that is, it is not in our best interests to just survive. We need to protect ourselves from the unexpected by our efforts to be prosperous. For example, I was content in my current situation in the above story, and I was managing the struggle well. But the unexpected fatigue that eventually set in became the catalyst that ended the match. The outcome might have been very different had I had more wealth on my side. Some examples of wealth in this context include more sleep, more training, more conditioning, a better attitude, and so forth. I could have accumulated all of these things by better preparing myself days, weeks, months, and even years before this day occurred. I could have conquered my struggle by defeating my opponent with these other assets that I was lacking. **In short, I should have respected finance more! The essence of prosperity is to stay as far away from the edge of survival as you can, for this is one place where second chances rarely exist. If you fall over its edge, then death might be inevitable.**

CHAPTER 16

The Three Major Wealth-Management Possibilities

Three major possibilities existed in the story from chapter 15. First, I could have minimized my wealth, particularly my energy, and then I could have been defeated (which would have equated to death in a real-life encounter). Although this possibility wasn't my intention, it was my result. The second possibility was that I could have survived the final round, and we both would have tied. This is what I tried to do, as demonstrated, but I didn't account for the unexpected fatigue.

There is a third possibility though. That is, as noted above, I could have accumulated more assets through wealth maximization to increase my odds of not falling off the edge of survival. It is here that I could not only have stayed alive but might have also defeated my opponent. The faster I could have defeated my opponent, then the faster I could have eliminated the risk of losing (or death).

This example is a microcosm of how wealth management generally works. That is, whether intentional or not, there are three major wealth-management possibilities (see also Exhibit 16.1). **First, you can minimize your wealth below the level of your bare minimum survival essentials necessary to survive (this will now be referred to as *the edge of survival*). Second, you can live on the edge of survival and have just enough wealth to survive. Finally, you can maximize your wealth above the level of your bare minimum survival essentials necessary to survive.** With this last possibility, you will enter prosperity where you will rise above the edge of survival. Let's take a closer look at these possibilities!

Exhibit 16.1

*The Three Major Wealth-Management
Possibilities*

1. Minimize wealth below the level of the bare minimum survival essentials necessary to survive (this level is also called *the edge of survival*). This possibility will eventually lead to death without the intervention of another entity or a positive change in wealth.
2. Live on the edge of survival, which is where an entity has just enough wealth to survive. This possibility is too risky as the probability of death is still too high.
3. Maximize wealth above the level of the bare minimum survival essentials necessary to survive. Prosperity begins after the edge of survival is passed. It yields the highest probability of staying alive over time.

The first major wealth-management possibility directly conflicts with the goal of survival. A survivalist knows all too well that someone may need every available resource to manage her or his struggle to stay alive. Every object, as useless as it may be in a normal day in civilization, may become the tool that saves your life in a survival scenario. For example, if you were stuck on a raft in the middle of the ocean but were able to salvage some old containers, then you might be able to collect rainwater to drink (you can't drink ocean water, or you will dehydrate and die). You might also be able to use the containers to bail water out of the raft to keep it from sinking. A quick death might have occurred if you had thrown away useful objects like these in this survival scenario. In short, minimizing wealth, especially in a survival situation where every asset counts, may be considered equivalent to suicide.

The first major wealth-management possibility also directly conflicts with the goal of prosperity, particularly economics and finance. If a financial entity minimizes wealth, then it is essentially not trying to maximize its desirable lifespan or the quality of its life. Let's take an extreme fictitious example: one of the wealthiest people in the world decides one day to slowly minimize his wealth. As he is very rich, he may not feel the pain of asset depletion for a while. He will eventually get to a point where his quality of life is affected. This is especially true when the luxury items start to go: no more luxury boats, cars, houses, or planes. In the last stages of minimization, this ex-rich person will now start depleting his long-term and then short-term reserves (basically working backward from the Survival-Prosperity Sequence). Finally, assuming he wants to continue this path, he will end up in survival mode with only the wealth necessary to survive. If this person continues any further along this nonsensical path—he has essentially chosen suicide.

Without any survival essentials, or any money to buy them, his life is now in jeopardy. Assuming he refuses to work, take gifts from others, or receive any form of intervention, then he will not have any income to restore his original situation. As blood circulation and air are generally free, without money, he will probably die in a range of about three days (assuming he can't get access to water) to a month (assuming he can't get access to food). Folks, you have just witnessed how one of the wealthiest people in the world can die without wealth in a short time if he freely chooses to minimize his wealth. Imagine how much faster this process would be if the person were already starting close to or at the edge of survival, which is the predicament of the majority of the world's population right now. **Living in absolute poverty is living below the edge of survival, which may be only a short distance from death.** As you can see, minimizing wealth is not a good option!

The second major wealth-management possibility is to live strictly in survival mode with only the bare survival essentials needed. It should be very obvious from our earlier analysis that this is not an ideal position to be in. Yes, it is true that being on the edge of survival is better than being either dead or very close to death, as in the case of wealth minimization. Yet, living day to day is indeed still a dangerous approach. It is here where the probability of dying increases as you move past the edge and head in the direction of wealth minimization. You can live to an old age by just scraping by if you're lucky. However, you are vulnerable when you don't plan for the future and the problems it may bring because you are susceptible to being controlled by the unexpected.

Note that living on the edge of survival is different than being broke. Being broke equates to not having any wealth, including the bare necessities of life. When you are broke, similar to when you minimize your wealth below the edge of survival, you cannot sustain being alive for long without the intervention of others or a favorable change in your income position. On the contrary, you can technically live with just the bare minimum survival essentials for your entire lifetime (again, if you are lucky).

The third major wealth-management possibility is to seek out prosperity by maximizing wealth. Through the pursuit of this possibility, you are automatically conceding that survival is insufficient. Striving for more wealth equates to striving for a better, securer life. This point will be demonstrated more throughout part 2.

The above statement works well for the majority of the population. However, a potential problem may occur when we talk about the superrich. One might wonder how more wealth could help extremely rich people have a better, securer life if they already have all of that. In this special case, you can see that they already have wealth way beyond the point of maximizing their short- and long-term survival essentials and luxuries of every sort. It is here where a new concept is called for.

The *prosperity tipping point* is where additional wealth will add little increased benefit to an entity. It is subjective, varies from entity to entity, and may change over time. One's financial or economic strategy may change at this point from maximizing wealth for its own use to maximizing wealth for someone else's. In other words, the prosperity tipping point is where philanthropy may become a major part of someone's wealth-management strategy. Some people may have a higher prosperity tipping point because they may prefer a more luxurious lifestyle. Other people may have a lower prosperity tipping point because they may need few or no luxuries.

To conclude, minimizing wealth is contrary to the goals of survival and prosperity. This option was only analyzed here to demonstrate its potentially fatal effects. Additionally, maintaining only the proper amount of survival essentials is not ideal. Survival may be the only choice when facing deadly struggles with a bare minimum of wealth. However, when the right opportunity appears again, the safest way to secure a longer, higher quality life is to focus on the goals of prosperity. *By maximizing wealth, you increase your chances of staying alive and well, both in the present and in the future.*

CHAPTER 17

Survival Resurfacing

It is to be clearly understood that the Survival-Prosperity Sequence is not completely rigid. Sometimes several steps can be accomplished all at once—for example, if a poor person suddenly becomes rich for whatever reason (like receiving an inheritance or winning the lottery). Other times, entities try to skip steps, but this can land them in trouble. For example, this can occur when someone uses her income to save for her retirement instead of paying for her immediate survival essentials (like her water or grocery bills).

Although the various steps of prosperity in the Survival-Prosperity Sequence are flexible, the survival step is not. The survival step must continuously resurface in the beginning of every one of the Major Scientific Phases of Prosperity. New entities that are created in each phase must first survive before they can be awarded an admission ticket to the first step of prosperity of the next phase. If such an entity cannot survive the initial present struggle, then all future plans are irrelevant.

In the first Survival Test before the very first Major Scientific Phase of Prosperity, the individual must fight hard. The success of this step is absolutely crucial to all other phases. If individuals don't survive, then other larger entities cannot be created. Generally, wealth can start to be accumulated when a person's immediate struggles are overcome. Two people may arguably be in a comfortable position to start a family with the accumulation of even a small amount of long-term emergency reserves.

A family must survive as a new entity once it is formed. This new Survival Test, part of a new Survival-Prosperity Sequence, will determine whether or not it can advance into the next Major Scientific Phase of Prosperity: group finance. A family was considered a personal financial entity in *The Necessity of Finance*. However, for the purposes of this book, it will be more convenient to consider the family as being in the same category as other groups and organizations (both informal and formal). Also, please note that although groups of one exist, group finance mainly pertains to groups with more than one individual.

The survival step resurfaces before the second Major Scientific Phase of Prosperity because the new group has many new struggles to overcome. Unity becomes a more difficult task with every increase in the number of people in the group. A new family, just like any new group or organization, must find a way to work together. This task can be considered as vital as managing a deadly struggle. Groups jeopardize their existence when they don't function well because of disagreements.

The end may be near when each vital member of a family, particularly the head of a household, does not fulfill her or his basic responsibilities. Principle 177 of *The Most Important Lessons in Economics and Finance* sums up this point clearly: *"If a man cannot provide for his family, then he may lose it"* (Criniti, 2014, 210). At the breaking point, a family and other groups will eventually separate into individual members. If this regression happens, then the group dies, and the individual members will only be concerned with their own survival and prosperity goals. Essentially, this equates to a regression in their Survival-Prosperity Sequence.

If a group survives its initial struggles, then it can proceed to prosperity. If the group becomes extremely prosperous, then its population may increase. This may continue to occur if the group merges with other groups and becomes a nation. As you can infer already, prosperous group entities eventually converge with others to form this progressive cycle of growth and consolidation. Many small businesses that have become large corporations know this cycle very well. They may have merged with and/or acquired other businesses many times in their life cycle in order to reach their larger growth level.

A group may eventually become a united national entity if it is very successful. The survival step will then surface again before the third Major Scientific Phase of Prosperity because the new economic entity will have many new struggles to overcome. With more people involved, more disagreements may arise about how the nation should be managed, which can lead to political instability and even civil wars. If the nation cannot manage to unite its people and its goals, then it may die. Its original groups then will regress back to Phase 2, and they will only be concerned with their own survival and prosperity goals.

However, if a nation survives, its next focus would be to maximize its wealth. Humans have entered Phase 3 hundreds of times in our history, as demonstrated by the quantity of nations that we have today. It is the last step of this phase that is highly relevant to our current struggles. *If the history of prosperity in our civilization is any indication of our future, then we are progressively preparing to attain the last two Major Scientific Phases of Prosperity in the same way that we attained the first three.* The world has now been mapped, colonized, and filled up with various prosperous nations that are intrigued about where to go from here. Phase 4 is probably very close, considering that the general prosperity patterns have been demonstrated time and time again. The Survival Test will have to resurface if that time comes. That is, the world will need to learn to survive together with united goals. The other options are not that pretty! Keep this point in mind, as it will be an underlying theme in parts 3, 4, and 5 of this book. Finally, in the future, if we are prosperous enough to be promoted to Phase 5, the survival step will have to show its face once more.

CHAPTER 18

The Greatest Options of the Wealthy

The preface included a brief explanation of the title of this book. It is now time to explore this aspect further. The major misinterpretation that many people may have by just reading the title and not the book is to assume that my conclusion is that all rich people survive better. That would be an incorrect assumption. *The actual meaning of the title is that more wealth provides more options for the wealthiest entities to survive better; it does not necessarily mean that those entities will choose the best options.* In other words, being wealthier increases their probability of continuously surviving and prospering by providing them the greatest options to obtaining survival essentials. Of course, the option of the rich to choose luxury items can also be extremely beneficial. However, by at least having the option to accumulate the right survival essentials now and later, they automatically have an advantage over those entities that do not have that option. **In short, the richest entities can enhance their probability of survival if they are able to successfully manage their wealth.**

The major reason that wealth provides *better options* to survive as opposed to a *guarantee* is because wealthier entities, for various reasons, can make decisions that conflict with the goals of survival and prosperity. This point is best illustrated with Principle 189 from *The Most Important Lessons in Economics and Finance*: "*You can't run away from yourself.*" Here it states, "**Until you know yourself truly and, with much courage, stand to confront your own weaknesses, then you may never be able to financially prosper to your maximum potential. No matter how fast or where you go, your problems will always follow**" (Criniti, 2014, 222).

Despite the quantity of their wealth, some people may have an assortment of problems that need to be addressed before they can understand and incorporate the goals of finance into their daily actions. For example, consider compulsive gamblers. Many people in this world work hard all week long only to immediately spend their paycheck at the casino. They may not even save enough money for the necessary monthly bills, including food. These people may live their whole lives in this state. How can they ever maximize their wealth if they have become their own biggest impediment to this goal?

Similarly, if they were wealthy and had the same gambling problem, then it might be only a matter of time before they would go broke. They might have been wealthy once, but they chose to destroy their wealth instead of choosing prosperous existences. As discussed in chapter 16, choosing a wealth-minimization strategy may eventually lead to death. This example illustrates how someone wealthy may choose not to exercise her or his option to survive and prosper, which is indeed a choice!

Many other personal issues can become road blocks to managing wealth properly including alcohol abuse, drugs, emotional problems, ignorance, indifference, irresponsibility, insatiability, peer pressure, restlessness, and so forth. It is not necessary to go into detail to show that these and other issues can lead to wealth-minimization strategies. The obvious speaks for itself! Further, someone's destructive past may be irreversible, despite future efforts to be prosperous. For example, a serious gambler might have damaged her financial position so badly that it may be almost impossible for her to reach prosperity, even if she stopped gambling forever. She may owe too much money to too many people, and she may be forced to live out her days just paying off the interest.

The above examples demonstrate how individuals may choose not to make good survival and financial decisions. But what excuse do bigger entities have? To answer this question, you must recall that groups are made up of individuals. Thus, they also inherit all of their personal problems. A catastrophe can result for larger entities if any of those problems is found in their wealth managers. In addition, the agency problem probably accounts for many of their downfalls. The agency problem occurs when an agent of any entity has a chance to prioritize its own financial goals before the prosperity goals of the entity it represents. For example, an executive of a large company may make decisions to maximize his wealth at the expense of the wealth of the company. If not corrected, this behavior may eventually lead to the company's death because it may lose all of its wealth.

Incredibly, some wealthy people lack knowledge in, as well as an appreciation of, economics and finance, which would definitely have an effect on their ability to exercise their greatest options to survive and prosper. For example, some wealthy people may invest everything they have into businesses that defy all of the lessons of finance. Contrary to what they may think, a business is not guaranteed immortality simply because it is initially wealthy. It, too, must bow to the timeless lessons of wealth management or risk perishing.

It should now be very clear that wealthy entities have no guarantees that their wealth will allow them to survive and prosper for the remainder of their lives. Despite this limitation, money and other forms of wealth can provide the richest with the greatest options to manage their struggles to stay alive. Human entities have the choice to use their wealth to supply almost all of their needs and wants, which is an achievement unmatched by any other known living entities. An entity that manages its wealth carefully can increase its chances of longevity and a quality existence for itself and its loved ones. We will soon look at how this process works for all entities in the Major Scientific Phases of Prosperity. But first, in the next chapter, we will examine a hypothetical example of both a rich and a poor individual. This very detailed chapter will be the cornerstone to understanding the significance of the relationship between wealth, survival, and prosperity. *If this strong connection can be demonstrated for the basic unit of all population sizes—that is, the individual—then it must be applicable to more numerous and more complex populations.*

CHAPTER 19

The Survival of the Richest Individuals

The first and second Major Scientific Phases of Prosperity deal with two different types of financial entities: individuals and groups. This chapter focuses on the first financial entity, the individual, which is the most basic unit that can manage wealth. A complete understanding of the importance of individual wealth management is crucial in order to understand the relationship to larger units, for example, a nation. Thus, let's take our time with this first one!

In this chapter, I use two fictitious examples to demonstrate the first Major Scientific Phase of Prosperity. These examples show how more wealth can increase the probability of various entities continuously surviving and prospering by providing them the greatest options to obtaining survival essentials. Importantly, an individual starting without any wealth or financial support from another should obtain a reasonable amount of prosperity before starting a family (considered here as the most basic form of a group). If a family is started before at least one of the parents is financially prepared, then that family is at an increased risk of having longer and more severe struggles.

Our first example is a twenty-eight-year-old rich man named Jack Smith. He has a fiancée named Jill and plans on marrying her at the end of this year. He has a dog, Sparky, and no children, although he plans on having many when he is married. Let's see how his money can be used to help him survive, prosper, and be promoted faster to the family phase of prosperity (in Phase 2). We will need to continuously reference the survival essentials noted in chapter 12 throughout this analysis. Let's start with our primary physical immediate survival essentials in their respective order.

First, although it sounds a bit strange, Jack can buy quality air in various ways. He can do this easily by installing a high quality HVAC (heating, ventilation, and air conditioning) unit. Next, he can also purchase expensive filters for the unit and change them frequently. With these filters, he can protect the quality of air in his house from bacteria, bad odors, dust, dust-mite debris, mold spores, pet dander, pollen, pollutants, smog, smoke, and viruses. He can also purchase many carbon monoxide and smoke detectors to protect against the risk of deadly air. Further, Jack can buy a house in a location with low pollution, such as in a lightly populated mountainous area. The many surrounding trees may help to improve the quality of the air he breathes.

Second, Jack can buy things that will assist in proper blood circulation. In general, this effect can happen automatically by the proper use of the other items that he can buy that we will be discussing, such as food, water, and exercise equipment. However, in an emergency, if Jack or his future family had blood-circulation problems, for example, a clogged artery, he can also pay for the necessary doctors and drugs to correct these issues. Circulatory-related surgeries are generally very success-ful these days but can be very expensive. No problem, money will take care of it for them—he can buy the best doctors from anywhere in the world!

Jack Smith can buy the second primary physical immediate survival essential: thermal balance of the body. He can obtain this in various ways. To start, he can buy a house in the middle of the tropics where the everyday weather pattern automatically supplies a consistent comfortable temperature. This can also be his vacation home if he wants, in addition to having a primary residence somewhere consistently cold. In that case, he will need more clothes first. No problem! He can buy any kind of clothes he wants, even the warmest, most expensive furs that exist. But clothes will not be enough for the cold climate that he may live in.

Consequently, he could buy a stone mansion that is well in-sulated from drafts. In this mansion, he could also have the best heaters in every room. He may also prefer several fireplaces in case the electric goes off. Also, he will need good air condition-ers for the hot summer. He can buy central air conditioning to cool the whole house. He may also want to include many ceiling fans in each room for extra comfort. These items above, bought with his money, can help to provide him and his future family with the right tools needed to keep their bodies at the required thermal balance in order to live, regardless of outside weather conditions.

Jack can use his money to buy the third primary physical immediate survival essential: relief of immediate life-threatening bodily injuries. If an emergency occurs, he can buy the best doctors in the world for him or any member of his family, even his dog. If he is rich enough, he may even be able to afford to keep a full-time personal doctor, a nurse, and an emergency helicopter to take him immediately to the nearest hospital if a serious injury were to occur. He could also be able to buy prescription drugs and physical therapy to help with recovery.

Jack can use his money to buy the fourth primary physical immediate survival essential: quality water. Many people assume that quality water should never be a problem, considering the total amount of water in this world. That is a major fallacy! Only a tiny percentage of existing water is good enough for human consumption. The rest of the accessible water is either polluted or salt water, which we cannot drink without proper filtration. Money can fix that though. Money will allow Jack to have the best water supply and filtration systems. He can start with buying access to fresh water, and then he can buy a home filtration system. For safety, he can also buy a filtration system that attaches to every sink, which can help to catch any remaining contaminants traveling from the outside pipes to each faucet.

Next, Jack can use his money to buy the fifth primary physical immediate survival essential: conservation of energy. Losing energy may not be much of a concern for him because he can always buy the most nutritious food. However, ignoring that aspect, let's admit what else he can do with his money: save his energy by outsourcing various tasks. In other words, he can save energy by paying others to do his laborious jobs for him. He can pay someone to clean, to collect his food, to cook, to educate his future children, to fix his house, to manage his home and office, to mow his lawn, to pay his bills, to serve his meals, to take care of his future children and his dog, to transport him places, and even to change the television channel for him. Imagine how much energy he is saving by not having to do these tasks (and many others not listed)!

Of course, it can be argued that storing all of this energy may make him overweight. In addition, he may be accumulating too many calories from eating many delicious meals every day. These events may have a negative effect on his survival rate, which is why it is important for the wealthy to manage their wealth properly in order to maintain a healthy lifestyle. Nevertheless, this point doesn't eliminate the fact that wealthy people at least have a choice to conserve their energy in various ways. How they approach it is up to them!

Next, Jack can use his money to buy the sixth primary physical immediate survival essential: a means to relieve bodily waste products, such as by defecation and urination. This topic is a crucial aspect of survival that cannot be ignored, regardless of how disgusting it may be. Money can buy better sewage systems that take waste away from the house. Money can buy the best and biggest bathrooms, with the best toilets and the softest toilet paper. Also, in emergency situations where people cannot eliminate waste properly from their bodies, the best doctors and nurses can be hired to remedy the situation. For example, if Jack or a member of his family were to have part of his colon removed as a result of colon cancer, then he may need someone to help him change his colostomy bag for the rest of his life. If the proper procedures are not followed, the waste can enter the bloodstream and can quickly lead to a deadly infection. These medical procedures can be a lifetime expense that only money can easily remedy. For example, a full-time nurse may be necessary.

Jack can use his money to buy the seventh primary physical immediate survival essential: quality food. Many modern people suffer from inadequate nutrition. Without enough money, they are forced to buy cheap, inferior-quality food, such as various fast foods. Even if they can afford the raw ingredients to cook a decent meal, their work may not afford them the time. In contrast, Jack can afford to eat healthy all day and every day. He can buy the freshest foods, from meats to produce. He can even buy the farm to supply it.

Next, he can have the best chefs cook his food for him using the healthiest methods. He can even afford to track his nutritional intake with the latest technology and buy any food or dietary supplements to meet his nutritional deficiencies. If he were to travel—no problem! He can afford to eat customized dishes at the best restaurants anywhere. Also, let's not forget that his food will be even healthier since he has the cleanest water supply. The quality water that washes and cooks his food and cleans the silverware used to serve it will enhance the quality of his food.

Finally, Jack can use his money to buy the final primary physical immediate survival essential: quality sleep. To start, money can buy the biggest and best bedrooms, which are insulated from any outside disturbances that can affect sleep (for example, a neighbor's barking dogs). If too much light is a problem, he can buy the most efficacious tinted windows and window shades. Next, money can buy the best beds, blankets, pillows, sheets, and accessories needed for the most comfortable sleeping experience possible. If all of the above don't work, then he can hire a medical professional to further analyze the problem.

We will now see how Jack's wealth can help him to obtain the best secondary physical immediate survival essentials. Please recall that some of the items on the list may be debatable and that the list may be incomplete. First, to a degree, money can buy customized beauty. Plastic surgery procedures have improved immensely over the years. Thus, with money, you can turn an old person into one many years younger. You can also turn a man into a woman and vice versa. From hair transplants to face and tummy tucks, wealth makes more options available to the rich.

Jack also can afford to spend more quality time with friends and family. He has the optional luxury to attend expensive social events and to travel frequently with whomever he pleases. Thus, it can also be argued that money could buy companionship.

To a degree, fitness and good health can also be bought. For example, Jack can create a fitness room in his home filled with very expensive exercise equipment. He can also pay a personal physical trainer to help educate and motivate him into better condition. As noted above, he also can afford to eat better-quality meals. In worst-case scenarios, he also can pay for expensive but necessary surgeries that may improve his health, such as a heart or a liver transplant.

Sanitation also can be bought in many ways. First, he can buy proper waste-disposal systems as noted above. He also can buy full-time maids and the products needed for them to ensure that his home is always clean. Excessive trash removal also can be very expensive. Fortunately, this is not a problem for Jack. Money also can buy great showers to keep his body clean as well as great washing machines to clean the clothes he wears.

Finally, Jack's sexual activity may be enhanced by buying medications or medical procedures (although they are probably not necessary for someone his age). Additionally, Jack can enhance the quality of his relationship with Jill, and probably their sex life, because he can afford to spend more free time with her.

We will now see how Jack's wealth can help him to obtain the best mental immediate survival essentials. Considering the complexity of this subject, this analysis will take a different approach. First, we will look at the primary and secondary mental immediate survival essentials collectively. Second, for the sake of convenience, I will subdivide these essentials into three categories: intelligence, emotions, and all other mental immediate survival essentials. In general, out of the three categories, it is easiest to demonstrate how wealth can be used to increase intelligence.

To start, wealth can buy the maximum amount of the various forms of education currently available. This assumes that one has the time and mental capability to absorb it. With the right amount of money, you can even hire the best teachers from around the world for any subject. For example, wealthy people have top-quality access to knowledge on finance, self-defense, wilderness survival, or any other area that they think will increase their survival intelligence. They also can afford to earn the highest degrees at the best private schools. If necessary, they can even hire the best private tutors.

We will now take a look at how wealth can buy the other categories of mental immediate survival essentials: emotions and all other mental immediate survival essentials. Admittedly, this topic is very controversial and is the most difficult to prove. Thus, it is more conservative to state that at least many of these essentials may be able to be bought at least indirectly—and arguably directly, to a certain degree. Considering the complexity of this subject, this discussion will be kept relatively brief in order to avoid going outside the scope of this book.

How can an emotion be bought? This can happen in a variety of ways but usually requires effort on the part of the one spending money. It is much easier if he knows what can make someone react emotionally. If the desired emotion is happiness, some examples may include a new house, a new car, a vacation, a meal at someone's favorite restaurant, flowers, and even a simple birthday card.

Some other mental immediate survival essentials may be bought. For example, with wealth, you have the option to buy things that will put someone in a better mood, thus, paving the way for humor. It is much easier to smile and laugh when you don't have the immense financial stress that plagues so many working-class adults these days. With money, you can buy access to live comedy clubs and the funniest television channels and movies anytime you want, and you may even be able to pay for your own private, professional joker.

With money, you can buy a motivational coach to help motivate you. You also can buy private self-defense lessons to become more aware of your surroundings, calmer in the presence of a struggle, and mentally stronger. The above options are not guaranteed to work, but they certainly are options that those without money don't have. In short, money can give the wealthy Jack Smith and his future family options to enhance their internal wealth. It is their choice whether they will decide to use them.

We will now take a look at the essential survival tools that Jack can buy. Please refer to the list in chapter 12 for easy reference since we will go through it in that exact order. These various tools are meant to help attain the immediate survival essentials needed to survive. Please note that other items that are not on this list may be necessary. Additionally, some items on the list may be irrelevant to his exact survival situation. It should just be used as a general guide. Special notes are put in parentheses wherever necessary.

With his wealth, he can buy the best axes; bags; beds; blankets; books; clothing; communication means (cell phones, the Internet, satellites); containers; cooking pots; cords; disinfectants; kitchenware; knives; lighting sources; a means to start and maintain a fire; medical kits; music; navigational equipment (a Global Positioning System, or GPS); security (such as alarm systems, security guards or even a whole security force, and trained security dogs); shelters (for example, homes of every kind); transportation means (that is, airplanes, boats, cars, and helicopters); wash kits; weaponry (anything from a simple gun to an arsenal of weaponry); and other miscellaneous personal items that can increase his odds of staying alive during a survival situation. The only thing on the original list that is excluded here is money, as he already has that. It can be argued, however, that he can obtain more money through the interest that can be earned with his existing money when it is well invested.

To conclude this analysis of the wealthy Jack Smith, there is hardly anything that his money cannot buy! We barely discussed the endless luxury items or the quantities of short- and long-term emergency reserves that he can buy. If he is wealthy enough and can manage his wealth properly, he can secure the survival and prosperity goals of his whole future family for many generations to come. Let us now discuss our final example for this chapter: John Jones. In this example, we will analyze this argument from a poor man's perspective.

To make comparison with Jack Smith easier, let's make some assumptions. First, we will assume that Jack and John are the same age. Next, we will assume that the two individuals have the same culture, ethnicity, race, and religion. They also live in the same region of the same nation and, thus, both must follow the same laws. *These assumptions will ensure that primarily their wealth is in the spotlight.*

John Jones has no children or pets because he cannot afford them. John has had a steady girlfriend for three years named Jane. He wants to marry her, but he can't afford to yet. Jane knows his situation very well, and she has actually considered leaving him many times. A lack of money is a major cause of their arguments, which in turn have also caused a serious strain in their relationship. Jane wants to ensure that her future husband will be able to take care of her and Tim, her four-year-old child from a previous relationship.

John lives with Jane in a tiny, two-story row home in a very poor downtown area of a big city. Jane is a stay-at-home mom, while John has been working a full-time job in a factory for eleven years. John is still barely making ends meet despite many years of hard toil put in at his company. Frankly, John barely has enough income to support himself, yet he still gives Jane any little extra money that he has. To better understand his predicament, let's discuss the primary physical immediate survival essentials in their respective order in the same way that we did for Jack Smith.

First, John can't buy the quality air that can help him live a healthier life. This sounds strange, so let's walk through the argument. Since he can't afford to move anywhere else, he is forced to live next to an old refinery in a high-traffic area of a very polluted part of the city. Thus, he must inhale various forms of pollution daily, especially from the buses that make frequent stops on his corner. He can't take a break from the continuous bombardment of low-quality air since he can't afford to go on a vacation to a place with low air pollution. Further, he cannot afford an air conditioner to help filter out the bad particles. This is especially dangerous for Jane's son, who is allergic to pollen and ragweed.

Second, John can barely afford to buy things that will assist in ensuring proper blood circulation and better health in general. Although John was loyal to his company for many years, he had a very weak insurance plan with extremely high premiums. He barely used his insurance for anything because he was afraid of its extremely high copays and deductibles. John canceled his plan two years ago when it became unaffordable. This was poor timing because his health has only deteriorated since then, especially his high blood pressure. John is in a very bad predicament due to the excessive risk that he is taking. Without any health insurance, one major health problem can negatively affect his whole life savings and any plans that he may have to start a family.

John's bad financial predicament is demonstrated by his low ability to obtain the second primary physical immediate survival essential: thermal balance. John lives in an old house that has inadequate insulation and improperly working heaters. Thus, he is forced to rely on some old blankets to keep him warm in the winter. In addition, he usually has no heat in January and February because he spent too much money during the holidays, and thus, he cannot afford the gas bill. As noted already, he also doesn't have air conditioners in his house, as that would be too expensive. Due to the above issues, John and his future family have a high risk of getting hypothermia in the winter and hyperthermia in the summer.

Since, as noted already, John does not have health insurance, he could not afford to send himself to the hospital if an immediate life-threatening bodily injury were to occur. He would be forced to deal with the emergency by himself, unless he received intervention from charities or another kind entity. This is a serious risk that could compound his problems. *In an emergency, having health insurance could be the difference between life and death.* Unfortunately, his lack of wealth leaves him with few options.

Next, John is forced to drink public water since he cannot afford fancy bottled water or a high-tech water filtration system. Although legally safe to drink, chlorine, fluoride, and other elements still may affect the quality and/or taste of the water. Additionally, he has old water pipes in his house. Thus, the water that comes out of his faucet may contain bad elements like rust.

John's bad financial predicament is demonstrated further by his low ability to obtain the fifth primary physical immediate survival essential: conservation of energy. Contrary to Jack Smith, John cannot afford to pay anyone to work for him. He must do all of his laborious jobs by himself. He must use his energy to clean, to collect his food, to cook, to educate and take care of his future children, to fix and to manage his home, to pay his bills, to transport himself, and so on. Most importantly, John must use the majority of his energy for his work and its commute to bring home his only income source. His lack of money is draining his energy from an overwhelming number of sources.

John works overtime every day without taking any sick days or vacations. Even if he could afford it, he never has the time to go to the doctor for his deteriorating health. This problem has affected many other aspects of John's life. You see, his first fiancée left him because they never got to spend any time together as he was always at work. This issue is starting to resurface as Jane and he are often arguing over his catch-22. That is, she complains that they don't have enough money while also complaining that they don't spend enough time together. If he resolves one problem, it appears that he will be left with the other. If he had more money, this mess could get cleaned up really quickly!

John's bad financial predicament is also demonstrated by his low ability to obtain the sixth primary physical immediate survival essential: a means to relieve bodily waste products. One tiny bathroom is slowly becoming insufficient with the three people in his small house. This is especially true as Jane spends much time in there washing her toddler. The line to get into the bathroom often causes high stress and arguments. To complicate matters more, the mechanical pieces inside the toilet and the inner wax ring at its base are in need of replacing. John can fix it, but he hasn't had the time. Thus, there is always the added risk that the toilet may not work when needed. Finally, the sewage pipes in the house are very old and have backed up on several occasions, which caused flooding. This has forced everyone at various points to use public restrooms.

Next, John and his potential family suffer from malnutrition. Jane can only afford to buy food with the money from John's paycheck because she doesn't have any other income. As this is usually inadequate, she is forced to buy cheaper, inferior-quality foods. Their fresh fruit and vegetables are limited because produce is more expensive these days. She also has a frequent habit of taking her child out to lunch at fast-food places to buy him cheap hamburgers and french fries. She also uses the microwave often because microwaveable dinners are usually very cheap. Inexpensive candy and soda are also a major part of their diet.

Finally, John suffers from insufficient sleep for various reasons. First, his mattress is old and uncomfortable. He feels more pain when he wakes up than before he went to bed. His noisy neighborhood often disturbs his sleep. In addition, John has recently acquired new friends: bed-bugs. These pests have made his life miserable because they feast on everyone night and day. This situation appears hopeless because he does not know how to deal with this problem, and he does not have the money to pay a professional.

We will now briefly discuss how John's lack of wealth is becoming an obstacle to obtaining some secondary physical immediate survival essentials. First, all aspects of his beauty have been affected by his lack of wealth. As beauty starts from the inside, John's difficult situation has negatively affected his emotional state. His stressful existence is very noticeable in his body language. Additionally, John wears old raggedy clothes because he can't afford new ones. He doesn't wash his clothes much because he doesn't own a washer and a dryer, and he has limited money for the Laundromat. His unsanitary lifestyle has also resulted in his having few friends. Actually, many of his coworkers often complain that he is dirty and smelly.

As already noted, his lack of wealth affects his sanitary concerns and his health in various ways, especially as he does not have health insurance. Since he doesn't have money for the gym or to buy physical fitness equipment, he can only afford to exercise by any means that is free. Finally, his sexual activity has been reduced to almost zero from lack of wealth. John and Jane's relationship is on the brink of collapse. They do not have much time to see each other anymore because of his intense work schedule. They certainly could use a little time off together, such as a romantic night out, but they don't have any money for that either. As their future is looking grim, Jane has been considering someone else to fill John's shoes. She still loves John, but she knows that without any money, their circumstances will probably get worse, especially if they ever have children.

We will now see how John's financial situation affects the attainment of his mental immediate survival essentials. Considering the complexity of this subject, this analysis will use the same approach as the one used for Jack Smith above. We will start by first looking at intelligence. John could get a better job if he could get a college degree. However, he does not have the time or the money to pay for school. He has tried to get a loan but was denied because of his low income and his lack of a qualified cosigner. It is not that John is biologically unintelligent. The real problem is that he does not have the right opportunities for a better education to increase his intelligence level because of his financial troubles. In addition, John could only afford to send his future children to free public schools. Private education of any kind would not be an option.

Finally, John's financial situation also affects his attainment of the other categories of the mental immediate survival essentials: emotions and all other mental immediate survival essentials. In brief, his lack of wealth has made his life extremely unpleasant. His relationship with Jane is on the rocks because they don't get to spend any time together. The little time they do spend with each other is spent talking about the bills and daily problems, which usually results in very bad arguments. Little Tim has also become irritable as a result of witnessing these daily quarrels.

Although money can't solve all problems (at least not yet), it may improve many aspects of John's life such as buying things that could lead to a positive impact on his psychological state. For starters, having enough money to ensure that he has better quality physical immediate survival essentials could lead to less stress. If he had extra money, then John could work less. Even one day off a week might make a big psychological difference on everyone. As you can see, a family's issues with insufficient wealth unavoidably affect every member in some way.

We will now take a look at the essential survival tools that John can buy. Please refer to the list in chapter 12 for easy reference since we will go through it in that exact order. These various tools are meant to help attain the immediate survival essentials needed to survive. Please note that other items that are not on this list may be necessary. Also, some items on the list may be irrelevant to his exact survival situation. It should just be used as a general guide. Special notes are put in parentheses wherever necessary.

Poor John can only afford some of the following items. Most of what he already owns are old items salvaged from Goodwill and discount stores. With his limited wealth, John may or may not be able to afford inferior versions of the following: an ax; a bag; a bed; blankets; books; clothing; a communication means (he has no cell phone or access to the Internet); a container; a cooking pot; a cord; disinfectant; kitchenware; a knife; a lighting source; a means to start and maintain a fire; a medical kit; music; navigational equipment (he has no GPS); security (he can't afford an alarm system or even a dog); a shelter (his old house is quickly deteriorating); a transportation means (he doesn't have a car, so he must take public transportation everywhere); a wash kit; weaponry (he has none other than his own body); and other miscellaneous personal items that can increase his odds of staying alive during a survival situation. The only thing that was excluded from the original list was money, and he barely has that.

To conclude this analysis of poor John Jones, there is hardly anything that he can buy. He has no luxury items and barely any emergency reserves. He doesn't have an educational fund to go to college or a retirement fund for himself. He doesn't even have enough money to marry Jane. Simply, he lives day to day, floating back and forth between the Survival Test and Prosperity Step 1 in the Survival-Prosperity Sequence. He may be trying his best, as he has a strong will to live, but that may not be enough. He cannot afford any kind of insurance, especially health and property insurance. Thus, one little accident could eliminate all of his wealth and ruin his chances of having a family. Additionally, if he ever lost his job, then John's situation would automatically go from bad to worse. His situation is very dangerous indeed!

In summary, despite the many similarities between Jack Smith and John Jones, one difference appears to have affected almost every aspect of their lives: their wealth. As Jack is very wealthy, he has many more options to obtain all of the survival essentials in addition to every luxury item possible. Jack's money also provides him with the option to marry Jill and raise a family without any financial stress. On the other hand, John has the exact opposite situation. He barely has enough income to pay for basic survival essentials. He also has no money for luxuries or even simple quality time with Jane. *If his situation does not improve soon, then he risks losing Jane, her son, and the potential family they could have created.*

Obviously, these two hypothetical examples cannot be expected to explain every situation out there. My former experience as a personal financial planner has taught me that no two individuals' situations are alike, despite their appearances. However, these opposite examples do highlight the necessity of personal finance. **No matter what example we would have used, there is no escaping the conclusion that wealth can play a significant role in so many crucial aspects of an individual's life.**

It also is important to note that Jack Smith could decide to minimize wealth for whatever reasons, for example, by gambling. *He could throw away his only chance of being prosperous and force himself to struggle for life. But that would be his choice: a choice that may not be available to a person who is just surviving—for example, John Jones!* It also is important to mention that some poor people in John's predicament may learn finance and practice its lessons well. They may not give up on maximizing their wealth and fighting their way into prosperity (hopefully in an ethical manner). As their struggles are great, this drive is highly commendable.

This chapter may be long and dry. However, thoroughness is necessary to fully understand this crucial argument. Please hang in there, as these concepts are vital to understanding the bigger arguments presented in parts 3 and 4. In the next chapter, we will briefly analyze the other type of financial entities: groups.

CHAPTER 20

The Survival of the Richest Groups

As you saw in the previous chapter, a very prosperous individual can easily form the most traditional group: the family. Jack Smith should have little trouble being promoted to Phase 2 of prosperity. On the other hand, John Jones still has many more personal financial obstacles to overcome before that can ever occur. This chapter will continue to demonstrate how more wealth can increase the probability of various entities continuously surviving and prospering by providing them the greatest options to obtaining survival essentials. However, the focus here is on the entity in the second Major Scientific Phase of Prosperity: groups. As we already walked through a detailed example of both a wealthy and a poor entity in the last chapter, we will now take a different, more condensed approach.

Although groups of one exist, the groups that we are mainly concerned with in this chapter range from small families to more formal larger groups, such as giant corporations. It is not necessary to walk through the survival essentials point by point as we did in the last chapter because groups are just an extension of their individual members. A lack of wealth could kill a group the same way it could kill an individual, regardless of the reasons that it was formed. Once the group dies, it will break down into its individual members who will then worry only about their own survival and prosperity. The process for survival and prosperity of a group is generally the same as for individuals. Thus, this chapter mainly consists of some general commentary on the differences.

To start, generally a group's individual members may be at different stages in their personal Survival-Prosperity Sequence. For example, a new employee of a large company may be in survival mode, just taking any job available to make ends meet. On the other hand, the CEO of the company might be making a substantial amount of money in base salary in addition to all of the stock options and other benefits that she has. In this example, you can see one member of the group is barely surviving while another member is prospering well.

These differences in wealth in a group can have a huge effect on the internal wealth of its members. For example, the more prosperous member may be less motivated to work harder and smarter. The new poorer employee with a family, depending on his income, may be prepared to do whatever it takes to feed his family even if it requires putting in much overtime. On the other hand, there are also examples of hard-working, wealthy

CEOs and lazy, poor, new employees. Either way, the disparity of wealth among members can and usually does play a large role in the employee's contribution as a member.

Wealthier groups remain wealthy when they take all of their individual members' financial goals into consideration. A group that has members who are having a hard time obtaining even the basic survival essentials while others are prospering well does not have a long-term approach to management. For example, a business can't expect an employee to perform her job well if its office is located in the middle of a war zone (unless security is its business). Every member should be provided a comfortable, secure working environment. How could someone be expected to perform her job to her fullest potential without at least the basic relevant survival essentials available, or at least enough money to obtain them? If her basic needs are met, then she would be in a better position to increase her productivity. The final result could be positive for everyone in the company.

Income disparities may always exist in a business because certain high-salaried jobs may require more skill and experience. However, this does not mean that the employees with little or no experience should be paid a salary that is inconsistent with their basic survival needs. Any group is only as strong as its weakest links, especially when those weakest links are very poor. If the weakest links are strengthened, then the group may increase its chance of succeeding. Additionally, in a positive working environment, group members have a better opportunity to increase and sustain their internal wealth, whether it is in the form of intelligence, emotions, or something else. This kind of environment will motivate employees to work there for many years.

Finally, a poor member can join an already established rich group. This may at first seem like it contradicts the Five Major Scientific Phases of Prosperity model. However, this problem must be looked at from the big picture. It is the prosperity of the group's *original members*, whether from their own means or from a third party, that has helped to create and promote the group to a separate phase. Once a group is established, it can then add new individual members from all levels of prosperity at any time. The group's collective wealth may provide an opportunity for a poorer member to make a living and to be promoted to a higher personal prosperity step. Additionally, the group's collective wealth may be what is keeping the group alive. This same idea can be applied to other entities in the higher Major Scientific Phases of Prosperity. For example, nations may have poor and rich member groups and individuals. Nations can even have many different types of groups, including very complex ones like C corporations and special-interest groups. Further, a united planet may have poor and rich member nations, groups, and individuals. *In short, as the population increases in the higher phases, smaller entities can be included into the larger, united whole.*

The groups with the most wealth will increase their chances of surviving better for the long-term while groups operating at the edge of survival are at an increased risk of dying. One major negative financial event could put poor groups in a position where they may become insolvent. This could be caused by carrying too much debt or even just by having a horrible financial manager. Regardless, the countless examples of extinct businesses continue to demonstrate one major theme: the necessity of finance.

CHAPTER 21

The Survival of the Richest Nations

The message of this chapter can be paraphrased in the words of Nelson Mandela, one of the greatest political heroes in the world's fight for individual freedom. Regarding the financial status of many people in South Africa during apartheid, he wrote in his famous book, *The Struggle Is My Life*, "The people are too poor to have enough food to feed their families and children. They cannot afford sufficient clothing, housing and medical care. They are denied the right to security in the event of unemployment, sickness, disability, old age and where allowances are paid they are far too low for survival" (Mandela, 2013, 75).

Later on, Mandela similarly concludes, "The Freedom Charter asserts that there should be houses, security and comfort for all. We demand that the government provides these basic necessities of life. The shortage of housing, water and work opportunities, the forced removal of people and the destruction of their houses: these are our problems" (Mandela, 2013, 381).

Generally speaking, groups expand in the following order: immediate families, bands, tribes, chiefdoms, and nations. Economics, the third Major Scientific Phase of Prosperity, pertains to the largest of all of these groups: nations. Instead of focusing on just a small minority, the quotes above from Mandela snapshot one nation's historical battle to allow opportunities for its *entire people* to survive and prosper. The story of South Africa during apartheid is an excellent example of how the perception of a nation's wealth can be misleading. South Africa appeared very wealthy to the international community on the surface, but the real truth was underneath the facade. The racial inequity of apartheid eventually started to rip the country apart.

If you can understand how a nation is born—that is, from the assembly of groups of individuals with shared survival and prosperity goals—then it will be easier for you to understand that the greatest obligation of a nation is to help meet these goals for all of its people. A nation can never maximize its potential wealth by neglecting the interests of all of its citizens. This point was summarized in Principle 40 of *The Most Important Lessons in Economics and Finance: "The ideal goal of an economic policy for a nation is to maximize the wealth of its entire people and not that of a specific financial entity"* (Criniti, 2014, 71). Amazing things can happen when a nation is united and focused on achieving its common goals.

What is true for Mandela's South Africa is certainly true for any poor nation—that is, a nation is fighting for survival when the majority of its people are not capable of obtaining basic quality survival essentials (see chapter 12). If a poor nation cannot survive, then it leaves an open door for other wealthier nations to come in and exploit it at will. This matter is analogous to a wealthy corporation executing a friendly or a hostile takeover of a weaker, desperately poor company.

It is the nation's responsibility to ensure that enough wealth exists for its people to continue strong as one united entity. If a nation breaks down, the individuals and groups may welcome a friendly, wealthier foreign nation to rule them because at least it will allow them to survive. However, this option is generally always bad for a people in the long term. Foreign rulers usually exploit the wealth of the people they are ruling. The wealth is then extracted and transferred to the foreign country. This has been done many times throughout history, and it has often resulted in a violent reaction by the oppressed nations.

Let's briefly take a look at some examples of how more wealth for a nation can also increase the probability of it continuously surviving and prospering by providing it the greatest options to obtaining survival essentials. First, wealthier nations generally have better access to water through several methods. Their wealth can afford the best water-treatment plants throughout the land. Their specialists then test the water before releasing it to their citizens. Good water means a healthier nation. Wealthier nations may also buy real spring water from poorer nations to ship back home. Wealthier nations can also afford to buy expensive salt-water distillers that will convert ocean water to fresh water. As the world is made up almost entirely of ocean, this option for wealthier countries can result in their survival if all of the fresh water is used up. On the other hand, poorer countries do not have this option. If that event were to occur, their people may quickly die without intervention from richer nations.

Next, wealthier nations have better access to food. A nation can maximize its agricultural needs with proper equipment and skills. Wealthier nations can also afford to buy large quantities of exotic foods from foreign nations. The obesity problem today found in many wealthier nations is strong evidence of their excess food supply. In all of today's wealthiest nations, you can buy food that was originally grown in almost every part of the world. The abundance of food in wealthy nations has made cooking a hobby rather than just a necessity. The endless cooking shows and culinary classes available demonstrate the large supply of not only just food but also quality finished meals.

On the other hand, poor nations have little to no food. How can these nations ever prosper if they can't even pass the Survival Test? If their people are starving, then they must dedicate all of their energy to just staying alive. There is no time for supporting specialists and taking their wealth to the next level.

Wealthier nations can also use their money to buy the fifth primary physical immediate survival essential: conservation of energy. Losing energy may not be much of a concern for them because they can always gain more with better access to food and water. However, ignoring that aspect, with their money they can save their energy spent on various tasks that they can outsource. In other words, they can save energy by paying other nations to do their laborious jobs for them. They can pay other nations to collect and grow their food, to manufacture all of their products, and, simply, to do any of the services that they don't want to do.

Comparing these facts with our Jack Smith example, we can see that wealthy nations share many similarities with wealthy individuals. *If a nation can save more energy by not having to do basic survival tasks, then more time is freed up to do more higher-level specialist jobs, such as rocket science.* On the other hand, poor nations do not have this option. They may be forced to take on the undesirable jobs from the wealthier nations in order to survive. However, if a poorer nation can find and manage a specialty product or service well, especially one that the wealthier nations will purchase, then they too may prosper one day.

It is not necessary to provide an extended analysis for obtaining all of the survival essentials listed in chapter 12 for nations in the way that we did for individuals. In order to keep this book at a reasonable length, I think the above analysis is sufficient. It should be very clear by now that a nation with wealth can choose to buy quality survival essentials for the short- and long-term in addition to any other desirable luxury items. Thus, it can buy the best infrastructure, medical services, security (such as military and police), technology of all kinds, transportation systems, weapons, and so forth, available. **It is important to remember though that just like an individual or a group, in general, if a wealthy nation decides not to continue to maximize wealth, then it automatically, by default, chooses to increase its chances of moving in the direction of the edge of survival, and ultimately, closer to death.**

CHAPTER 22

Maximizing Guns, Germs, Steel, and Other Forms of Wealth

This book cannot be published without acknowledging and providing some commentary on a great related book by the university professor Jared Diamond—*Guns, Germs, and Steel: The Fates of Human Societies*. As the book is very detailed, it is best to present Diamond's conclusions in his own words: "My main conclusion was that societies developed differently on different continents because of differences in continental environments, not in human biology. Advanced technology, centralized political organization, and other features of complex societies could emerge only in dense sedentary populations capable of accumulating food surpluses—populations that depended for their food on the rise of agriculture that began around 8,500 B. C. But the domesticable wild plant and animal species essential for that rise of agriculture were distributed very unevenly over the continents..." (Diamond, 1999, 426).

Diamond's book is very important for our analysis because it demonstrates how the richest countries got there in the first place. For example, he tries to explain why the Europeans were the ones who were able to colonize the entire Americas and Australia rather than any other competing human group or nation. His attempt to attack this problem from a nonracist, truthful viewpoint led to his startling conclusion noted above. In short, modern civilization can be traced to the Fertile Crescent area, where early farmers had the best wealth available out of all of the competing existing human societies. That is, they had the best access to the most valuable crops (for example, wheat) and the most valuable large domesticated animals (for example, cows), which led to the creation of the largest populations of that era. Subsequently, they were the first to begin learning how to live together with more people.

Considering the Fertile Crescent's central location to the three major continents of Africa, Asia, and Europe, it was these three areas where people began migrating first. Further, they took with them their accumulated wealth. Their increased food supply led to more specialists, more organized writing, and more tools. It also eventually led to guns, steel, and the ability for their descendants to carry an antibody to many deadly microscopic diseases, like the Black Plague. Meanwhile their technical knowledge was accumulating over centuries throughout various areas of these three continents. By the time the Europeans began their world conquest, their accumulated wealth of military weapons and knowledge were very difficult for the native peoples of most other continents to compete with. Simply, it's not that the Europeans were biologically smarter—they just had a great head start!

If you can accept at least most of what Diamond's conclusions are (hopefully you will want to read his book first), then it may be easier for you to see the parallels with our former analysis. Diamond's main conclusions speak to the essence of survival and the organization of prosperity depicted in this book. Humanity probably started out with all groupings equally in survival mode. Eventually, some humans became prosperous first, which was most likely because of a combination of having access to the best wealth available and their good management of it. We have learned earlier that prosperous individuals multiply as they advance through each of the Five Major Scientific Phases of Prosperity. Diamond's conclusions and my own are very similar because our current human state of almost entering Phase 4 of prosperity can be directly traced back thousands of years ago to the smallest groups beginning their ascent to prosperity in the Fertile Crescent. *Specifically, the events that occurred there are evidence of the order of the Survival-Prosperity Sequence for the first three Major Scientific Phases of Prosperity.*

Inevitably, some human society would have taken the lead in prosperity, whether it started in the Fertile Crescent or somewhere else. That is, some small group of humans eventually would have accumulated more wealth relative to other groups. This leads me to what I see as a major shortcoming of Diamond's book. That is, although a connection to wealth management is implied throughout, the book fails to clarify and elaborate on the relationship between the conclusions and the three sciences from which the whole book's argument is based on: economics, finance, and survivalism. **In particular, stronger nations derived their power over others mainly from properly managing all of their wealth, particularly their survival essentials.** Let's explore this aspect further.

Diamond recognizes that animals and crops, a major foundation to his argument, can be considered wealth: "The Fertile Crescent's biological diversity over small distances contributed to a fourth advantage—its wealth in ancestors not only of valuable crops but also of domesticated big mammals" (Diamond, 1999, 141). Additionally, in regard to the Europeans' colonization of Africa, he admits, "In short, Europe's colonization of Africa had nothing to do with differences between European and African peoples themselves, as white racists assume. Rather, it was due to accidents of geography and biogeography—in particular, to the continents' different areas, axes, and suites of wild plant and animal species. That is, the different historical trajectories of Africa and Europe stem ultimately from differences in real estate" (Diamond, 1999, 400–401). Here he is again talking about wealth, particularly real estate, to explain away the book's conclusions. Further, certainly guns and steel are assets, and germ warfare can be considered an asset too.

When you put this all together, it is difficult to escape the conclusion that the book is missing an analysis from the proper context in which it belongs: from the perspective of economics, finance, and survivalism. The lessons from these fields, more than any other subjects, should be able to best attack his book's problems. In addition, *Guns, Germs, and Steel* failed to give a good explanation of the role money has played in the human story of wealth management. As you will see in part 3, the creation of money was a new force in evolution that cannot be ignored. The major flaw noted above was indirectly acknowledged by Diamond in his 2003 afterword: "THE THIRD RECENT extension of *GGS*'s message to the modern world was to me the most unexpected one. Soon after the book's publication, it was reviewed favorably by Bill Gates, and then I began receiving letters from other business people and economists who pointed out possible parallels between the histories of entire human societies discussed in *GGS* and the histories of groups in the business world" (Diamond, 1999, 433).

Despite the above limitations, many aspects of Diamond's book were well researched. However, by bringing *Guns, Germs, and Steel* into the realm of the sciences of prosperity, we can have a better understanding of its problems. *The Survival of the Richest* can actually be viewed as an extension to Diamond's theories. ***That is, as his book helps to explain our prehistory and our history, the concepts used in this book can help to explain our prehistory, our history, our present, and our future.***

I end this chapter with some final questions and analogies to reflect on. First, let's start with some questions. How can a lightweight fighter defeat a much stronger and heavier sumo wrestler? How does a tiny local mom-and-pop business turn into a giant multinational company? How was a relatively small country such as ancient Egypt able to accomplish so much for its era? How did a relatively small economic entity such as ancient Rome create one of the greatest land empires? How did a relatively small nation such as Great Britain once create one of the greatest sea empires? How did a relatively small nation such as Japan become a great competitor to its giant neighbors on all sides? How can humans, a much weaker, slower species than many in the living family, become the dominant species on this planet?

To answer these questions, we must understand the greatest assets of wealth: our survival essentials. We have learned from our former analysis that the ability and the determination to obtain and to manage the right resources can increase the probability of achieving the survival and prosperity goals for any economic and financial entity. Even the smallest entities can become greatly enhanced if they apply the lessons of economics and finance well.

Finally, let's view Diamond's conclusions through a unique analogy. Instead of comparing the wealth of the early European colonizers to those whom they colonized, we will try a different approach. To increase the validity of this analogy, we will want to completely eliminate any elements of racial superiority from our argument. The best apples-to-apples comparison should be made by imagining what it would be like for the same nation to combat *itself* from an earlier time frame. Here we can assume that the average citizen is almost entirely biologically the same. Since there is now no room for racism in this argument, we can look more clearly at wealth management's role in history. This exercise will require some imagination though!

First, let's pretend that the conquistadors of the Spain of 1492 discovered another nation that was identical to the Spain of 2016. What would have been the outcome if combat were to ensue between the two groups? Very few would argue with the obvious truth that the modern version of Spain would annihilate the older version. Despite the fact that Spain is no longer as rich as it was in 1492 (at least compared to other European nations of that time), Spain's increase in technology and the knowledge to use it over the past five hundred-plus years has made it *relatively* richer today than before. Modern Spain has weaponry such as machine guns and bomb-dropping airplanes that would easily defeat its older version.

How about the United States of America of 1776 versus the United States of America of 2016? How about Great Britain of 1776 versus Great Britain of 2016? How about China of 1776 versus China of 2016? We can do this exercise with all of the richest nations from every continent and keep coming to the same conclusion: the modern, wealthier nation is much more powerful and would most likely win the war. *This demonstrates clearly, with racism eliminated from the equation, that the origin of national power is mainly connected to how well a nation manages the wealth it has access to.* If we could bring great ancient nations to the present and teach them modern technology, then they would quickly adapt, if it were necessary. Obviously the ancients were capable, as they were human, too, but they just were lacking the technological wealth to compete.

To sum up this chapter, the proper management of the accumulation of *accessible wealth* has led the wealthiest nations to their current position of power. If modern poor countries want to learn how to be prosperous like them, then they must first understand the role wealth plays in survival and prosperity. Next, they must manage their wealth in accordance with the principles of economics.

CHAPTER 23

Surviving an Economic Collapse

All nations have a risk of dying at some time. But all of the many ways to destroy a nation have something to do with wealth. If a nation were demoted to the survival step from a once-prosperous position, then it needs to be prepared for tough times. But how do individuals survive when the nation it belongs to is barely alive?

In an economic collapse, wealthy individuals and groups are usually still in the best position to survive. They may have accumulated enough wealth that they can provide themselves the proper amount of survival essentials for a sufficient time period to wait out the catastrophe. The poor may have a more difficult time, as the economic struggle may aggravate their already-challenging individual positions. But there is some good news!

Contrary to what many doomsday preppers may say, the conclusions of this book actually have some positive messages for any potential economic Armageddon. Two major things can help individuals survive a major economic collapse. First, if everyone has an emergency reserve, then it will relieve some pressure until the situation is hopefully rectified. But for how long should your emergency reserve last? In *The Most Important Lessons in Economics and Finance*, I proposed a twelve-month emergency reserve broken down as follows: "…at least six months of current living expenses in cash equivalents (e.g., a checking account in a bank), three months in actual cash stored somewhere fire-proof and safe, and three months in gold…" (Criniti, 2014, 177). If you want to add even more protection for a major economic emergency, then I would add to the above an additional one-year minimum emergency reserve of the survival essentials listed in chapter 12, for example, a one-year supply of food, water (or at least an alternative plan to obtain more, such as by collecting rainwater), and so forth. You could have more than a one-year supply of survival essentials but having less than this minimum is very risky.

If everyone in a given country were to take these measures, then the whole country would be better prepared to handle an economic catastrophe. Usually in these situations, the nation just needs a little time for the economic managers to reorganize their strategies. They may need to borrow or print more money. They may even need an entire economic facelift with a totally different strategy, for example, to shift from communism to free-market capitalism. The individual just needs to ensure that he or she has enough survival essentials to survive until the political smoke clears.

The second major thing that can help individuals survive a major economic collapse is to recognize the value in human co-operation and unity. Many doomsday preppers plan on isolating themselves and taking care of only their families. This is a short-sighted approach though. **It should *never* be forgotten that what took us to our current state of civilization is our proper management of wealth *together*. Collectively we have created civilization, and collectively we can destroy it. Thus, in a worst-case scenario, collectively we can *recreate* it!** Humans can fix almost any situation, as long as we keep united. It may take a little time, and thus, the reason for the individual emergency reserves. However, people should not hurt others and steal from one other. This can lead to a downward spiral of other problems.

We are our best assets! If we create animosity among our neighbors, especially for reasons that may be out of our control, then we divide ourselves and lower our collective probability of returning civilization to its former state. None of us, regardless of our occupation, can restore an economy alone. Simply, it would require too much knowledge and labor for any single person or even a small group. The above points could help us keep our focus and our sanity if we ever were to unfortunately experience an economic collapse.

CHAPTER 24

The Survival of the Richest Planets

I have included the next two highly subjective chapters because I feel that some commentary may help you to better understand the origins and the future of prosperity. Humans have made many advances in astronomy over the past several hundred years, especially the past fifty years. Scientists have been using the most amazing telescopes to try to discover similar planets. Although they have made some progress, many details are still very fuzzy. However, it has become increasingly clear that our planet is unique in many ways. In particular, it has an abundance of life of all kinds. From the water that flows over the majority of the surface to the highest trees, Earth is extremely special!

Earth is probably one of the wealthiest planets, if not *the* wealthiest planet, due to its extreme diversity of life and its creations. From the perspective of the living, our planet is certainly rich compared to any of the planets known at the time of this writing. The large majority of our survival essentials are only located here, which makes this planet even more valuable to us. It also has a large selection of resources, both organic and inorganic, which can be put to various uses.

Many scientists believe that the diversity of our rich atmosphere led to the creation of life—for example, the right mixtures of hydrogen, nitrogen, and other gases. At the moment, Earth has millions of living species in a wide range of sizes. Life here is found above, under, on, and near water. We also have many kinds of metals, minerals, and weather patterns. We have deserts, mountains, and valleys. How many other planets that we know of have even close to this diversity of living and nonliving things? So far the count is zero. How many other planets that we know of have technology like ours—or technology at all? Again, the current answer is zero. That is, we don't yet know of any other planet that has cars, the Internet, or rockets. This makes Earth uniquely wealthy. Earth started out diverse, and its accumulation of so much wealth over billions of years has made it even more diverse.

Although this subject may be premature, many scientists have little doubt that the facts of history are becoming increasingly more convincing—the only way to solve many of the world's existing problems is to understand how we solved our past ones. Hopefully, at this point of the book, you are convinced that the human survival story has illustrated that wealth management has led us to our current position. It should also be clear that much of our progress, whether figuring out how to survive giant predators or how to live in Arctic climates, usually had the most success when parts of humanity were unified. That is, cooperation among humans has always been one of our biggest assets. If this is true, Earth's present major problems may only be resolved the same way. The general historical pattern of prosperity depicted in this book is unarguable: individuals became groups; groups became larger; and larger groups became nations. This pattern, formed over tens of thousands of years from humanity's rising, provides a clear indication of the next logical phase of prosperity: the unifying of nations to become a unified planet.

It is our duty to preserve and manage well *all* of the wealth that exists on this planet. Other similar planets may exist somewhere in this universe. If those planets have living entities that are similar to ours, then coexistence may not be possible and conflict may ensue. Our planet is at risk of colonization by aliens if we ever encounter hostile life with more advanced wealth than us. The unity of nations can ensure a well-prepared planet in the face of uncertainty, from meteorites to alien attacks. We must admit that we have already entered the space era. Thus, we must be prepared to deal with the unconceivable, even if it may currently sound weird.

I understand that to some this all may sound like science fiction and laughable to a degree. However, it is not far-fetched when you think about how little the most technologically advanced civilizations knew about the rest of the world only about five hundred years ago. The span of human history from 1492 until now is relatively short compared to the period from the origins of humanity. In that year, long-separated human groups from different continents accidentally rediscovered one another. In the Age of Discovery, conflict was inevitable almost every time a new place was discovered. The group wealthier in technology usually was the victor, and much bloodshed was the result.

These situations dealt with humans versus humans. Imagine what would happen if we were to encounter a nonhuman? It is a far-fetched scenario, but it is still a possibility that we must admit to if we are to continue to explore other planets. What if our wish comes true, and we find life somewhere else? Are we prepared to defend ourselves and our planet if necessary? What other living Earthling will defend our planet: ants, bears, lions, snakes, tigers, or maybe the wolves? The last question was rhetorical because the next possible options are far behind us in that regard, as you will see in parts 3, 4, and 5. If we do encounter hostile aliens, would they really care about national differences? They probably would consider us all the same enemy, and they would attack us equally.

In short, as we close out Phase 3 of prosperity, humanity must reflect on the reasons why we should continue into Phase 4. Although much of this topic will be covered in later parts of this book, hopefully the one conclusion that you have derived, or will eventually derive, is that the unity of all nations may help us to resolve many of our most immediate problems as well as many unexpected ones, such as potentially deadly alien encounters or an android rebellion (more on this latter struggle in part 3). *As always, those who prepare for all potential future struggles are generally in the best position to handle them.*

It is important to remember though that just like individuals, groups, and nations, in general, if the inhabitants of a wealthy planet like Earth decide not to continue to maximize wealth, then they automatically, by default, choose to increase

Earth's chances of moving in the direction of the edge of survival, and ultimately, closer to death. As demonstrated earlier, more wealth provides more options for the wealthiest entities to survive better; it does not necessarily mean that those entities will choose the best options. If life on our planet is to continue to prosper, then we must exercise our options for better survival and do it together!

CHAPTER 25

The Survival of the Richest Universe

Why are humans so determined to explore space and to look for other planets? Why did we put humans on the moon? Why do we have the International Space Station above us? What is the purpose of space telescopes? Why do we have rovers on Mars? Why did we send space probes to every planet in our solar system? Many of the common answers to these questions can be traced to our insatiable desire to learn more and for the good of humanity. But are these explanations sufficient?

I think that our determination to colonize space is also related to our wealth-management goals. I view our various space odysseys as a search for more resources. There may be more places that we can claim, more raw materials that we can use, and more knowledge that we can gain. All of this can be labeled as being in the name of survival and prosperity. How many planets exist out there? How much wealth can we absorb from them to increase our chances of surviving better? Can extraterrestrial life add value to our existence?

Obviously we have a long way to go before we can conquer the universe. We need to finish Phase 3 of prosperity, survive, and then advance to the top of Phase 4 first. In parts 4 and 5, we will discuss humanity's current major priorities that need to be resolved before we can take on our next challenges. It may be best to not get ahead of ourselves. However, although this topic may make many people feel uncomfortable, it doesn't hurt to at least admit that this is where we appear to be heading.

It is becoming increasingly more apparent what humanity's destiny may be as we continue to reflect on the many struggles that our ancestors encountered during their expansion from the family unit to the globalized world. The human story forces me to wonder whether it is possible that we are here not only to manage this planet but also the whole universe. The real "masters of the universe" may be accurately titled the true "universal managers." If we ever get that promotion, then we will certainly have a huge responsibility. Imagining such an unbelievable role that we may play one day forces us to recall our simple beginnings here, surviving and prospering together on this wonderful planet, Earth!

CHAPTER 26

Conquering Struggles with Wealth

The Role of the Struggle

Maybe the musician Seal was correct in his popular song "Crazy" when he sang, "But we're never gonna survive unless we get a little crazy" (Seal, 1991). As life is crazy and unpredictable, it can be argued that we need to manage our struggles accordingly. Unquestionably, life is difficult for the large majority of entities on this planet. The level of difficulty generally depends though on the size and the quantity of the struggles that one must overcome. This may explain why some people seem to have an easier life than others.

Struggles may exist to make life difficult and to keep it challenging. It can be argued that struggles exist to force us to find out who really wants to live. But certainly everyone—even the richest people—must face struggles, externally and internally, at various points in their lives. That is, everyone must confront hardships in order to stay alive. Since the beginnings of academic biology, the words "struggle" and "survival" have always been mentioned in the same breath but without much further analysis. This is unfortunate because the struggle plays such an ***inseparable role*** in survival (and in the sciences of prosperity as this book demonstrates) and in biology. This is the reason why the struggle was included in the definition of survival in part 1. **In essence, it would be unnecessary to learn survivalism if struggles did not exist because nothing could stop us from dying. Whether we like it or not, our struggles are a part of who we are and who we could become. Struggles are indeed an inevitable part of life!**

The actor Sylvester Stallone in *Rocky Balboa*, the sixth movie in the *Rocky* series, has a great line that sums up the role of the struggle and the characteristics of a survivor. Stallone's character, Rocky Balboa, a fictitious boxing champion from South Philadelphia, was giving a lecture to his son who was developing the wrong attitudes about life. He said, "You, me, or nobody is gonna hit as hard as life. But it ain't about how hard you hit. It's about how hard you can get hit and keep moving forward" (*Rocky Balboa*, 2007). *Life certainly does hit hard, and may I add, consistently. But it is our ability to manage these hits, both the present ones and the ones that we may take later, that can position us for greatness in the endless fight to survive.*

The Role of the Fight

This brief section was added just to note the important relationship between the terms *fight* and *struggle*. The *fight* can have many different meanings in normal conversation, depending on the context. However, for the purposes of this book, it may be very useful to view it as *a powerful approach to survival*—for example, as used in the expression "fight to survive." **That is, the fight can refer to an intense, relentless management of the present struggle to stay alive for a living entity.**

Some people may halfheartedly manage their confrontations with hardships. In contrast, fighters are a special breed of individuals who focus all their energy on reducing or eliminating each struggle. Although it certainly helps, you do not have to be physically strong to be a fighter. Comprehensive mental toughness is the true starting line for the ultimate warrior.

True fighters do not give up, regardless of the struggle! In other words, it is all or nothing for them: conquer the struggle, or die trying. They courageously confront adversity with a relentless commitment to survive. Fighters truly have a special place in survivalism, as generally they are the ones who transition into *survivors*. Their strong will to live is a useful tool to help them to survive, and eventually, to prosper.

The Role of Wealth in the Human-to-Human Struggle

The great irony of wealth is that it can help us to lessen or eliminate so many major struggles, but lack of it can prove to be one of the greatest struggles of all. In this section, we will take a closer look at the role that wealth plays in various struggles. I have specifically selected two major national leaders who became internationally famous for their parts in world history. They were chosen because they represent two completely opposite struggles: one for evil and one for good. Adolf Hitler, the Nazi dictator during World War II, was chosen because his struggle was a racist one that had no benefit for the collective whole of humanity. Nelson Mandela, a leader in the struggle against South African apartheid, was chosen because his struggle ultimately was to eliminate racism and to unite humanity. Interestingly, both of them wrote a famous book about their struggles: Hitler's *Mein Kampf* (this translates from German as *My Struggle*) and Mandela's *The Struggle Is My Life*. Although they both had completely different struggles, they both undeniably shared a major one within their lifetimes: a lack of wealth.

First, let's have both Hitler and Mandela state their struggles in their own words before adding commentary. Hitler's greatest struggle was to become anti-Semitic. "My views with regard to anti-Semitism thus succumbed to the passage of time, and this was my greatest transformation of all. It cost me the greatest inner soul struggles, and only after months of battle between my reason and my sentiments did my reason begin to emerge victorious" (Hitler, 1999, 55). On the other hand, Mandela's struggle involved providing equal individual freedom for all South Africans (and eventually for all of humanity): "For my own part I have made my choice. I will not leave South Africa, nor will I surrender. Only through hardship, sacrifice and militant action can freedom be won. The struggle is my life. I will continue fighting for freedom until the end of my days" (Mandela, 2013, 210).

The differences between Hitler and Mandela are very obvious. But what did these two have in common? Yes, they both enjoyed boxing, and they both were jailed for their chosen struggles. Yet despite their completely different goals, they both endured major financial struggles in their lifetime. If they had never been able to successfully manage their own financial struggles, then they might never have been able to advance their chosen causes.

Two statements from Hitler provided information about his poor childhood and his early adult life. First, he wrote, "Poverty and hard reality now compelled me to take a quick decision. What little my father had left had been largely exhausted by my mother's grave illness; the orphan's pension to which I was entitled was not enough for me even to live on, and so I was faced with the problem of somehow making my own living" (Hitler, 1999, 18). Next, he described his tough early years in Vienna as a starving artist: "Five years in which I was forced to earn a living, first as a day laborer, then as a small painter; a truly meager living which never sufficed to appease even my daily hunger" (Hitler, 1999, 21).

Mandela explained the financial hardships that he encountered later in life while fighting for his cause: "I have had to separate myself from my dear wife and children, from my mother and sisters, to live as an outlaw in my own land. I have had to close my business, to abandon my profession, and live in poverty and misery, as many of my people are doing" (Mandela, 2013, 210).

The major reason that I have chosen to discuss Hitler and Mandela was to demonstrate that wealth can be used to fight almost any struggle, both for evil and for good causes. Both of their causes (one that brought some of the greatest destruction to humanity and another that helped foster some of the greatest construction) were promoted by wealth. That is, we can establish a direct link between two of the greatest competing human-to-human struggles in history and wealth (especially money). Although there are many ways to show this link, to keep this part brief, let's just hear it directly from each leader!

In the early days of Hitler's movement, his group needed money to survive, or it could not continue to function. Hitler acknowledges this when his movement was able to receive some funding (a donation of three hundred marks): "This relieved us of a great worry. For at this time the financial stringency was so great that we were not even in a position to have slogans printed for the movement, or even distribute leaflets. Now the foundation was laid for a little fund from which at least our barest needs and most urgent necessities could be defrayed" (Hitler, 1999, 355–356). Hitler indirectly admits here the necessity of finance. Just think that World War II possibly might have never occurred without those three hundred marks!

Mandela's organization also needed money to fight for its cause: "Our political struggle has always been financed from internal sources—from funds raised by our own people and by our own supporters" (Mandela, 2013, 299). It may be argued that these are just two examples. What about all other political organizations and their agendas? The answer will always be the same. Every political struggle can only be conquered if its organization first has wealth, particularly in the form of money.

Mandela can also give us more insight on this issue. He dealt first hand with it in order to give his struggle the international attention it needed. He wrote, "I must add that, whilst abroad, I had discussions with leaders of political movements in Africa and discovered that almost every single one of them, in areas which had still not attained independence, had received all forms of assistance from the socialist countries, as well as from the West, including that of financial support" (Mandela, 2013, 300).

In short, this section was added to elaborate on wealth's major role in a specific part of survival: the struggle. *By comparing the leaders of two of the greatest competing struggles in history, my intention was to demonstrate the effect of wealth on human-to-human struggles. In both cases, Hitler and Mandela would not have been able to properly manage their struggles without wealth—particularly, money.* All political goals and charitable causes follow the same pattern—that is, more wealth can increase their chances of success. Contrary to common beliefs, money is not the real root of evil and of good causes. Instead the economic or financial entities that use money to help fight their battles are the real root of evil and of good causes.

In the next section, we will now take a more comprehensive view of the role that wealth plays in many other types of struggles.

The Role of Wealth in Other Various Struggles

We learned in chapter 8 that an individual or a group can survive an almost unlimited supply of potential survival scenarios. Any one of the many forces of nature, alone or in combination with others, can represent the major cause of an entity's struggle to stay alive. I will now briefly review that exact list of major deadly struggles and demonstrate how each struggle can be reduced or eliminated with wealth. Many examples of wealth are derived from the survival essentials listed in chapter 12. For the sake of brevity, I will list only some of them for each struggle; however, probably many more exist.

Please recall that the original list of struggles was incomplete. Nonetheless, it is still sufficient to show the effects of wealth. Regardless of the entity types discussed in part 2, the right wealth can always help us better manage our struggles. The following are some examples of major deadly struggles and the corresponding wealth that a living entity can manage to help stay alive:

1. Accidental personal injury (such as falling down a manhole): a communication means, a hospital, a medical kit, medical knowledge, a rescue team, and transportation
2. Aging: a communication means, companionship, fitness equipment, good health, a hospital, a medical kit, medical knowledge, and transportation
3. Alcohol or drug abuse: a clinic, medical knowledge, medicine, and a therapist
4. Alien invasion: a communication means, navigational equipment, security, transportation, weaponry, and a unified human race
5. Android rebellion: a communication means, counter technology, navigational equipment, security, transportation, weaponry, and a unified human race
6. Animal attack: a medical kit, medical knowledge, self-defense knowledge, and weaponry
7. Being stranded in the wilderness: a communication means, quality food, a medical kit, medical knowledge, a rescue team, a strong shelter, transportation, quality water, and wilderness survival knowledge

8. Broken heart: companionship, music, a positive attitude, and a therapist

9. Burglary: a communication means, security, self-defense knowledge, and weaponry

10. Car accident: a communication means, a hospital, a medical kit, medical knowledge, transportation, and a rescue team

11. Child abuse: companionship, medicine, a positive attitude, security, and a therapist

12. Dehydration: a beverage, a communication means, a hospital, a medical kit, medical knowledge, transportation, and a rescue team

13. Depression: companionship, music, a positive attitude, and a therapist

14. Disease (mental or physical): a communication means, a hospital, a medical kit, medical knowledge, medicine, and transportation

15. Near drowning: a blanket, a communication means, dry clothes, a hospital, a medical kit, medical knowledge, a rescue team, and transportation

16. Earthquakes: a communication means, a hospital, a medical kit, medical knowledge, a rescue team, a strong shelter, and transportation

17. Economic issues: an emergency reserve, a good economic manager(s), money, a positive attitude, and a unified nation

18. Electrocution: a communication means, a hospital, a medical kit, medical knowledge, a rescue team, and transportation

19. Electromagnetic pulse (EMP): an alternative communication means, emergency reserves, security, and counter-technology such as Faraday cages

20. Embarrassment: companionship, humor, a positive attitude, and a therapist

21. Extreme loneliness: a book, a communication means, and companionship

22. Financial issues: an emergency reserve, a good financial manager, money, and a positive attitude

23. Fire: a communication means, fire fighters, a hospital, ladders, a medical kit, medical knowledge, a rescue team, smoke detectors, a sprinkler system, a strong shelter, and transportation

24. Gangrene: a communication means, a hospital, a medical kit, medical knowledge, a rescue team, and transportation

25. Genocide: a communication means, hospitals, medical kits, medical knowledge, a positive attitude, rescue teams, security, self-defense skills, shelters, transportation, weaponry, and a unified international support system

26. Global warming: a communication means, medical knowledge, cooler shelters, helpful technology, and transportation

27. Heart attack: a communication means, a hospital, a medical kit, medical knowledge, a rescue team, a therapist, and transportation

28. Heat-related illnesses (lack of or overabundance of heat): a communication means, a hospital, a medical kit, medical knowledge, a rescue team, and transportation

29. Inadequate sleep: bed, blankets, clothes, pillows, a shelter, and sleep

30. Lack of shelter: clothes and a shelter

31. Landslide: a communication means, a hospital, a medical kit, medical knowledge, a rescue team, a shelter, and transportation

32. Life imprisonment: companionship, a positive attitude, a purpose to live, and the will to live

33. Loss of all reasons to live: a positive attitude, a purpose to live, and the will to live

34. Low self-esteem: knowledge, a positive attitude, and a therapist

35. Malnutrition: quality food and water

36. Maritime disasters: a communication means, quality food, a medical kit, medical knowledge, a rescue team, a shelter, transportation, and quality water

37. Meteorite strike: an alternative communication means, counter technology, emergency reserves, security, telescopes, and large-quantity transportation methods (may need to relocate everyone)

38. Plane crash: a communication means, quality food, a means to start and maintain a fire, a medical kit, medical knowledge, a rescue team, a shelter, transportation, and quality water

39. Poisoning: a communication means, a hospital, a medical kit, medical knowledge, a rescue team, and transportation

40. Predation: a communication means, security, self-defense knowledge, and weaponry

41. Rape: companionship, medicine, a positive attitude, security, self-defense knowledge, a therapist, and weaponry

42. Sexual frustration: sexual companionship and a therapist

43. Shock: a communication means, a hospital, a medical kit, medical knowledge, a rescue team, a therapist, and transportation

44. Starvation: a communication means, quality food, a hospital, a medical kit, medical knowledge, transportation, a rescue team, and quality water

45. Stroke: a communication means, a doctor, a hospital, a medical kit, medical knowledge, a rescue team, a surgeon, a therapist, and transportation

46. Suffocation: quality air, a communication means, a hospital, a medical kit, medical knowledge, a rescue team, and transportation

47. Suicide attempt: companionship, a hospital, medicine, music, a positive attitude, a psychologist, and a therapist

48. Terrorist attack: a communication means, hospitals, medical kits, medical knowledge, a positive attitude, rescue teams, security, self-defense skills, shelters, transportation, weaponry, and a unified nation

49. Torture: apathy, a communication means, a hospital, a medical kit, medical knowledge, a positive attitude, security, self-defense skills, transportation, and weaponry

50. Violence: a communication means, a hospital, humor (to avoid it), a medical kit, medical knowledge, a positive attitude, security, self-defense skills, transportation, and weaponry

51. Volcanic eruption: an alternative communication means, counter technology, emergency reserves, security, and large-quantity transportation methods (may need to relocate everyone)

52. War: apathy, a communication means, hospitals, medical kits, medical knowledge, a positive attitude, rescue teams, security, self-defense skills, shelters, transportation, a unified nation, and weaponry

53. Weather-related issues: a communication means, a hospital, a medical kit, medical knowledge, a rescue team, a strong shelter, and transportation

CHAPTER 27

The Survival and the Prosperity by a Third Party

This book presents a perfect opportunity to expand on a concept called *financial survival by a third party* that was originally introduced in *The Necessity of Finance*. My original term mainly referred to individuals in modern civilization who survive without money because they are supported by another economic or financial entity. Some examples include, but are not limited to, dependent children or parents, pets, prisoners, and welfare-dependent citizens. It is now necessary to introduce a more comprehensive term called *the survival by a third party*, which will apply to all entities: individuals, groups, organizations, nations, and planets (this last one was included just to be thorough). It can also be applied to all forms of life, as you will see in part 3.

We will first want to know more about the party members in order to better understand the terms in this chapter. The first party refers to the entity being supported with wealth, usually in the form of money. The second party is the entity from which the first party obtains its wealth (excluding money), usually for a price. This entity is generally the seller of a product or a service, for example, the grocery store or the electric company. The third party is the entity who pays for the products and/or services from the second party, directly or indirectly, on behalf of the first party. Money is definitely involved when there is a third party. For example, a teenager buys lunch at the pizzeria with money that was given to her by her parent. She is the first party and the pizzeria is the second. The parent who gave the child money to buy the food is the third party. It is the parent who indirectly allowed this event to occur. Alternatively, the parent could have bought the pizza from the pizzeria directly and then allowed the child to eat it.

Finally, sometimes the first party is directly supported by a second party. In the above example, the kind owner at the pizzeria could have given the lunch to the teenager for free. No money was involved here, and thus, the third party (the parent) did not need to be involved with the transaction. The wealth was directly transferred from the second party to the first party for free. This situation could be called *the survival by a second party*. Any of the methods above still has the same effect: one entity helps another to stay alive through its wealth.

The survival by a third party is when an entity is surviving because another entity is providing a part or all of its present required wealth. The third party providing the support can also take the form of any entity type, such as an economic or a financial entity. For example, a person can survive because a third party, his nation, is paying for all of his living expenses. Alternatively, it is possible for a nation to survive because a third party, a wealthy individual or group of individuals, is paying for all of its expenses.

I noted in *The Necessity of Finance* that needing money to survive has become an inescapable reality of modern civilization: **"Every individual, group, organization, and country (in the case of economics) in modern civilization needs money, and consequently wealth, to survive"** (Criniti, 2013, 45). Every human entity needs money: from the homeless man to a nation's richest citizen; from the smallest tribe in Africa to the smallest corporation on Wall Street; and from the largest nonprofit organization to the largest nation. This fact was not always true, but it certainly is now. The only exceptions to this rule seem to be in the cases of the survival by a second and a third party. The first party entities initially may appear to not need money. However, when you trace the roots of their existence, you will find another entity that is somehow paying for their survival essentials, including their clothing, food, shelter, and water.

The process of getting a job to provide someone income is properly labeled by the layman as "making a living." Essentially, laborers enable themselves to continue to live through their efforts to make money. The money provides an opportunity to buy survival essentials. **The fact is that it costs money to be alive.** The amount of money needed is *the cost of living.* Make no mistake—a person with no money, no other forms of wealth with a monetary value, or no form of income (like a job) can only survive one other way: through the support of another. If a person has none of the above resources and cannot survive by a third (or a second) party, then his situation looks very grim. With each passing moment, he may be moving in the opposite direction of the edge of survival, and inevitably, closer to death.

Considering what we have learned in this book so far, it is a good opportunity to introduce a new related concept: *the prosperity by a third party*. In the survival by a third party, the third party is only paying for an entity's basic living expenses. That is, an entity only has enough support to cover basic levels of survival essentials. This entity is not provided with any emergency reserves or any kind of luxuries. On the other hand, the prosperity by a third party is an extension of this concept.

The prosperity by a third party is when an entity is prospering because another entity is providing a part or all of its present and/or future required and nonessential wealth. The difference between the two concepts can be made clear with two examples. If you provide an alley cat with food, an outdoor shelter, and water every day, then this is the survival by a third party. Without your support, this cat will need to find another way to survive. However, if you provide this cat with a caregiver, her own house, many exotic cat toys, and a large trust fund to ensure that she is taken care of properly for the rest of her life, then this is the prosperity by a third party. Dependent children can also fit in this category if the parents help them become prosperous. With this new concept, it is clearer to see that a wealthy entity has a choice to increase the probability of another entity surviving better for as long as its money can afford to support the other entity.

We need to clarify some more details about our new terms. *The total survival by a third party* and *the total prosperity by a third party* occur when an entity provides total support for another entity. An entity also can have limited support from another entity. We can call these specific situations *the partial survival by a third party* or *the partial prosperity by a third party,* depending on how much and the type of support provided to another. For example, with the partial survival by a third party, a third party may provide another person's food. The first party would be responsible for obtaining the rest of his basic survival needs. Alternatively, with the partial prosperity by a third party, a third party may provide additional support to help another prosper—for example, by paying for all of her college expenses or a new car. The first party would be responsible for obtaining the rest of her prosperous items.

The above terms are very important, especially as we move into the next parts of the book. It will be easier to show how wealthy people are also given the option to assist other forms of life (including plants and animals) to survive better. This power is so unique that it is forcing us to rethink what we know about the evolutionary process (as we will see in part 3).

CHAPTER 28

Part 2 Summary

This part of the book demonstrated a direct relationship between survivalism and the sciences of prosperity via the management of wealth. Prosperity is essentially an extension of survival, and it pertains to the duration and the quality of our lives in the present and in the future. The extended definition of survivalism is the science of the management of the present struggle to stay alive (through the management of wealth) for a living entity. The extended definition of finance is the science of (the management of all struggles to stay alive through) the management of wealth for a (living) financial entity. Other prosperous sciences were extended similarly to show the direct link with wealth. The Five Major Scientific Phases of Prosperity listed in chronological order are finance (starting first with personal finance and then with group finance), economics, planetonomics, and universonomics.

A new entity must progress through the Survival-Prosperity Sequence in each phase, which includes a Survival Test that must be passed before an entity can enter that phase of prosperity.

Whether intentional or not, there are three major wealth-management possibilities. First, you can minimize your wealth below the level of your bare minimum survival essentials necessary to survive (this is referred to as the edge of survival). Second, you can live on the edge of survival and have just enough wealth to survive. Finally, you can maximize your wealth above the level of your bare minimum survival essentials necessary to survive.

In this part, it was also demonstrated how more wealth can increase the probability of various entities continuously surviving and prospering by providing them the greatest options to obtaining survival essentials. The role of the struggle and the fight were also analyzed, as well as how wealth can reduce or eliminate a variety of deadly struggles. Finally, we explored the concepts of the survival and the prosperity by a third party.

In short, ignoring the combined lessons of the sciences of survivalism and prosperity equates to potentially welcoming either a lifetime of many struggles or a fast-approaching death for *any* entity. Alternatively, embracing the combined lessons of the sciences of survivalism and prosperity equates to potentially welcoming a lifetime of fewer struggles and a longer, quality life for *any* entity. In the next part, we will see the implications that our conclusions have on biology and, ultimately, our future!

PART 3
The Reunion Party: Biology, Economics, Finance, and Survivalism Come Together

CHAPTER 29

A Divided Family Reunited

A long time ago, the unofficial (and later the official) versions of economics, finance, and survivalism started veering off from general biology, which occurred mostly unnoticed. However, these four sciences have gone as far as they can go before their inevitable collision that is occurring today. It is often forgotten that the main subject of study in economics and finance is living human entities, which are a specific aspect of biology: the science of life. What else would be the significance of wealth management if it had no relationship to us?

Survivalism is also related to biology because its science pertains to life trying to avoid death. Further, as this book has painstakingly demonstrated, survivalism and prosperity are absolutely interconnected through the management of wealth. I showed earlier that you must survive before you can prosper, but let's not forget that you must first be alive before you can worry about survival. Hence, the above statements establish a direct link from biology to all of the Major Scientific Phases of Prosperity. Biology is the true root of survival and prosperity!

Aside from the major direct link noted above, biology also has many other links to the sciences of prosperity. For example, modern biology (and science as a whole) owes one of its greatest discoveries to academic thinking about wealth management. That is, Charles Darwin's theories of evolution, particularly of natural selection, may never have existed if he hadn't read a book called *An Essay on the Principle of Population* by an early economist named Thomas Robert Malthus. Darwin was influenced by Malthus's ideas so much that he established a direct link between human population issues and the evolution of populations for all species. In *On the Origin of Species*, Darwin wrote: "Hence, as more individuals are produced than can possibly survive, there must in every case be a struggle for existence, either one individual with another of the same species, or with the individuals of distinct species, or with the physical conditions of life. It is the doctrine of Malthus applied with manifold force to the whole animal and vegetable kingdoms; for in this case there can be no artificial increase of food, and no prudential restraint from marriage. Although some species may be now increasing, more or less rapidly, in numbers, all cannot do so, for the world would not hold them" (Darwin, 2006, 490).

Darwin was also no stranger to wealth, as he was from a very wealthy family in England. He wrote in the last pages of *The Voyage of the Beagle*, published many years before his major theory was introduced to the world, "To hoist the British flag, seems to draw with it as a certain consequence, wealth, prosperity, and civilization" (Darwin, 2006, 431). Although certain parts of this statement may be highly debatable, unquestionably, he is recognizing that there is at least some connection between wealth, prosperity, and civilization. It is important to note that the above statement was made after almost five years of sailing around the world and seeing firsthand the effects of wealth on various human civilizations. Make no mistake: for his era, Darwin was very knowledgeable about the subject of wealth!

Darwin often made other connections to economics in his explanations of biological concepts: "The advantage of diversification in the inhabitants of the same region is, in fact, the same as that of the physiological division of labour in the organs of the same individual body—a subject so well elucidated by Milne Edwards. No physiologist doubts that a stomach by being adapted to digest vegetable matter alone, or flesh alone, draws most nutriment from these substances. So in the general economy of any land, the more widely and perfectly the animals and plants are diversified for different habits of life, so will a greater number of individuals be capable of there supporting themselves" (Darwin, 2006, 523). This line of thinking undoubtedly originated with early economists. In particular, it was the famous economist Adam Smith who expanded on the concept of the division of labor in his pioneering work, *The Wealth of Nations*, in 1776. Malthus read Smith, and Darwin read Malthus. Again, for his era, Darwin was very knowledgeable about the subject of wealth!

There are many other examples of analogies made in biology to that of the sciences of prosperity. For the sake of brevity, only a few more significant ones will be mentioned. First, we will start with Herbert Spencer, a famous philosopher and one of the biggest early advocates of the theory of natural selection. In his momentous two-volume book called *The Principles of Biology*, he used economic terms and analogies on many occasions. In particular, he often referenced the phrase "division of labour." But Spencer also openly makes analogies to business and capital allocation. For example, in volume 1 of *The Principles of Biology*, he wrote, "In brief, the rate at which a man's wealth accumulates, is measured by the surplus of income over expenditure; and this, save in exceptionably favourable cases, is determined by the capital with which he begins business. Now applying the analogy, we may trace in the transactions of an organism, the same three ultimate elements" (Spencer, 2014, 129).

In another case, Spencer makes an analogy of wealth management to the internal processes of an individual. For example, in volume 2 of *The Principles of Biology*, he wrote, "Diminished expenditure in any direction, or increased nutrition however effected, will leave a greater surplus of materials. The animal will be physiologically richer. Part of its augmented wealth will go towards its own greater individuation—its size, or its strength, or both, will increase; while another part will go towards more active genesis" (Spencer, 2014, 475). In other words, by managing our internal wealth better, we could have enough energy to stay alive and healthy in addition to having enough excess nutrients to fund our reproductive goals (this part could represent prosperity). Through these and other examples, it becomes apparent that Spencer started to recognize similar patterns between biology and prosperity.

So far, I have only given examples of biologists from the nineteenth century making connections between biology and the sciences of prosperity. To see the pattern more clearly, let us see if these connections are still relevant today, which is approximately one hundred and fifty years after the above referenced statements were made. To start, we will need to take some clues from Edward Wilson, one of the most famous biologists of the contemporary era. If anything, we will discover that the connections between the sciences have only strengthened.

For starters, the term *diversification*, a key concept in economics and finance, has been embraced more since its usage by Darwin and Spencer. Biologists have now applied this idea to life via the concept of biological diversity or *biodiversity* for short. Note how Wilson elaborates on this concept: "...as a purely incidental effect, highly diversified groups have better balanced their investments and will probably persist longer into the future. If one species comes to an end, another occupying a different niche is likely to carry on" (Wilson, 2010, 130). The connection between diversification and better-balanced investments are a product of the sciences of prosperity. What is the reason for this analogy?

Later on, Wilson concludes, "BIODIVERSITY is our most valuable but least appreciated resource" (Wilson, 2010, 281). He mentions key economics and finance buzz words here, such as *valuable* and *resource*. Has Wilson been reading economics and/ or finance books? The answer is probably yes. He knows very well, as many other biologists are gradually learning today, that the major way to protect nature is to start understanding more about money and wealth management. In order to protect the diversity of life on this planet, he admits, "It is within the power of industry to increase productivity while protecting biological diversity, and to proceed in a way that one leads to the other" (Wilson, 2010, 299).

Wilson's conclusions are very similar to the general message of this chapter: "Even now, with the problem only beginning to come into focus, there is little doubt about what needs to be done. The solution will require cooperation among professions long separated by academic and practical tradition. Biology, anthropology, economics, agriculture, government, and law will have to find a common voice" (Wilson, 2010, 312). However, many biologists are learning that the loudest common voice is amplified by the speakers of money.

Many biologists and nature lovers worldwide have come to the above conclusions as a result of frustration with many other failed methods to accomplish their increasingly urgent goals. They have tried rationalizing, even pleading, with others and have made little progress. They have tried marches and protests to governments, also with little progress. They also have tried educating the masses on the importance of biodiversity, again only to be met with little progress. But many biologists and scientists are now learning that the best way to preserve a species or an entire forest of species is through wealth management. As we will see more clearly in future chapters, money can buy the protection of other living species. **At a minimum, money will at least buy enough time until the rest of the human population fully learns what many scientists have already known: that our whole planet, including *all* of the life in it, is extremely valuable to us.**

CHAPTER 30

The Survival of the Fittest

An Overview

One of the most misinterpreted theories in science is Charles Darwin's theory of natural selection, which was later relabeled "the survival of the fittest" by Herbert Spencer. Over the years, many scientists and nonspecialists have helped to confuse this concept. In order to understand the new paradigm that will be introduced later, we will need to go back to the drawing board and review what Darwin and Spencer originally meant. First, I think it's appropriate to explain the main characters and their relationship to one another.

Charles Darwin hardly needs an introduction. Although he did not invent the idea of evolution, he did explain its process best with his theory of natural selection. His theory shook every aspect of the academic world of his time, and it is still shaking it today. Darwin took his time forming his very disturbing conclusions. Actually, he finally published his book after about twenty years of reflection, mainly because of the pressure of another man's work.

Alfred Russel Wallace, a biologist who studied the natural history of the Malay Archipelago, came to roughly the same conclusions as Darwin. Darwin did not want to risk losing credit for his life's work, so he finally published his theory in a book called *On the Origin of Species* in 1859. However, Wallace has been given equal credit for the discovery. Despite Wallace's independent contribution, which certainly should be acknowledged here, it is more useful for us to reflect on the theory from the perspective of Darwin as his arguments and terminology were more influential to academia overall.

Herbert Spencer is another key participant in our discussion. Although his name is relatively obscure today, he was viewed as one of the most intelligent people of his era. Darwin even spoke highly of him. For example, in *The Descent of Man*, he wrote, "Our great philosopher, Herbert Spencer..." (Darwin, 2006, 835). Later in *The Expression of the Emotions in Man and Animals*, he wrote, "All the authors who have written on Expression, with the exception of Mr. Spencer—the great expounder of the principle of Evolution—appear to have been firmly convinced that species, man of course included, came into existence in their present condition" (Darwin, 2006, 1265). As you can see, Spencer was a prominent intellect of his time who was respected even by Darwin. Thus, any elaboration that he gave on Darwin's theory could not be ignored. As it turned out, Spencer did more than just elaborate on Darwin's theory; he gave it a nickname, and he praised it.

In Spencer's *The Principles of Biology*, a huge two-volume work published between 1864 and 1867, he analyzed Darwin's conclusions in detail. Although this work was about all aspects of biology, the impact that natural selection must have had on his thinking becomes apparent by the excessive number of times that he mentioned Darwin and his theories. In volume 1, Spencer provides an explanation of natural selection and the new term he gives it: "This survival of the fittest, which I have here sought to express in mechanical terms, is that which Mr Darwin has called "natural selection, or the preservation of favoured races in the struggle for life." That there is going on a process of this kind throughout the organic world, Mr Darwin's great work on the *Origin of Species* has shown to the satisfaction of nearly all naturalists. Indeed, when once enunciated, the truth of his hypothesis is so obvious as scarcely to need proof. Though evidence may be required to show that natural selection accounts for everything ascribed to it, yet no evidence is required to show that natural selection has always been going on, is going on now, and must ever continue to go on" (Spencer, 2014, 444–445).

It is important to understand that Darwin openly welcomed and interchangeably used Spencer's expression "the survival of the fittest." In his sixth edition of *On the Origin of Species*, he wrote, "I have called this principle, by which each slight variation, if useful, is preserved, by the term Natural Selection, in order to mark its relation to man's power of selection. But the expression often used by Mr. Herbert Spencer of the Survival of the Fittest is more accurate, and is sometimes equally convenient" (Darwin, 2003, 61). The title of his fourth chapter in the above-noted edition further demonstrates Darwin's acceptance of Spencer's term: "Natural Selection; or the Survival of the Fittest."

In his *The Descent of Man*, Darwin again uses the term interchangeably: "Thus a very large yet undefined extension may safely be given to the direct and indirect results of natural selection; but I now admit, after reading the essay by Nageli on plants, and the remarks by various authors with respect to animals, more especially those recently made by Professor Broca, that in the earlier editions of my 'Origin of Species' I probably attributed too much to the action of natural selection or the survival of the fittest. I have altered the fifth edition of the Origin so as to confine my remarks to adaptive changes of structure" (Darwin, 2006, 863).

Although Spencer agreed with most of Darwin's conclusions, he also added his own contribution. That is, in addition to natural selection, which he titled "indirect equilibration," Spencer concluded that the individual's ability to adapt to the situation should be recognized. In volume 1 of *The Principles of Biology*, he called this process "direct equilibration" and highlighted the relationship between the two processes: "What is ordinarily called adaptation, is, when translated into mechanical terms, direct equilibration. And that process which, under the name of natural selection, Mr Darwin has shown to be an ever-acting means of fitting the structures of organisms to their circumstances, we find, on analysis, to be expressible in mechanical terms as indirect equilibration" (Spencer, 2014, 466). This is the crux of Spencer's modified theory: natural selection plus self-adaptation (or indirect plus direct equilibration respectively) equals the evolution of a population.

Problems with Its Related Terminology

Undoubtedly, Darwin brought a clearer understanding of the origins of life to the world. His contributions to science should be respected and appreciated by any seeker of the truth. However, if we are ever going to take our understanding of his theory to a higher level, then we must fully understand its inherent weaknesses. In this section, we will discuss several problems related to the terms "natural selection" and "the survival of the fittest," some that are derived from others' misinterpretations of them and some that are directly inherent in the concepts.

First, the most common mistake that people make is to assume that Darwin's theory, and Spencer's nickname for it, refers to the survival of the most physically fit. The population that is the strongest or that has the best endurance is not guaranteed to be the population that gets to continue to live in the face of a struggle. The dinosaurs are the perfect examples of this truth. The age of the dinosaurs saw most of the biggest and the strongest living species ever on the planet. If the survival of the fittest meant the survival of the biggest and the strongest, then they would still be here!

The actual meaning of the word "fittest" was almost equivalent to the usage of "fit" when referring to a puzzle piece. In other words, the life-forms that best *fit in* or adapt to an environment may be the ones that can live and reproduce there. Sometimes the smallest and the weakest ones fit best in a given environment. We find that this is what happened when we again refer to the dinosaurs. The big and strong died, and our ancestors, supposedly small and weak ancient mammals, survived.

Next, the word *selection* in the concept of "natural selection" is problematic. As you will see in a future chapter, several other selection processes exist besides natural selection. However, the term "natural selection" puts Darwin in a very difficult position of explanation. It is easy to understand how humans can select with artificial selection, but when we refer to natural selection, who is the "nature" that is doing the selecting? Is it a superior being or a nonliving entity like an earthquake? These challenging questions are probably why Darwin was quick to accept the alternative term used by Spencer.

The word *survival* in the phrase "the survival of the fittest" is also problematic. The survival of the fittest generally helps to explain the evolution of a larger population. However, after getting this far in the book, you should have concluded that survival is relative to both an individual and other population sizes, including very large ones. An individual should always be trying to survive, whether alone or as part of a large group. Although Darwin and Spencer acknowledged the individual's adaptation to the environment, I think their analysis of the individual's role of survival was insufficient. In particular, the concept of "survival" and its related term the "struggle" were never analyzed as they have been in this book. The full discussion of modern human survivalism as presented earlier was absolutely necessary as a basic foundation to demonstrate how survival can also apply to every individual of any species. Further, the role of individual survival is the key ingredient in the theories of evolution that will be proposed later. We will discuss the individual more in several other later chapters.

The next issue to be addressed is with the use of the word *fittest* again. In its original usage, the term puts too much emphasis on the role that the reproduction of a population plays in evolution. Somehow the individual's survival goals and its contribution to evolution seem to be out of focus again. This consistent theme of deemphasizing the individual resurfaces again with the concepts of "natural" (as in "natural selection") and "evolution." We will come back to these topics in the next few chapters with a more extensive discussion.

To conclude this chapter, Arthur Koestler—and a statement by C. H. Waddington with which he agrees—can best explain much of what has been discussed in this section so far: "…in the present form of the orthodox theory the very term 'selection' has become ambiguous. It once meant 'survival of the fittest'; but, to quote Waddington for the last time: 'Survival does not, of course, mean the bodily endurance of a single individual, outliving Methuselah. It implies, in its present-day interpretation, perpetuation as a source for future generations. That individual "survives" best which leaves most offspring. Again, to speak of an animal as "fittest" does not necessarily imply that it is strongest or most healthy or would win a beauty competition. Essentially it denotes nothing more than leaving most offspring. The general principle of natural selection, in fact, merely amounts to the statement that the individuals which leave most offspring are those which leave most offspring. It is a tautology'" (Koestler, 1989, 159–160).

CHAPTER 31

Biology's First Predicament: Defining Nature

Who Is Nature in Natural Selection?

Darwin's version of natural selection is still the backbone of much of what is taught by professors and textbooks in modern biology. However, in everyday conversation, the modern words *nature* and *natural* are not always used in the same manner as Darwin intended. Darwin's main use of the term *natural selection*, as noted in his quote from chapter 30, was to simply distinguish something else from the selection powers of humans. Edward Wilson explains Darwin's theories as they relate to humans and nature in his introduction to Darwin's work: "If instead of nature, human beings are the agent that decides which varieties in the population best survive and reproduce, then the result is still evolution, but evolution by artificial selection. The result has been the amazingly diverse domestic breeds of plants and animals created by human beings during the past 10,000 years. In *On the Origin of Species* Darwin stressed the close parallel between natural and artificial selection, making it a cornerstone of his argument for the occurrence of evolution in nature" (Darwin, 2006, 438).

But what is that something else that exemplifies nature? First, in *On the Origin of Species*, Darwin explains that climate is one of the strongest natural selection forces: "Climate plays an important part in determining the average numbers of a species, and periodical seasons of extreme cold or drought, I believe to be the most effective of all checks" (Darwin, 2006, 493). Second, recalling Darwin's quote from chapter 29, his "nature" could also refer to the whole animal and vegetable kingdoms, from either the same or different species. From his statement in *On the Origin of Species*, Darwin's "nature" could also be a female superior being: "Nature may be said to have taken pains to reveal, by rudimentary organs and by homologous structures, her scheme of modification, which it seems that we wilfully will not understand" (Darwin, 2006, 754). Darwin's "nature," never officially defined, remains generally understood, yet it is still ambiguous. From his various writings, you can infer that his view of nature includes almost everything that is not human.

In contrast, in his interpretation of natural selection, Spencer was much more specific about what nature was. He included a great chart that breaks down the process at the back of Volume 1 of his *The Principles of Biology*. Essentially, the natural selection process included almost everything organic and inorganic: "The astronomic, geologic, and meteorological changes that have been slowly but incessantly going on, and have been increasing in the complexity of their combinations, have been perpetually altering the circumstances of organisms; and organisms, as they have become more numerous in their kinds and higher in their kinds, have been perpetually altering one another's circumstances" (Spencer, 2014, 464–465). Despite the above statement, Spencer sometimes appeared to have a similar viewpoint to that of Darwin that nature and humans are different. That is, human (artificial) selection is separate from natural selection: "We have numerous cases, among both plants and animals, where, by natural or artificial conditions, there have been produced divergent modifications of the same species; and abundant proof exists that the members of any one sub-species, habitually transmit their distinctive peculiarities to their descendants" (Spencer, 2014, 239–240).

Ultimately, regardless of Darwin's and Spencer's final definition for nature, clearly defining the term can certainly be an opportunity for improving our understanding of the process of natural selection. Many modern biologists still view humans as separate from nature in their teachings of artificial selection. As you saw in the above quote from Edward Wilson, nature was contrasted with human beings while discussing the concept of natural selection. However, later he appears to say the exact opposite: "Humanity is part of nature, a species that evolved among other species" (Wilson, 2010, 348). At a general level, he specifically admits that species are also natural: "Fifth and final principle: the exact limits of the higher taxa are arbitrary. The species themselves, the atomic units, are natural—more or less" (Wilson, 2010, 153). **If humans are a part of nature like** other species, then artificial selection must be a part of natural selection and not its opposite. This conclusion may appear insignificant, but it is not.

Human societies may continue to feel disconnected from nature for as long as they are taught that they are separate from it. However, the exponential rise in popularity of modern nature and wilderness survival shows demonstrates our strong desire to be properly reconnected. *Subconsciously we know the truth: we are not just human, but we are also human nature.* To understand this point better, I would first like to give some examples of how the word *nature* has been used in various literatures.

In *Robinson Crusoe*, Daniel Defoe uses God and nature in the same sentence: "I have been in all my Circumstances a *Memento* to those who are touch'd with the general Plague of Mankind, whence, for ought I know, one half of their Miseries flow; I mean, that of not being satisfy'd with the Station wherein God and Nature has plac'd them; for not to look back upon my primitive Condition..." (Defoe, 2008, 164). The debate of the role of God and nature still occurs today. Are God and nature the same thing, or are they separate? I think the lack of a good answer to this question is what caused Darwin much difficulty in his natural selection term, and as noted earlier, it is probably a reason he adapted Spencer's expression so quickly.

Jack London was famous for writing novels about nature and survival almost two hundred years after *Robinson Crusoe*. Here is a sample of his multiple uses of the term in one sentence: "One cannot violate the promptings of one's nature without having that nature recoil upon itself. Such a recoil is like that of a hair, made to grow out from the body, turning unnaturally upon the direction of its growth and growing into the body—a rankling, festering thing of hurt" (London, 1998, 178). Also, many survivalists frequently acknowledge humanity's integration with nature. For example, the theme of unity especially penetrates into the heart of bushcraft: "Remember, the essence of bushcraft is not mere survival, but to be at one with nature" (Mears, 2003, Author's Note).

Even in *The Elements of Style*, one of the oldest and most popular style guides for English writing, writers are cautioned about the ambiguity associated with the word *nature*: "**Nature**. Often simply redundant, used like character...Nature should be avoided in such vague expressions as "a lover of nature," "poems about nature." Unless more specific statements follow, the reader cannot tell whether the poems have to do with natural scenery, rural life, the sunset, the untracked wilderness, or the habits of squirrels" (Strunk and White, 2000, 53).

The first edition of the US Navy's *How to Survive on Land and Sea* book provides a military example of nature: "Take advantage of all natural facilities at the station, such as streams, swamps, rough and wooded country or cliffs, in planning the field exercises" (Aviation Training Division, 1943, 229). So nature here appears to be the same as the geological factors that Spencer mentions.

Additionally, is food a part of nature? Food can be viewed as a transition from what can be considered external nature to what can be considered internal nature. In volume 2 of *The Principles of Biology*, Spencer elaborates on this discussion: "Food is a foreign substance which acts on the interior as an environing object which touches it acts on the exterior—is literally a portion of the environment, which, when swallowed, becomes a cause of internal differentiations as the rest of the environment continues a cause of external differentiations" (Spencer, 2014, 382).

As you can see from this discussion so far, defining nature is complex because it appears to include so many things. Yet, at the same time, the main element that is generally *excluded* is humanity. I would now like to paint an imaginary picture for you to confirm what you probably already know about nature.

An Imaginary Picture of Nature

If you go to any art gallery to look at a picture of nature, then you will generally see a wide variety of images. For example, a beach scene might look like the following:

Large palm trees are stretched over the sand gazing at the ocean. Below the palm trees are shadows, which are a product of the giant sun at the top of the image. The sky includes many shades of blue and is dotted with various tiny white clouds. The ocean has a wide range of progressively deepening light greens that transition into several small white waves on the beach. Two small children are on the beach using buckets to build sand castles while their parents are behind, watching them from inside a swinging hammock. Meanwhile, some other activities are unfolding in the background: colorful fish swim in the almost clear ocean; large seagulls are flying in the air; and small crabs are stretched out on the beach.

Most people would agree that the scene described above represents many aspects of nature: the living animals (including the human children and parents), the ocean, the palm trees, the sand, the sky, and the sun. Thus, the big question is this: "What in this image is not natural?" The answer should be nothing. Simply, this whole environment can be said to be "natural."

The above conclusions can be drawn not only from beach environments. If you name the place, you should be able to find nature everywhere inside. Please recall from chapter 10 some examples of various survival environments. These include, but are not limited to, being adrift at sea, caves, concrete jungles (this term works for many urban survival areas), deserts, forests, islands, jungles, mountains, plains, polar regions, rain forests, swamps, and valleys. An artist can paint a different pretty picture of nature with any one of these environments!

The picture of the beach described above was pretty. But nature can be ugly too! Severe weather can be incorporated into the scenery in the above various environments. Some examples of the scary side of nature include, but are not limited to, avalanches, blizzards, cyclones, droughts, earthquakes, floods, hailstorms, heat waves, hurricanes, lightning strikes, monsoons, thunderstorms, tidal waves, tornadoes, and tsunamis. With any one of these environments, an artist can paint a different hostile picture of nature. Although they are still natural settings, these are the pictures that most artists prefer not to paint!

Our usage of the word *nature* today in various settings also supports the wide variety of applications. Let's talk some more about this. Being "natural" is big business today. Many businesses are targeting the human desire to return to nature by using this buzzword to market their products. Some examples include natural beauty care, natural building supplies, natural drinks, natural energy resources, natural foods (including natural pet foods), natural hair care, natural medicine, natural music, natural personal care, natural sensations, natural smells, and so forth. This list seems to increase almost daily because natural versions of products and services can always be found. The reason for this will be elaborated on next.

Reformed Nature: Nature Is Everything

The ultimate conclusion of this chapter is that nature is everything, which will be represented by a new concept called *reformed nature.* As can be demonstrated by any artistic picture of nature, everything in the scenery is natural: the geological features, the living, the stars, and the weather. Every living thing from the microscopic to the largest living creatures is a part of nature, which includes us. Humans probably have been separated from nature because our activities and our inventions are very different. Hence, this line of logic dictates that we must be different from the rest of nature. That is partially true. We certainly are different, but we are not separate from nature. *Those children and their plastic buckets made by other humans were just as much a part of the beach picture described above as everything else. A product should not be considered unnatural because a human made it. This is the giant fallacy of our era.*

Very few would argue that a beaver and its dam or a hermit crab and its new found home in an old seashell are not a part of nature. However, if a human intervened and built a steel dam for the beaver or a plastic shell for the hermit crab, then the scene might not be perceived as natural anymore. This conflicts with the conclusions of evolution when applied to man. If all other living things and the things that they create are natural, then why shouldn't we consider humans and our creations natural as well? Humans are interconnected in the tree of life. We do not live on a separate tree. The productions of our species like the productions of all others should also be considered natural. That would be more consistent with the way biology looks at all life. In other words, if all animals are natural, and humans are animals, then humans must also be natural.

Deep down, I think Darwin also knew that humans are a part of nature. His book *The Descent of Man* demonstrates how humans evolved from the same tree of life as all other life-forms. If all other life is natural, as can be inferred from his description of natural selection, and if humans evolved from other living species, then it can also be inferred that natural selection somehow should include humans. Yet, in its traditional sense, it never does. "Artificial selection" is the term used for human selection, and it is meant to be a separate process. This is an issue that will be confronted later when we look at the evolutionary selection processes. Many missing truths may be discovered if we can find a way to bring back our species into the concept of natural selection where it rightfully belongs.

If nature is everything, this also must include every human product and service; hence, our wealth must be natural too. With nature taking the shape of everything in our universe, we will need to organize it better to understand evolution. Reformed nature could be broken down into two major categories: *living nature* and *nonliving nature*. Living nature can then be broken down further into *human living nature* and *nonhuman living nature*. Additionally, *nonhuman nature* can refer to any form of nature that is not human, whether living or nonliving.

Our new categories of nature can help us to compare evolution in new ways to determine if there are any unique relationships. Darwin's theory only applied evolution to the living aspects of nature. If we now apply our understanding of evolution to the nonliving aspects, then we can find out some amazing things. In particular, it will be shown that nonliving nature does highly evolve under the guidance of the right species of living nature. We must understand the concept of evolution better in the next chapter before we can explore this subject more. But first let's conclude this chapter with an interesting discussion of one more related aspect about nature!

Who Is More Powerful: Humans or Nature?

We must now turn to address an ancient argument that is probably as old as humanity. Who is more powerful: humans or nature? Let's first take a look at various viewpoints on this topic throughout the ages before we derive any conclusions.

Some people believe that nature is more powerful than humans. First, the survival expert Tom Brown Jr. believes that nature is stronger: "In fact, the moment you begin to resist nature is the moment you will begin to lose. Nature is much too powerful an entity to overcome. No amount of modern technology can prevent a volcanic eruption. No person alive can turn back a thunderstorm" (Brown, 1983, 18–19).

Cody Lundin in Season 2 of the *Dual Survival* reality television series (found in Disc 2 of the DVD set in a section titled "Adrift") appeared to have a similar view. At the end of the show, Cody explained, "There is no system to survive. Nature tells you what she wants, and you can listen to her and live, or you can ignore her and die" (*Dual Survival*, 2013).

Next, Adolf Hitler had similar conclusions: "The ultimate wisdom is always the understanding of the instinct—that is: a man must never fall into the lunacy of believing that he has really risen to be lord and master of Nature—which is so easily induced by the conceit of half-education; he must understand the fundamental necessity of Nature's rule, and realize how much his existence is subjected to these laws of eternal fight and upward struggle" (Hitler, 1999, 244–245).

Even Charles Darwin agreed that nature is more powerful, as that was a cornerstone to his argument. If humans can make evolution occur by artificial selection, then nature can surely do better: "As man can produce and certainly has produced a great result by his methodical and unconscious means of selection, what may not nature effect? Man can act only on external and visible characters: nature cares nothing for appearances, except in so far as they may be useful to any being. She can act on every internal organ, on every shade of constitutional difference, on the whole machinery of life. Man selects only for his own good; Nature only for that of the being which she tends" (Darwin, 2006, 503).

Some viewpoints on this topic appear to be somewhat intermediate. First, survival expert John Wiseman views nature as neutral: "People often view an alien environment as an enemy and feel they must fight it. This is not the way to survive – fight it and you will lose! There are dangers against which precautions must be taken, but nature is neutral. Learn to live with each climate and to use what it offers" (Wiseman, 2009, 64). This viewpoint appears very similar to that expressed in the US Army *Survival* field manual: "You can remain alive anywhere in the world when you keep your wits. This is a major lesson in survival. Remember that nature and the elements are neither your friend nor your enemy—they are actually disinterested. Instead, it is your determination to live and your ability to make nature work for you that are the deciding factors" (US Department of the Army, 1970, 3–4). This viewpoint tends to lean more toward humanity being more dominant than nature *if* it can learn how to control it.

This whole argument takes a different direction though, when we consider what we have learned about nature in the previous section. If nature is everything including humanity, then what are we really comparing ourselves to anyway? **The truth is that we are an extension of nature, and thus we shouldn't compare ourselves to all of nature, only to all nonhuman aspects of it.** Thus, the whole argument above can now be reframed. *What is more powerful: human nature or nonhuman nature?*

After reviewing the facts, I can draw the following conclusions. In the beginning of humanity, what we will call the "General Control Scale of Nature" tilted in favor of nonhuman nature. Humans had little control over any of the other aspects of nature. The General Control Scale of Nature started to tip very slowly in the direction of human nature when we started to make fire and become very successful at hunting a wide range of animals. This gradual process of humanity gaining dominance over nonhuman nature took much time.

Debatably, the equilibrium point on the control scale might have occurred somewhere during the early parts of the Industrial Revolution to the period after World War II (and possibly even today). Although many may disagree with this point, few will probably disagree that humanity has certainly gained significant control over nonhuman nature compared to where we began. This progress is not to be underrated. A significant upward trend appears to have occurred over tens of thousands of years, particularly in the past few hundred years, as humanity has gained control over nonhuman nature. For example, from the perspective of human nature versus the rest of living nature, it should be clear that the battle has been more or less won for some time now. Most remaining problems from the living parts of nature now mainly include the microscopic (bacteria and viruses) and ourselves (human warfare). Thus, the major part of nature that has not been conquered is the nonliving. However, as you will see in chapter 37, humanity has continuously made significant progress against that part of nature as well.

In short, the General Control Scale of Nature is starting to tip in favor of humanity gaining control over the nonhuman aspects of nature. If the past is any indication of the future, the scale may eventually reach its other extreme (see Exhibit 31.1). Humanity or our evolved descendants may eventually control every aspect of nonhuman nature and then accurately be given the title "masters of the universe."

Exhibit 31.1

The General Control Scale of Nature

The three scales below demonstrate that the General Control Scale of Nature is starting to tip in favor of human nature versus nonhuman nature. The first scale depicts the early stages of our existence, when human nature had little control over nonhuman nature. The second scale depicts human nature gaining much control over nonhuman nature over the course of thousands of years. The scale may have attained equilibrium in the years starting approximately around the Industrial Revolution until the present. The final scale depicts human nature or its evolved descendants potentially having total control over nonhuman nature in the future.

Scale 1: In the Beginning—Nonhuman Nature Has More General Control

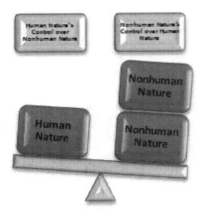

Scale 2: Debatably the Present—An Equilibrium May Have Been Established

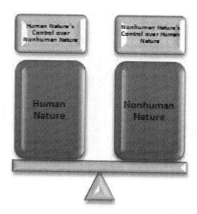

Scale 3: In the Future—Human Nature Might Have More General Control

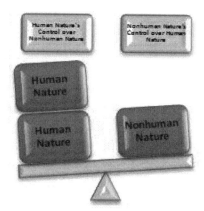

An alternative way to view this argument is to envision human nature as the student of nonhuman nature. In this view, humanity has never been at odds with nature. Instead, the struggles of humanity since the beginning may be compared to the training program of a great master. A great student is an extension of his instructor because the knowledge flows from one person to the next. This may explain why it is often said that great teachers retire once they recognize that their best student has excelled them. For example, there has always been speculation that this is what happened to Andrea del Verrocchio after he saw an angel painted better than his own work by one of his greatest students, Leonardo da Vinci, while the pair were working on del Verrocchio's *The Baptism of Christ*. Maybe he recognized that his life's work as a teacher was now complete. He had passed all his knowledge on to someone else who could now do better than him.

In hindsight, if you were the teacher of one of the greatest artists this planet has ever seen, a Leonardo da Vinci, what use would there be to search for another great student? Is it possible that we can make an analogy between this situation and that of nature? Can it be that the hypothetical great master of the nonhuman aspects of nature is passing the stick to its greatest student: us? Is human nature the chosen student who will soon take over the role of the master of nature? Another similar analogy could be how the head of a very large family selects her or his best child to be the next leader. In either case, one thing is for sure: nonhuman nature certainly appears to have invested much time in helping to make us better; we might even be its greatest investment!

CHAPTER 32

Biology's Second Predicament: Defining Evolution

A General Overview of Evolution

Darwin didn't invent the concept of evolution or its application to life. However, he did provide some of the best theories on how it occurs for Club Life, in particular, the theories of artificial selection, natural selection, and sexual selection. Before him, many didn't believe that life evolved at all. It was Jean Baptiste Lamarck and his theories that gave evolution its biggest push. In particular, he was famous for explaining how a giraffe got its long neck by stretching, over time, to eat from higher trees.

But Lamarck, like most naturalists before Darwin, still believed in spontaneous generation. That is, he believed that all species originally appeared out of nowhere, like a magician pulling a rabbit out of an empty hat. One minute there was nothing, and the next minute, *poof*, a giraffe or another living creature appeared. Darwin's theories eventually led to the scientific dismissal of this belief in the creation of life. Other major figures also played a vital role in the extinction of spontaneous generation, particularly Gregor Mendel, the founder of genetics, and Louis Pasteur, whose conclusions on the microscopic revolutionized biology.

From Darwin to the present, the general view of how life evolves by most biologists is basically "descent with modification." Traditionally, evolution occurs by a mixture of Darwinian processes such as those mentioned above and genetic processes like gene mutation of the descendants. These selecting forces are an extremely important part of the evolutionary process that we will cover in a later chapter. However, the current way evolution is taught needs a significant overhaul because there are still major gaps in the theory. In order to better demonstrate an alternative paradigm, first we will need to revisit the original meaning of evolution.

Evolution in its simplest form just means change. It is sometimes forgotten that other nonliving parts of nature can evolve, or change, too. For example, heated water can evaporate and evolve into a gas. A glacier can evolve into different shapes based on many factors. A machine can evolve into a better version over time. The screen on a television can evolve when you change the channel. The common denominator in all of these evolutionary events is *change.*

Somehow over the years in the process of explaining how evolution occurs in life, the term itself has become ambiguous. When a biologist refers to the change of living populations from the beginning of time, it is called "evolution." However, when referring to the changes that happen inside an individual, it usually goes by some other fancy similar name, for example, a "gene mutation." The confusion is somewhat understandable because many of the changes that occur in an individual may not be inherited by its descendants. For example, if a person's body positively changed as a result of exercising at the gym, then that does not mean that his children will inherit stronger bodies. They will also need to exercise to keep in shape.

However, the genetic change that may occur in an individual *during its lifetime* that may be passed along to its descendants is generally ignored in current biology. The common thought is that we are all born with a fixed number of genes that don't change. These genes are mixed in the next generation to cause evolution. This certainly is a large part of the story but not the whole truth. We must understand the origins of life on this planet better in addition to exploring some basic math concepts to derive a more comprehensive view of evolution. More on that in a moment! First let's take a closer look at what the current school of thought is for evolution.

Simply, most biologists today believe that individuals don't evolve and that only populations evolve. Even the great biologist Edward Wilson wrote, "Evolution is absolutely a phenomenon of populations. Individuals and their immediate descendants do not evolve. Populations evolve, in the sense that the proportions of carriers of different genes change through time. This conception of evolution at the population level follows ineluctably from the idea of natural selection, which is the core of Darwinism. There are other causes of evolution, but natural selection is overwhelmingly dominant" (Wilson, 2010, 75).

This is very similar to an article posted by the University of California Museum of Paleontology, Berkeley. A specific section of it, titled "Misconception: Individual Organisms Can Evolve during a Single Lifespan" includes this information: "Evolutionary change is based on changes in the genetic makeup of populations over time. Populations, not individual organisms, evolve. Changes in an individual over the course of its lifetime may be developmental (e.g., a male bird growing more colorful plumage as it reaches sexual maturity) or may be caused by how the environment affects an organism (e.g., a bird losing feathers because it is infected with many parasites); however, these shifts are not caused by changes in its genes..." (University of California Museum of Paleontology, Berkeley, 2016).

Campbell Biology, one of the leading biology textbooks used by students today, also has a similar view on evolution. In the ninth edition, chapter 23 "The Evolution of Populations" states, "One common misconception about evolution is that individual organisms evolve. It is true that natural selection acts on individuals: Each organism's traits affect its survival and reproductive success compared with other individuals. But the evolutionary impact of natural selection is only apparent in the changes in a *population* of organisms over time" (Campbell et al., 2011, 469).

Instead of the above current academic views, there remains an alternative paradigm on evolution that should be considered. If you follow the next argument through, then you will have a better comprehension of the various theories that will be offered in later chapters. Simply, as I will show you below, the missing link in the view of evolution of life has always been the forgotten individual!

The Forgotten Individual

From my perspective, two major types of evolution, not just one, occur by external and/or internal forces: the evolution of an individual and the evolution of a population. The evolution of a population has been the focus of much attention since the time of Darwin. He provided the explanation of how life evolved from simpler organisms. Initially, as noted previously, much labor was put into dispelling the theory of the spontaneous generation of a population. We now know that populations of species were not created independently out of thin air but that they evolved from the same tree of life over a long period of time. However, a different form of spontaneous generation still exists—that is, in the individual.

Darwin's only illustration from his *On the Origin of Species* book demonstrates how natural selection causes species to evolve. But this diagram is a zoomed-out version of evolution that focuses on many generations of evolution. Darwin states: "The intervals between the horizontal lines in the diagram, may represent each a thousand generations; but it would have been better if each had represented ten thousand generations" (Darwin, 2006, 524). This macro view helped Darwin tackle his immediate goals, but there was a cost to this perspective: the zoomed-in view of his tree was not fully explored.

While biology has been focused so long on the big picture of evolution, the small picture has been put on the back burner. To a degree, this may be excusable because much time was needed to determine if Darwin's theories were accurate. But biology is well beyond that point now! We must now revisit the basics to find the forgotten individual. Somehow the individual unit was not completely understood and incorporated into the evolutionary process.

To be more direct, in general, a population can't evolve unless an individual evolves. First, let's start with a definition: a population is the number of individuals in a group in a specific location. Next, a truth often forgotten by many biologists is that a population of only one individual is still a population. Thus, a new evolved population is automatically created when its first individual member has evolved. *Mathematically speaking, without skipping numbers, it is impossible to count to a whole number higher than one without starting from one first.* One always comes first, and that is why it is one. In other words, first always must be before second, third, or billionth.

For example, the first zebra somewhere, that creature with some variation of a striped coat, had to exist before a large population of related zebras could have come into existence. This point can also be explained in a genetic format. If a population derived its evolved genes from an ancestor, where did that individual ancestor receive her or his evolved genes? Somebody, someone, some individual, no matter how far back in the ancestral line, had to be the *first* person to have a uniquely evolved gene—that is, a gene that was never created before—before it could be inherited by anyone.

This point can be understood better if you can imagine going back to the very first living creature, which supposedly was a simple, asexual, unicellular organism. This first individual would have been the first *group of one* and, consequently, also the first *population of one*. This so-called *universal common ancestor* has been acknowledged by many biologists all the way back to the nineteenth century. Actually, in *On the Origin of Species*, Darwin wrote, "Therefore I should infer from analogy that probably all the organic beings which have ever lived on this earth have descended from some one primordial form, into which life was first breathed" (Darwin, 2006, 756). Let's assume that this universal common ancestor did exist, and let's also assume, for simplicity's sake, that it only had one gene. Unless this organism changed in some way, it doesn't matter how many external forces of nature acted on it; any of its children would essentially be biologically the same.

Simply, the evolution of an individual automatically starts the evolution of a population. However, the evolution of an individual must occur *before* the evolution of a population larger than one. In the simple beginnings of life, if our original ancestors were exactly the same, then we would have stayed the same—unless someone evolved. For example, if our universal common ancestor didn't change biologically, then its offspring would have stayed the same—unless its offspring evolved. *Nevertheless, before the population evolved, someone had to evolve a new trait from one direction of the family tree, either from the universal common ancestor or from one of its descendants.*

You may ask, "What if more than one common ancestor existed?" The conclusion is still the same in that case (although it is highly unlikely that it occurred this way). For example, for the sake of simplicity, let's pretend that there were three asexual, unicellular common ancestors, each with only one gene. How does a more complex population of species occur—for example, an asexual, unicellular organism with two genes? At least one of those three ancestors, or their descendants along the way, must invent the second gene before it can be spread to the rest of a population. Further, this one gene is all it takes to evolve an organism, as Edward Wilson admits: "One gene can change the shape of a skull. It can lengthen lifespans, restructure the color pattern on a wing, or create a race of giants" (Wilson, 2010, 86). **That one gene does not appear out of nowhere, like a rabbit out of a magician's empty hat. In the same way, the various populations of species did not spontaneously appear out of nowhere on the first day of life. This is what I meant earlier, that spontaneous generation in the individual still somewhat exists.**

The gene in the individual must have experienced its own evolutionary process in a similar way to that of the evolution of our current species as a whole. Like all great inventions, the first great rocket into space did not appear out of nowhere. It started evolving through the scientists' experimentation of earlier primitive forms. Similarly, genes had to undergo their evolutionary process *inside the individual.*

The first-life forms were most likely asexual: generating offspring without a partner that are genetically identical to the only parent. This point would only strengthen the role that each individual ancient ancestor must have played in evolving populations. Unless one parent or its descendants changed, the same biological outcome could have occurred for its descendants until perpetuity, generally regardless of the external forces of natural selection.

It may be easier to understand the above newer paradigm of evolution by comparing it to a deck of playing cards. Let's assume that our deck has fifty-two blank cards—that is, each card is the same. Could you imagine playing any kind of game with this deck? How boring it would be! Almost every game imaginable will come to the same conclusion. You need variety to make the game fun. But how do you get variety if all of the cards are the same?

Here comes the fun part! Let's pretend that we now have a deck of living playing cards. Let's pretend that the cards are asexual and that each card can produce only one offspring. However, each parent card must die simultaneously as its offspring is produced. Assuming that each card reproduces, there will always be fifty-two cards. The death of a parent card happens simultaneously with the birth of a child card.

If every card was the same initially, then the deck will always be the same unless one of the fifty-two cards changes. That is, the population of this deck will always be blank cards regardless of what external forces are applied. We can shuffle them, stack them, toss them against the wall, or throw them off a plane. Population evolution will never occur unless a change occurs in at least one of the individual cards. But how do we get the cards to change into colors, numbers, and/or suits? There is generally only one way (unless we directly change their DNA, but more on that later): somehow a card will have to evolve on its own!

If just one card were to change into, say, a red ace of hearts, then the total card makeup would now be different. At least three evolutions would have occurred in this card—that is, there would be changes in its color, number, and suit. Each of the cards in the deck also would have to evolve separately to create more variety (since we are assuming that they are all asexual). These evolutions could eventually go on until we have the deck of cards that we are used to today with two colors, four suits, and thirteen different cards in each suit. Each card would have to evolve *at least* three times to acquire its proper color, number, and suit (assuming at least one separate evolution for each of these characteristics per card). In other words, *at least* 156 evolutions total (the calculation for this is fifty-two cards times at least three evolutions per card) in the individual cards would have to occur in order to make a standard deck out of all blank cards (ignoring jokers, wild cards, and other possible miscellaneous cards).

The above example could be analogous to having multiple universal common ancestors. In this case, we would have fifty-two original ancestors, which is much more than the three hypothetical ones mentioned earlier. Most biologists probably would agree that this would be fifty-one more than what actually occurred. Nevertheless, this example gives an illustration of a much more complicated original scenario, but we can always make it easier. Let's try using a simpler card example and see what happens!

We will now pretend that our card deck has only one card called a *one of circles*. The card is a plain, colorless circle with only the number one on it. It is also asexual and can produce only one offspring. However, each parent card must die simultaneously as its offspring is produced. Assuming that each card reproduces, there will always be only one card. The death of the parent card happens simultaneously with the birth of the child card. The only way to evolve the population of these cards is to have one individual card change. Some card, whether the first card or its one thousandth descendant, must change in some way to put a halt to its perpetually identical biological descendants.

Thus, to get a population of cards with a higher number on it, like maybe a card with a two on it (or what we could call a *two of circles*), at least one individual card somehow would have to evolve this number at least one time.

The one-card example above can be analogous to the same scenario that might have happened for the supposed universal common ancestor. Let's pretend, for simplicity's sake, that this organism was just a plain, colorless circle with one gene, which we can also call the *one of circles*. To create a second gene, its species will need to evolve like the *two of circles* in the one-card deck above. That is, this life-form or one of its descendants will need to evolve to create a second gene if larger populations of plain, colorless circles with two genes are to ever have a chance of being created (see Exhibit 32.1). *In short, the mass-production assembly line for future populations can never begin without the original template of the first, newly evolved individual form.*

Exhibit 32.1

The Evolution of an Individual Example

This is a hypothetical example of the evolution of an individual from the perspective of the ancient past looking toward the future. The first image depicts the first Universal Common Ancestor (assuming there was only one) with one gene (we can also call this the *one of circles*). The second image depicts the Universal Common Ancestor or any one of its descendants with two genes (we can also call this the *two of circles*). Under this model, assuming they were both asexual, only one of these individuals could have made this new gene. Regardless of who did it, an individual must have evolved first before a larger related evolved population could have occurred.

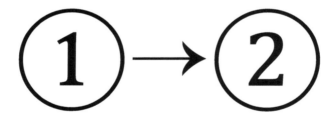

Please keep in mind that the above analogies may be limited for various reasons including the following points. First, we have limited knowledge about the universal common ancestor(s). Second, life is much more complex than these examples depict. Third, a variety of other unknown reproductive outcomes may have occurred in real life. Regardless of these limitations, the intuitiveness of these analogies has plenty of portable value to our discussion because they are based on the same general idea. Indeed, we can learn much from them!

The most important lesson is that the individual's contribution to evolution has been underrated. In particular, the internal processes of an individual, whether conscious or unconscious, must select the various attributes to create an evolved individual. This may sound very unorthodox, but I am not alone in this conclusion. In the nineteenth century, Herbert Spencer wrote in volume 1 of *The Principles of Biology*, "If a single cell, under appropriate conditions, becomes a man in the space of a few years; there can surely be no difficulty in understanding how, under appropriate conditions, a cell may, in the course of untold millions of years, give origin to the human race" (Spencer, 2014, 350). This statement appears to me to confirm Spencer's acknowledgement of an individual cell evolving on its own. Similar to our "one of circles" example, the cell that Spencer mentions, or at least one of its descendants, must have evolved on its own in order to begin the evolution of humanity. If you agree with this statement, then consider the following question: **Why should we suppose that modern generations of life can't evolve individually if earlier generations (or even the single-celled, universal common ancestor) were able to? Simply, evolution is**

always present in everyone, regardless of whether or not we are capable of consciously noticing it.

Spencer called the internal processes "direct adaptation," which was very similar to what Arthur Koestler called "internal selection" almost one hundred years later. Although they both also realized the importance of this process, Koestler, similarly to my above conclusion, went on to consider it a missing part of evolutionary theory: "In the orthodox theory, natural selection is entirely due to the pressures of the environment, which kills off the unfit and blesses the fit with abundant progeny. In the light of the preceding considerations, however, before a new mutation has a chance to be submitted to the Darwinian tests of survival in the external environment, it must have passed the tests of *internal selection* for its physical, chemical and biological fitness. The concept of internal selection, of a hierarchy of controls which eliminate the consequences of harmful gene-mutations and co-ordinates the effects of useful mutations, is the missing link in orthodox theory between the 'atoms' of heredity and the living stream of evolution. Without that link, neither of them makes sense" (Koestler, 1989, 132).

If the individual is selecting traits internally, then the conclusion can also result in evolution just like external nature's selection efforts. We will save more of this discussion for later when we discuss the evolutionary selection processes. However, for now, consider that the above arguments made about these internal selection processes are finally starting to be taken seriously by modern scientists (at least at the genetic level). According to the June 24, 2008, news release "Mendel Didn't Have the Whole Picture: Our Genome Changes Over Lifetime, Johns Hopkins

Experts Say," experts at the famous Johns Hopkins Medicine, one of the leading health-care systems in the United States, have concluded that our genome does change in our lifetime: "Contrary to conventional wisdom, it appears that while the overall health of our genomes is indeed inherited from our parents, chemical marks on our genomes' DNA sequences actually change as we age, driving increased risk of disease susceptibility for us and similarly for our close family members" (Johns Hopkins Medicine, 2008). Folks, if our genes change inside of our bodies during our lifetime, then only we could have done it. We can't blame an earthquake, a hurricane, a lion, the moon, or the stars. It is simply just us. Let's face it—we are evolving!

An argument to the above may be that we only demonstrated this theory with asexual individuals. However, if we added sexual individuals to our discussion, then we will find that little changes. Please take a look at the simple illustration of the traditional evolutionary model of descent with modification found in Exhibit 32.2. In this example, sexual individuals with different genetic traits mate, and their children combine their genetic material to evolve. It is true that evolution can work this way too, but this model works best at the more advanced stages of the tree of life, when a tremendous amount of diversity has already been created. Even still, the question is begged, who invented the unique traits of the parents before they were melded together into the child. For example, from where did Genes 1, 2, 3, and 4 in the exhibit *originally* derive? Individuals somewhere up in the ancestral line must have evolved each one of them first.

Exhibit 32.2

The Traditional Evolutionary Model

This is a hypothetical example of the traditional evolutionary model of a population. In this model, it is taught that only populations evolve and not individuals. The ancestors are at the bottom, and the descendants are at the top. This model shows changes to the population over time with the most recent at the top. Only four hypothetical genes are shown here in grayscale for simplicity. (Many academic variations use a variety of colors instead.)

Starting from the bottom, one male has Gene 1, and one female has Gene 2. (Each person has only one color to represent his or her gene.) They have two children, shown in the middle row, who now are each half Gene 1 and half Gene 2. (Each child has two different colors—one color for each gene.) The male child on the left has two sons with a female that has Gene 3. Their children at the top left corner are now mixed with Genes 1, 2, and 3. (Each child has three different colors—one color for each gene.) The female child in the middle row on the right has one son with a male that has Gene 4. Their only child is now mixed with Genes 1, 2, and 4. (He has three different colors—one color for each gene.) But where did each of these genes *originally* come from? For example, who first created Genes 1 and 2 from the couple at the bottom? Some forgotten individuals at some point in time in the past must have evolved each one of them.

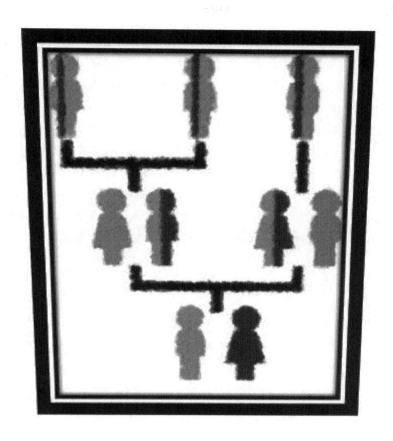

Using our earlier analogy, let's pretend that the first asexual universal common ancestor with one gene created the first two sexual offspring. They were identical in all respects to the parent except one was male and one was female. Basically, these organisms would have been equivalent to the first Adam and Eve. Here, like other examples, evolution could have also occurred either in the parent or in its children. That is, both the first sexual male and female must have either evolved separately on their own or from an asexual ancestor (assuming that asexual individuals evolved before sexual individuals). Either way, the individual is again responsible for the primary evolution before a larger population of both genders could have been produced.

If the first male and female above were to have the first sexual activity on our planet and reproduce, then their child could only be either a male or a female one-gene organism. The only way for the species to further evolve (for example, into a two-gene sexual organism) would be for either the parents or their children to evolve a second gene. Once that second gene was created, then it was available for use by all other descendants, including us. This process could have gone on until a sexual living entity had thousands of genes and became as complicated as many modern life-forms.

External natural forces have a large say as to which organisms continue to live and which ones die. However, in general, it is the individual who first must provide the original options for those external forces to select. This can be analogous to a restaurant that provides its menu to its customers. The restaurant represents the individual who must choose what items to sell. The customers would represent the external parts of nature acting on the individual. They have a significant influence on what the restaurant will serve by selecting what they like from the menu. Whatever the customers don't select should eventually be eliminated, as it may be unprofitable for the restaurant to continue to sell useless goods. Holding the raw materials to make these items may become very expensive and take up valuable space.

External nature chooses what items should continue to exist on the menu of various meals created by the restaurant. Essentially, the restaurant would not sell anything from the menu and eventually die if it did not have anything that its customers wanted. The restaurant, like the individual, must adapt to its environment. Thus, it must continue to evolve new items on the menu to keep up with the demands of its ever-changing customers.

In short, it is the internal nature of the individual that provides the initial evolved genes, the meals on the hypothetical menu. It is the external nature of the individual that provides the feedback and does the selecting to help evolve the later structure of that menu. *External nature has a higher probability of assisting the evolution of more diverse populations with every additional individually created evolution.* External nature may have an enormous number of potentially unique hybrid populations that it might help to create in order to demonstrate its true evolutionary powers, especially after the individual has already evolved tens of thousands of unique genes. But we should never forget the original evolved individuals that helped to build external nature's momentum! Now we will digress to discuss the Evolutionary Control Scale of Nature!

CHAPTER 33

The Evolutionary Control Scale of Nature

Now that we have a better understanding of nature and evolution, we will begin to explore their relationship to each other in more detail. You were introduced to the concept of the General Control Scale of Nature in chapter 31. The conclusion was that human nature has been progressively gaining general control over nonhuman nature throughout time. We can now apply this conclusion to evolution.

At the birth of humanity, humans had very little control over the evolution of living organisms. Early humans were limited in their influence over other parts of living nature as they were confined only to certain places on the continent of Africa at that time. One by one, many major predators started to come under our control as we became better hunters. Those early humans specifically singled out any imminent threats to their existence and figured out ways to eliminate them. Of course, they may have also done this simultaneously to satiate their hunger! After they annihilated any competing predators, they would have also enjoyed a good home-cooked meal. As humans spread all around the globe, they left plenty of evidence that they became the dominant predator: an archeological trail of fire and bones. For various reasons, humans were causing large quantities of extinctions to happen even before the written record existed.

As we will discuss more in a later chapter, the above mainly represents early humans conducting negative selection in the evolutionary process, which is a process that generally involved killing all life that they didn't want around. However, since the birth of humanity, humans have also been implementing positive selection in the evolutionary process. That is, they have also been selecting the life-forms that are most useful to them. In particular, humans have selected a very small segment of the many animals that they have encountered since the beginning to become their permanent clothing providers, entertainment, food sources, laborers, and pets. Some of our most precious animals that we have selected as useful include alpacas, bison, buffalo, camels, cats, chickens, cows, dogs, dolphins, donkeys, elephants, goats, goldfish, honeybees, horses, llamas, mice, pigeons, pigs, primates, reindeer, sheep, silkworms, squirrels, turkeys, yaks, and more.

Humans have also used positive selection to influence the evolutionary process of the plant and other kingdoms. This is particularly true for plants since the birth of agriculture. We allowed the ones that we liked the best to increase in population size. Some of our most precious plants that are still with us today include bananas, beans, coffee, corn, eggplants, manioc, millet, oats, olives, peas, poppy, potatoes, rice, sesame, squash, sugar cane, sunflower, teas, teff, wheat, yams, and more. The list of human-approved plants and their fruits is growing longer every day.

In short, we have been progressively influencing the evolutionary processes of various living organisms since our beginning. Through both positive and negative selection processes, the majority of known species that exist today are alive only because we allow them to be. However, as there are still millions of undiscovered species, particularly at the microscopic level, humans are not yet ready to claim that they are responsible for 100 percent of the evolution of all living things. Yet, when we look at the Evolutionary Control Scale of Nature (see Exhibit 33.1) since the birth of humanity, we can see a similar trend found in the General Control Scale of Nature. The timeline of our increase in control over the evolution of various living things seems to follow approximately the same time frame as our growing general control over nonhuman nature.

Exhibit 33.1

The Evolutionary Control Scale of Nature

The three scales below demonstrate that the Evolutionary Control Scale of Nature is starting to tip in favor of human nature versus nonhuman nature. The first scale depicts the early stages of our existence, when human nature had little control over the evolution of life compared to nonhuman nature. The second scale depicts human nature gaining much control over the evolution of life compared to nonhuman nature over the course of thousands of years (particularly starting from its early hunting and farming efforts). The scale may have attained equilibrium in the years starting approximately around the Industrial Revolution until the present. The final scale depicts human nature or its evolved descendants potentially having total control over the evolution of life compared to nonhuman nature in the future.

Scale 1: In the Beginning—Nonhuman Nature Has More Control over the Evolution of Life

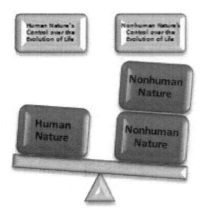

Scale 2: Debatably the Present—An Equilibrium May Have Been Established

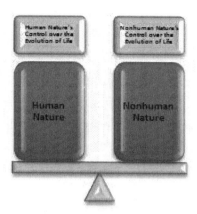

Scale 3: In the Future—Human Nature May Have More Control over the Evolution of Life

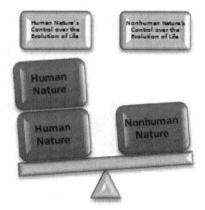

Compared to the little control humans had in the beginning, the scales of progress are starting to tip in favor of humanity gaining control over the evolutionary aspects of the whole of living nature. If the past is any indication of the future, the Evolutionary Control Scale of Nature may eventually reach its other extreme. Humanity or its evolved descendants may one day control every aspect of the evolution of living nature. Additionally, as it will be argued in a future chapter, we may one day control every aspect of the evolution of nonliving nature.

This is a good time to reflect on a point that I hinted at briefly before. That is, ignoring its inherited genes, hardly any evidence exists to demonstrate that an individual has ever evolved outside of its own internal selection processes by any part of external nature, both living and nonliving, except in the case of humanity. This point further strengthens the argument that an individual generally must evolve before larger populations evolve by highlighting the only rare exception known since the original common ancestor: human tampering. Although we still have plenty to learn about genetics, humans are currently capable of forcing an individual to evolve the way we want it to by manipulating its genetic code. We now may be able to do things in one generation that may have taken nonhuman nature millions of years to accomplish. That fact alone demonstrates the power that humans have gained over nature.

Not only do we have the ability to evolve populations, but we also can force an individual's internal mechanisms to evolve the way that we want by essentially hijacking that individual's DNA. I call this process *evolutionary intervention*, and we will discuss it in detail in chapter 35. For example, a mouse can be genetically modified to carry a green fluorescent protein that glows green under blue light. Most people would probably agree that if this mouse had a choice, then he or she would not have chosen to grow like this. By doing this, humans have been able to break the established pattern of evolution. Another form of nature, a human being, for the first time on record (ignoring the microscopic, particularly viruses, which we still don't entirely understand) has been able to hack into the personal evolutionary selection processes of the individual to direct its outcome against the will of the individual life-form. Here we have defied the general laws of evolution! This is not science fiction. Actually, we currently have the ability to do much more than the above example. The question is this: "What more are we capable of doing?" Hold that thought, as we will eventually get to it!

CHAPTER 34

Natural Luck

We are now almost ready to analyze the various natural selection processes that can result in the evolution of life. However, before we do that, we must investigate further what we mean by "selection." Ignoring this topic may lead to the same problems that Darwin ran into when discussing natural selection. In particular, what is this "nature" that does the selecting, and how can it select? Darwin later accepted "the survival of the fittest" as a synonym for the phrase "natural selection," but interestingly he still retained the word "selection" when referring to his two other concepts of artificial and sexual selection.

Darwin's original terminology problems revolved around two unaddressed topics. We already covered the first one, which is properly defining and analyzing the term *nature*. To recall, *nature* is everything, which includes humans too. That is why we must be specific about what part of nature we are referring to when we discuss it. We will now address the second issue, which is properly defining and analyzing the term *selection*.

In short, selection means choosing something. The person or thing doing the choosing is implied to have a choice. *Essentially, there are two major types of selection: pure selection and random selection. Pure selection pertains to the selector having full control over what is being selected.* If someone or something has control over the life or death of the living thing that was selected, then it could influence its destiny and possibly the destiny of its descendants. It may be able to control the evolutionary process by positively or negatively purely selecting another species.

Random selection pertains to the selector having limited control over what is being selected. Biologists have used the term "random" ambiguously since Darwin's time. As you will see though, the random part of the selection process has to do with luck. Something random that is selected could still imply a choice, but it is only a choice to select from unknown options. Only by retaining full control over the selection can the randomness be eliminated. In other words, random selection allows you to choose to select even though you can't fully choose what you are selecting.

For example, imagine if someone held out ten playing cards face down and told you to randomly pick one for a new card trick. You do not have full control over what card you can choose because you do not know what they are. All of these cards look the same to you. To review, you are selecting because you are able to choose something, but you have no control over what is really being selected. The card underneath could be any possible option available—you just don't know. This example further demonstrates that random selection gives someone a choice, but that choice is limited only to the action of choosing.

We can now introduce a more comprehensive term than *random*—*luck*. Luck has many usages…too many. I once asked someone to define *luck*. An hour later, I had about thirty or more personal examples of it, but I still had no definition. This person struggled so hard to define it, but the exercise only ended in frustration. Initially, I had the same problems too. However, over the years, I have concluded that the variety of usages of the word *luck* mainly shares one commonality: lack of control. **Luck is the parts of nature that a living entity has no control over.** It is irrelevant whether or not there is any selecting going on. However, the entity that randomly selects does not have any control over certain aspects of that selection. **In contrast, *skill* is the parts of nature that a living entity has control over, which we also can call *controlled nature.***

This different perspective on luck has important implications. First, the internal nature that we do not control, whether consciously or unconsciously, is now attributed to luck. Second, luck can now be either a living or a nonliving entity depending on what we are referencing in our usage of the term. For example, from the perspective of a pet rabbit, the human owner may be his luck. If the rabbit has good luck, then his owner will take good care of him. From the perspective of the owner though, the rabbit is not her luck, but rather he is her skill because he is a part of nature that she has control over.

Also, the combined relationship between lucky (uncontrolled) natural forces and skilled (controlled) natural forces should equate to 100 percent of all possibilities. In any particular situation, some parts of nature may represent skill while other parts of nature may represent luck. Thus, when survival experts say that you need good luck in survival situations, they are referring to you benefitting from the positive consequences of natural forces out of your control—for example, having good weather. Similarly, bad weather in a survival scenario can be properly called bad luck.

As was indicated in the last chapter, the progression of humanity has allowed us to have more control over the forces of nature. *From our perspective, luck is slowly dying as humans gradually acquire more general control and evolutionary control over all of nature.* Thus, our skills are progressively replacing what used to be our luck.

As a final point to our earlier discussion from this chapter, it is easy to understand the usage of the term *selection* when we are referring to a living thing making a choice. However, like the original problem with natural selection, it is challenging to explain who is doing the selecting when the term is applied to the nonliving. We are stuck in a difficult predicament considering that the nonliving are generally viewed as incapable of having a choice. For this situation, this riddle may only have one way out, which is to apply the term metaphorically when referring to the nonliving.

We shouldn't throw away everything that we have achieved just because we lack a better term to fill the void that the word *selection* leaves when applied to nonliving natural selection. It is more useful to keep the term *selection* and temporarily allow the nonliving to select and control. This allows us to retain all of the good things about natural selection at a meager cost. Consequently, we also may obtain more respect for the nonliving forces of nature, which are so powerful that they can actually give a great appearance of truly selecting!

CHAPTER 35

The Evolution of an Individual

An Overview

We must first learn more about how an individual evolves before we can understand how a larger population evolves. Remember, contrary to common teachings, we cannot change a whole population of a species without first changing the individual. Even in a high-tech genetics lab, we cannot clone quantities of an evolved species until we first have a template organism. This lesson hopefully will become clearer as we progress through our analysis.

At the most general level, an individual can evolve only in two ways: 1) it can learn how to evolve itself, consciously and/ or unconsciously; or 2) it can be evolved by someone or something else that knows how to do it. The first process involves internal natural selection while the second process involves external natural selection. (These two concepts will be explored in depth in the next section.) In the first process, individuals can evolve mainly through learning by self-education, by following another's instructions (being taught how to do it), or a combination of the two.

A common misunderstanding of the evolution of the individual begins in the early years of life. That is, many scholars have little trouble understanding that children and adults of living species can learn. However, many people view the idea of learning as nonsensical when the microscopic is included in the discussion.

Simply put, it is more sensible to take the perspective that individuals are learning from the moment they are created and debatably even before (in the latter case, the sperm may be learning before it fertilizes an egg). This conclusion also can be demonstrated mathematically. Let's pretend that a human lived to exactly one hundred years old. If you could agree that he learned from the moment of birth to his death, then you could say that he was learning for one hundred years. But was he learning in the small window of time before he was born?

The period from conception to birth, assuming a nine-month pregnancy beginning at conception, is roughly only 0.74 percent of his total lifetime. The calculation for this amount is as follows: 100 years × 12 months = 1,200 months + 9 months of pregnancy = 1,209 months of total life. Then 9 months ÷ 1,209 months = 0.00744 or 0.74 percent. In other words, most people would agree that the above human is capable of learning 99.26 percent of his life (100 percent minus 0.74 percent), which is obviously the large majority of his existence. It is the other less than 1 percent that sparks the debate. If a person is capable of learning for 99.26 percent of his life, then why could he not learn during the other fraction of a percentage of time?

The above analysis is important for our discussion because if you can take the position that we are learning from at least the moment of conception, then it is easier to understand that an individual has learned to evolve, consciously or unconsciously, from her or his very beginning. If you agree with the above statements for a human, then it should also be a conclusion that can be retrospectively applied to all species in the tree of life starting from our universal common ancestor (or possibly ancestors). This simple mathematical conclusion becomes more supporting evidence that the individual may be responsible for her or his entire evolutionary destiny.

For simplicity's sake, let's take the stance that the learning process begins as soon as the individual is given the genetic code by its parent(s). At the microscopic level, the new organism could learn automatically from the genetic instructions that she inherited. Next, she may choose to create any possible modifications from her inherited accumulated wealth passed down from her ancestors. The individual evolutionary selection process may then begin, which may never really stop either, although it may slow down at a certain point in her life. Finally, the individual may continue to evolve as she gets older by selecting or discarding various mutations.

To digress for a moment, please recall that evolution just means change. An individual may experience uninheritable changes and inheritable changes. Uninheritable changes may include things like the growth of a person's intellect from years of studying a specialty. The son of a great brain surgeon is not born with all of his mother's knowledge about brain surgery. Those mental changes would need to be personally acquired throughout his own experiences. It is the inheritable changes that are the subject of our inquiry. These changes represent what were passed along to the offspring via his genes. Although these changes represent what changes occurred in his ancestors, the individual may make the final decision through internal selection processes on what changes will be made to him.

Individuals, like the larger populations they can create, can evolve for the better or for the worse. They can also evolve back and forth, in theory at least, an infinite number of times from one state to the next as long as it doesn't kill them. For example, hypothetically, giraffes could have evolved large and small necks a thousand times, alternating back and forth each time, before they ended in their current state. Although this may be a rare possibility, the point is that the first new evolution for an individual (for example, the first invented long neck of a giraffe) is a very different thing than reverting to an already invented change (for example, a long-neck giraffe evolving back to a short-neck giraffe). It is the difference between the invention and the reinvention of the wheel. We will talk more about the role that the creative process plays in evolution in a moment.

To return to our original discussion at the beginning of this section, the second general way that an individual may evolve is if someone does it for him, which can occur by an external natural selection process that we can call *evolutionary intervention*. This very rare event in evolutionary history is when another living entity essentially creates evolution inside a living organism by modifying its genetic code. As mentioned in an earlier section, humans are now gradually becoming more capable of genetically modifying life. It is interesting that humanity probably is the first living entity to learn how to do this—that is, assuming that life began unassisted by a superior being. We will now briefly digress to further explore the concepts of external and internal natural selection, which should help us to better understand evolution.

External and Internal Natural Selection

The evolutionary selection processes of both an individual and a population can be divided into both external and internal natural selection. These two processes combined represent all of the selection efforts of nature. **External natural selection is a process that occurs when the external natural forces of an individual select the evolutionary outcome of that individual and/or its population. Internal natural selection is a process that occurs when the internal natural forces of an individual select the evolutionary outcome of itself and/or its population.**

The key to understanding these two concepts is to focus on the specific individual that is being selected (not the selector). All aspects of nature, whether external or internal, should be referenced in relationship to this person. This will help to maintain consistency in the analysis process and avoid confusion. It will also help to track the impact that various forces can have on the evolutionary process from the first individual to its descendants.

Exhibit 35.1 depicts the two separate natures of an individual baby ostrich. The dividing line between its external and internal nature, like that of any other entity, is at the first particle of space outside of the body. The internal nature (or what I will also refer to as "the wealth inside") includes the whole body from its internal organs to its most superficial parts. This is contrasted with external nature, which can be a variety of things, such as astronomical, geological, and meteorological factors. External nature can also include other living creatures either of the same or different species.

Exhibit 35.1

External and Internal Nature

Below is an example of the external and internal nature of a baby ostrich. The dividing line marks the approximate separation between the two major types of nature. All living things follow the same pattern.

Although separate processes, the external and internal natural processes often work in conjunction with each another. Their constant push-and-pull relationship demonstrates the continuous struggles that are inherent in life. Various forces are relentlessly selecting and/or deselecting themselves and other members of life to ensure that evolved individuals and their populations will continue to be created. In the next chapter, we will look more closely at the concepts of negative and positive selection to enhance our understanding of how this all takes place.

The Three Major Processes of Unique Individual Evolution

Now that I have presented an overview of how the evolution of an individual occurs in general, we can turn to the more specific. In particular, let's now focus on how an individual can evolve a new characteristic that is unique in its ancestral line. **There are three major processes of unique evolutionary selection in individual evolution:** *absolute creativity evolutionary selection, hybrid creativity evolutionary selection,* **and** *evolutionary intervention.* The individual controls its evolutionary process in the first two major processes (by internal reformed natural selection, a process explained more in chapter 36), consciously and/or unconsciously, while someone or something else controls its evolutionary process in the third major process (by external reformed natural selection, a process also explained more in chapter 36). These three separate major processes also can happen in conjunction with one another. Let's now take a closer look at each one of these processes!

First, the individual can create a new inheritable evolution that is completely unrelated to any of the previous evolutions that ever occurred in its ancestral line. This evolution will be called *absolute creativity evolutionary selection* to reflect the pure creativity of the individual. Future descendants might be able to choose later if they want to keep this unique change as part of their inherited genetic wealth. This is one of the most important evolutionary changes and certainly one of the rarest.

Please recall the example of the one and two of circles in chapter 32. If the first universal common ancestor had just one gene, then how did its offspring evolve to have two genes? As will be explained, the second major process that we will discuss cannot apply to this situation. This leaves absolute creativity evolutionary selection and the third major process of evolutionary intervention as the key potential suspects. If we assume that life arose without the assistance of a superior being, then the first individual probably created the evolutionary change on its own. It may have learned how to do this somehow, like how an inventor creates a new invention.

The great inventor Thomas Edison failed thousands of times before he invented the light bulb. Every failure was a learning experience for him that got him one step closer to his goal. Every invention in history has taken a similar path of learning, although some paths were quicker than others. Life-forms, including the universal common ancestor, might also have followed a similar pattern while inventing new genes.

In the case of the universal common ancestor, the major argument to these assumptions is to whom to attribute the change. In other words, did the parent evolve first, or did the child evolve later? Either one could be possible. However, either way, one of these individuals had to be the culprit who created the new evolution. Further, absolute creativity evolutionary selection could probably be attributed to so many other instances throughout evolutionary history. For example, some creature had to create the first eye, fin, leg, lung, and even brain. However, this process alone does not fully account for the many evolutions that have resulted in our present complex forms.

The second major process of unique evolutionary selection in individual evolution can be called *hybrid creativity evolutionary selection*. With this process, the individual learns how to create a new evolution by combining what it was taught to evolve by its ancestors. In other words, a person can combine her genes to create a unique pattern that has never been seen before. The result is a new evolution that shows similarities to traits from its earlier ancestors. More possibilities of unique combinations of genes exist when an individual has more inherited genes. In effect, a larger quantity of inherited wealth increases the chances of new evolutions that can occur from this process. Similarly, consider the almost infinite number of new colors that you can create with just a few basic colors. The potential for new hybrid colors increases with every new basic color that is introduced. In short, mathematics helps to explain why life started to become exponentially more complicated at its later stages.

Marine mammals are a good historical example of the second process. The marine mammals contain the DNA of both their former land mammal ancestors and also their ancient aquatic ancestors before they moved to land. Thus, they could have been able to tap into an accumulated variety of genetic instructions once their life was first being assembled, in order to slowly evolve into a unique hybrid that eventually returned to the water. Considering the existing variety of marine mammals, many individual evolutions probably had to occur, in conjunction with the forces that controlled the evolution of the larger populations, before their extreme forms (like dolphins and whales) could have been produced.

Marine mammals evolved from land mammals that slowly became new piscine creatures while retaining their mammalian evolutions from their ancestors. You can see hints of this process from studying the process of marine mammal change from the most mammal-like polar bears to the most fish-like whales. The animals in the intermediate stages (for example, sea otters) give the best clues to this process. Old genetic evolutions of their ancestry were combined with new ones to invent a unique hybrid. This event may be somewhat analogous to the invention of the wheel and the later invention of rubber, which eventually led to the invention of the rubber tire. A rubber tire is obviously a newer hybrid invention, but it might never have occurred without the wheel and rubber being separately invented first.

Hybrid creativity evolutionary selection is probably the most common for complex organisms, especially humans, and is essentially what many biologists have been calling descent with modification for the past 150 years and longer. It may appear as if evolution is only occurring from random pairings of previously created genes when you look at complex life-forms by their genes from the perspective of the present to the past. That is, external forces appear to be controlling this process and its outcome. However, only the individual can directly control its internal evolutionary selection processes (ignoring evolutionary intervention for now). This can only be fully understood when you reverse the looking glass and view evolution from the ancient past to the present.

Modern genealogy teaches us that if you want to learn about your ancestors, it is easiest to start building a family tree from yourself in the present and working your way backward in time. If you have ever completed your own family tree, then you know the usefulness of this lesson. It would be easy for things to become immediately confusing if you were to start from any point in the past (even within only a few generations). This lesson has also been absorbed in the mainstream genetics books starting from the time of Gregor Mendel's famous work on peas. But although this line of thinking has its benefits, it also has its drawbacks, especially when trying to understand how individual evolution first began.

Obviously humans are missing a large part of the evolutionary record. Many things could have happened that we might be unaware of. However, from some basic potential evolutionary models, we can obtain a better indication of how things unfolded from the point of our universal common ancestor. Reverting to examples from a prior chapter, if the universal common ancestor only had one gene, then it could use absolute creativity evolutionary selection to create a child with two genes. Its offspring might create another gene using the same process. Let's pretend that this goes on until its descendants have ten genes. The youngest descendant might then be in a position to create a new invention by a different process: hybrid creativity evolutionary selection. It might apply a unique combination of any of its inherited ten genes to create a similar, yet different, evolutionary invention (like our rubber tire analogy). This process of evolution only started to pick up momentum as its descendants gained more genetic material. *More genes equal more potentially unique genetic combinations.*

Also, consider the first universal common ancestor's position. What genetic material could it have combined if it didn't inherit anything from anybody? It could be argued that it combined various chemicals it inherited from the atmosphere to breathe life into it. This might be true, but this might lead us into a possibly infinitely unproductive analysis about the microscopic origins of the first life-form. It is easier for now to just assume that life began with only one whole very simple life-form. Thus, this first ancestor could only have learned on its own how to create an evolution. To put it bluntly, if all complex life learned by standing on the *shoulders* of its ancestral giants, then whose *shoulders* did the first ancestor stand on? There is actually one more option!

The final major process of unique evolutionary selection in individual evolution can be derived from *evolutionary intervention.* We have already discussed this above, so here I will just highlight its attributes. First, this is the only process in individual evolution where an external force can cause the individual to evolve against its will, which occurs when it programs it with the proper genetic instructions. As mentioned earlier, humans have made significant progress with this process over the years. The point of this major process is that someone else is taking control of an individual's evolutionary process. In this case, evolutionary intervention results in unique evolutions that are created in the individual. However, external forces can also create evolutions that are not unique.

Finally, it is important to mention that any one of the three major processes of unique evolutionary selection in individual evolution can occur at the same time. For example, an individual can use absolute creativity evolutionary selection in conjunction with hybrid creativity evolutionary selection to design a new evolution. In addition, it should not be ruled out that an individual whose evolutionary process is controlled by external forces could learn how to evolve into something of its own design. For example, let's assume that our genetically modified mouse who glows green under blue light realizes that its new evolution (which was created by humans) is detrimental to its existence. The mouse may be able to learn how to change the modification by either reverting to a safer evolution of its ancestors or by creating a new evolution that will result in a better adaptation to its environment.

CHAPTER 36

The Evolution of a Population

An Overview

The fully assembled electric light bulb did not miraculously show up one day at Thomas Edison's lab door. The fully detailed written theory of natural selection did not magically appear one day at the door of Darwin's study room. Similarly, other major complex inventions in history also did not show up at their inventor's door. In every case, the inventor must have learned how to create it first. A new necessity usually forces an inventor to find a solution, which is generally a difficult process that requires the complete focus of the individual. This process of learning to create can also occur in many other aspects of life, particularly, the evolution of an individual.

To recall, my proposed definition of life from chapter 4 includes thinking. An organism can think if it can make a decision. For example, by reproducing offspring, it is displaying its decision to have a child. However, the first evolved life-form demonstrated to the world that it could also think big—that is, it demonstrated that it could learn how to create a genetic change when it produced the first evolution. Eventually, many other individual life-forms learned how to create evolutions too, and this provided the foundation for the complexity of life that we know today.

Many biologists often forget that a population can include one or more individuals. Thus, an individual can be the first member of a population—even of an evolved population. An evolved population of one is immediately created once its first individual has been evolved. Individuals are the foundation and the building blocks of populations of all sizes. Thus, from this perspective, it is nonsensical to say that a population can evolve but individuals cannot. The last chapter was primarily focused on the processes that can *cause* an individual to evolve, which can also result in the creation of the first member of an evolved population. However, this chapter is primarily focused on the events that can *influence* individual evolution and the evolution of a large related population. Thus, the following analysis of population evolution will take more of a big-picture view of evolution.

You can only start to truly grasp how a large population can evolve when you fully understand the prior conclusions on individual evolution. All of the selection procedures taught in academia today could not possibly have helped to create even one evolved population if individuals did not learn how to evolve first. For example, by artificial selection, we have influenced the evolution of wolves into dogs for thousands of years. However, if wolves had never changed since that time, then they probably would still be exactly the same, and dogs would have never been invented.

But wolves did change a variety of times, and we certainly capitalized on those changes. Hundreds of dog breeds now exist, and this list grows bigger every year. The evolved population of dogs may be one of the easiest understood microcosms of how the whole of life has been evolved. A layman may have little trouble relating to this process because he can actually witness this evolution in his lifetime. Just one trip to an international dog show can demonstrate the powers of artificial selection in a short period of time. Dogs are truly one of the greatest displays of how humans can select a variety of individuals with unique evolutions and, consequently, help to create various unique, large, related, and evolved populations!

Business-minded dog breeders get excited every time a dog evolves a new marketable trait. They can then start playing match maker with another dog of their choice to influence the creation of a uniquely evolved larger related population. They can continue this process until the ideal population size of this unique breed is produced. It is amazing to consider how many individual evolutions of wolves and their dog descendants needed to occur for humans to help to evolve them into a strange new breed of poodles.

We will learn in this chapter about various selection processes that are used to help to create an evolved population. First, we will review the differences between negative and positive selection. Next, we will review the traditional evolutionary selection processes of how to influence the evolution of populations. Third, we will give these processes a modern upgrade while introducing the important concept of *reformed natural selection*. Finally, some additional processes will also be discussed. These various discussions will help you to better understand evolution and the significant conclusions of later chapters.

Negative and Positive Selection

The concepts of negative and positive selection can help to better explain how a large population can evolve through the various selection processes that will be discussed. We will start with positive selection, as it is the easiest to understand. **Positive selection is a process that occurs when a specific individual(s) of a species is (are) chosen to evolve a population. Negative selection is a process that occurs when a specific individual(s) of a species is (are) chosen not to evolve a population.** Let's take this one step at a time!

First, humans that select certain larger cows to help evolve a population of super cows are an example of positive selection for human artificial selection. Humans have also used this same process to help to create populations of honeybees that create sweeter honey. Further, humans aren't the only ones to positively select species. For example, a honeybee that selects a specific colored flower is an example of two different forms of positive selection that will soon be introduced: positive reformed artificial selection and positive traditional natural selection.

On the other hand, negative selection is usually much more brutal than positive selection because it usually requires killing those who don't meet the requirements of the selector. For example, human genocide is a form of negative selection as certain individuals who meet a certain criteria are labeled "not fit to live." The group with more power attempts to carry out its mission of eliminating the target group entirely. We will discuss this monstrous practice further in part 4. By default, the ones who were not selected may evolve into a larger population.

Other isolated examples of negative human artificial selection may include killing bacteria, bedbugs, cockroaches, and mice in a specific location. For example, if a house were infested with the above creatures, then an exterminator could be called over to eliminate all of them. Humans aren't the only ones who use negative selection though. Nonliving nature has been responsible for much of it throughout history. For example, extreme flooding and tsunamis are examples of negative nonliving natural selection. In these cases, it could be argued that anyone in the path of a nonliving natural disaster who couldn't survive it would be eliminated through negative selection (metaphorically).

You can also have both negative and positive selection forces working at the same time, such as in the Nazis' activities during World War II. In this case, certain blond-haired and blue-eyed Germans were positively selected, allowed to live, and encouraged to reproduce. However, the Nazis negatively selected certain groups like Gypsies and Jews by attempting to exterminate them all.

Positive selection is generally a more peaceful process than negative selection. In many cases of positive selection, both selected members and other members of a species that were not selected do not have to be harmed in any way. Actually, the other members may not even need to be contacted at all. For example, consider the honeybee mentioned above. If a honeybee likes a specific flower, then it helps pollinate it. That flower's pollen grains are given a free ride to the female organ of another flower, and now its reproductive process could occur. The bee's actions did not harm the positively selected flower, actually it helped it. Further, the bee's actions may have no harmful effect on the other flowers that were not positively selected. On the contrary, with many forms of negative selection, generally only the organisms that were not negatively selected may live or be unharmed in any way.

A few more points about these processes are in order. First, positive selection doesn't always translate to the evolution of a larger population. The individuals selected must positively self-select (more on this later) and survive to fulfill their required roles in the reproductive process in order to potentially increase the population. We will discuss survival's role in evolution in more detail in a later chapter.

Second, negative selection doesn't always require the selected to die, as commonly taught. Although many processes of negative selection are still brutal, nonlethal alternatives exist. Specifically, an individual can have its reproductive organs removed or rendered useless so it cannot have any offspring. On the positive side, this process of sterilization can at least allow the individual to live out its life. The effects of these actions on large population evolution are easily witnessed: all the sterile will die (in the fullness of time) having produced no offspring, and only the offspring of the other groups will remain. Many examples of negative selection are clear in the various eugenics movements of the twentieth century.

Controversially, homosexuality can be considered the most peaceful variation of negative selection. If two people of the same sex become monogamous life partners, then they can't create their own offspring together. Thus, they cannot create a larger evolved population (ignoring modern medical procedures like artificial insemination). This certainly may have an underrated effect on population evolution, which is a reason that the traditional sexual selection process was reformed in a later section.

Finally, negative and positive selection can also apply to the evolution of an individual too. However, the terminology needs some minor adjustments as noted next. **Positive selection is a process that occurs when a specific trait(s) of a person is (are) chosen to evolve an individual. Negative selection is a process that occurs when a specific trait(s) of a person is (are) chosen not to evolve an individual.** These processes basically follow the same general format as the negative and positive selection processes of the evolution of a population that was analyzed above. Any detailed further analysis of this would be beyond the scope of this book.

The Evolutionary Selection Processes: The Traditional Processes

An Overview
We will now analyze the traditional processes for evolving a population of more than one. This section has been included to provide a good historical context of this topic as well as to

build a foundation for the next section where these processes will be upgraded. We should discuss some more literature on natural selection or "the survival of the fittest" to sharpen your understanding of it. However, I would recommend that you first review chapter 30 to ensure that you understand the basics of this subject. In addition to natural selection, we will also review two other traditional processes of evolutionary selection: artificial selection and sexual selection.

The above three traditional processes of selection were all discovered by Charles Darwin. Darwin's concept of artificial selection was actually used as a starting point in his famous *On the Origin of Species* to explain natural selection. His tactic was to show that if humans can change a population of living things, then certainly nature can do it. The third process of sexual selection that Darwin discovered was a subject that appeared to fascinate him. Although he only discussed the term briefly in *On the Origin of Species*, he devoted almost the whole of the second part of his later book, *The Descent of Man*—the majority of the book—to unravel the riddle of this process. Obviously, this became a subject that he spent much time reflecting on. Let's now take a look at some literature on these three important concepts before providing some commentary. The best place to start is with the man who invented the terms.

The following quote was selected from Charles Darwin's *The Descent of Man* because it is a rare instance when he simultaneously integrates a discussion of all three of his major concepts. First, he describes sexual and natural selection together. In the last statement, although he doesn't state the term specifically, he implies the process of artificial selection. Further, although his arguments were sound and relatively clear, keep in mind that the exact definitions for these three concepts were very loosely defined in his works. He wrote, "Sexual selection depends on the success of certain individuals over others of the same sex in relation to the propagation of the species; whilst natural selection depends on the success of both sexes, at all ages, in relation to the general conditions of life. The sexual struggle is of two kinds; in the one it is between the individuals of the same sex, generally the male sex, in order to drive away or kill their rivals, the females remaining passive; whilst in the other, the struggle is likewise between the individuals of the same sex, in order to excite or charm those of the opposite sex, generally the females, which no longer remain passive, but select the more agreeable partners. This latter kind of selection is closely analogous to that which man unintentionally, yet effectually, brings to bear on his domesticated productions, when he continues for a long time choosing the most pleasing or useful individuals, without any wish to modify the breed" (Darwin, 2006, 1244).

As stated before, Herbert Spencer, with Darwin's approval, was famous for labeling natural selection "the survival of the fittest." He also added a process called "direct equilibration" to it to help make it more complete. Edward Wilson defines natural selection (and artificial selection simultaneously) in his glossary as, "The differential contribution of offspring to the next generation by various genetic types belonging to the same population; the mechanism of evolution proposed by Darwin. Distinguished from artificial selection, the same process but carried out with human guidance" (Wilson, 2010, 403).

Jared Diamond provides his interpretation of the natural selection process: "Darwin's phrase "natural selection" refers to certain individuals of a species surviving better, and / or reproducing more successfully, than competing individuals of the same species under natural conditions. In effect, the natural processes of differential survival and reproduction do the selecting. If the conditions change, different types of individuals may now survive or reproduce better and become "naturally selected," with the result that the population undergoes evolutionary change" (Diamond, 1999, 123).

Edward Wilson provides more elaboration on Darwin's process of artificial selection: "Artificial selection has always been a tradeoff between the genetic creation of traits desired by human beings and an unintended but inevitable genetic weakness in the face of natural enemies" (Wilson, 2010, 300). Further, Jared Diamond provides some elaboration of the process: "That's why Darwin, in his great book *On the Origin of Species*, didn't start with an account of natural selection. His first chapter is instead a lengthy account of how our domesticated plants and animals arose through artificial selection by humans...Those principles of crop development by artificial selection still serve as our most understandable model of the origin of species by natural selection" (Diamond, 1999, 130).

I provide my interpretation of these three traditional processes in the next part of this section, which also contains a simple evolutionary formula for each. Exhibit 36.1 consolidates all of the processes discussed in this book and their evolutionary formulas. This can be very helpful as a reference later.

Exhibit 36.1

The Reformed Natural Selection Formulas for Population Evolution

Please note that ">" signifies "selecting" and "=" signifies "the potential conclusion."

1. **The traditional natural selection evolutionary formula:**
   External nonhuman nature > An individual(s) of any species = An evolved population of the species
2. **The traditional artificial selection (can also be called human artificial selection) evolutionary formula:**
   A human individual(s) > Another individual(s) of any species = An evolved population of the species
3. **The first process of traditional sexual selection evolutionary formula:**
   An individual of any sexual species > Another individual(s) of the same sex of the same species (as a consequence of the traditional sexual process) = An evolved population of the species
4. **The second process of traditional sexual selection evolutionary formula:**
   An individual of any sexual species > Another individual(s) of the opposite sex of the same species (as a consequence of the traditional sexual process) = An evolved population of the species

5. **The reformed artificial selection evolutionary formula:**
   An individual(s) of any species > Another individual(s) of any species = An evolved population of the species
6. **The reformed sexual selection evolutionary formula:**
   An individual of any sexual species > Another individual(s) of either sex of the same species (as a consequence of the sexual process) = An evolved population of the species
7. **The descendant selection evolutionary formula:**
   An individual(s) of any species > Its descendant(s) = An evolved population of the species
8. **The monetary selection evolutionary formulas (four major variations although others may exist):**
   1) **Individual evolution: External reformed natural selection:**
      An individual(s) of any species (particularly humans) > Money as a tool > A trait(s) of another individual = An evolved individual
   2) **Individual evolution: Internal reformed natural selection:**
      An individual(s) of any species (particularly humans) > Money as a tool > Its trait(s) = An evolved individual
   3) **Population evolution: External reformed natural selection:**
      An individual(s) of any species (particularly humans) > Money as a tool > Another individual(s) of any species = An evolved population of the species

4) **Population evolution: Internal reformed natural selection:**

An individual(s) of any species (particularly humans) > Money as a tool > Itself to live and to reproduce = An evolved population of the species

9. **The technological selection evolutionary formulas (two major condensed variations although others may exist):**
   1) **For the evolution of the living:**

   Any living individual(s) (particularly humans) > Technology = An evolved living population (of one or more individuals) of the species

   And/or

   2) **For the evolution of the nonliving:**

   Any living individual(s) (particularly humans) > Technology = An evolved living individual(s) from a non-living individual(s) and an evolved population of a new living group with its own tree of life

10. **The self-selection evolutionary formula:**

An individual(s) of any species > Itself to live and to reproduce = An evolved population of the species

Traditional Natural Selection

Traditional natural selection **is a process that occurs when external nonhuman nature potentially evolve(s) a specific population by selecting an individual(s) of any species.** It is important to understand that this process includes all external natural forces except for humans. Darwin specifically wanted his process of natural selection to be different from the human process of selection. To be clear, it includes selection by all external organic and inorganic forces except humans. These forces include astronomical (e.g., meteors, stars, and/or the sun), geological (e.g., avalanches, earthquakes, and/or volcanic eruptions), meteorological (e.g., hurricanes, monsoons, tsunamis, and/or twisters), and organic (e.g., animals, germs, and/or plants). The traditional natural selection evolutionary formula can be expressed in the format below. Please note that ">" signifies "selecting" and "=" signifies "the potential conclusion."

Additionally, unless noted otherwise, any selection discussed from this point in the book can be a negative or a positive selection. The specific individual that is being selected may or may not be evolved. However, someone connected to the selection process must be evolved to potentially result in a population evolution. For example, a new environment may negatively select (metaphorically) certain unevolved individuals who could not survive its conditions. However, the remaining ones that were not selected could have evolved, which could have potentially resulted in an evolved population.

The traditional natural selection evolutionary formula:

External nonhuman nature > An individual(s) of any species = An evolved population of the species

Traditional Artificial Selection

Traditional artificial selection, **which will now also be referred to as** *human artificial selection,* **is a process that occurs when a human individual(s) potentially evolve(s) a specific population by selecting another individual(s) of any species.** The traditional artificial selection evolutionary formula can be expressed in the format below. Please note that ">" signifies "selecting" and "=" signifies "the potential conclusion."

The traditional artificial selection (can also be called human artificial selection) evolutionary formula:
A human individual(s) > Another individual(s) of any species = An evolved population of the species

Traditional Sexual Selection

Finally, the traditional sexual selection processes can actually have two variations as noted by Darwin's quote above. **The first process of** *traditional sexual selection* **occurs when an individual of any sexual species potentially evolves a specific population by selecting (usually negatively in this case) another individual(s) of the same sex of the same species (as a consequence of the traditional sexual process).** For example, a male can negatively select competing males to help create a population evolution in his favor. Alternatively, a female can negatively select competing females to help create a population evolution in her favor.

The second process of *traditional sexual selection* **occurs when an individual of any sexual species potentially evolves a specific population by selecting (usually positively in this case) another individual(s) of the opposite sex of the same**

species (as a consequence of the traditional sexual process). For example, a female can positively select evolved males to whom she is attracted. This may result in population evolution if reproduction occurs successfully.

The first and the second traditional sexual selection evolutionary formulas can be expressed in the format below. Please note that ">" signifies "selecting" and "=" signifies "the potential conclusion."

The first process of traditional sexual selection evolutionary formula:
An individual of any sexual species > Another individual(s) of the same sex of the same species (as a consequence of the traditional sexual process) = An evolved population of the species

The second process of traditional sexual selection evolutionary formula:
An individual of any sexual species > Another individual(s) of the opposite sex of the same species (as a consequence of the traditional sexual process) = An evolved population of the species

The Evolutionary Selection Processes: The Upgraded Processes

Reformed Natural Selection

Frankly, Darwin's traditional processes of artificial, natural, and sexual selection are long overdue for a modern upgrade. Since they were formed, many crucial events have happened to improve our understanding of the universe. Darwin and his contemporaries never got to experience the discovery of DNA, the Internet, the radio, robotic surgeries, the sight of men walking on the moon, television, and so much more. Few efforts have been made by scientists since then to find a better way to express his theories. Maybe this can be explained by the immense task of doing so or possibly by complacency. After all, they really are good theories that generally still hold true.

However, by striving to find a better way to express Darwin's theories of evolution in combination with others' theories—for example, Spencer's and Koestler's—we may be able to improve our overall understanding. In particular, my quest is not to eliminate the progress of Darwin and his followers but to search for a more unified way to explain all of organic evolution. With so much existing ambiguity in evolution, I needed to create the concept of *reformed natural selection*, which is derived from our earlier concept of reformed nature.

To understand our new concept, we need to revisit our analysis on what nature is in chapter 31. Darwin's term *nature* does not match our modern understanding or usage of it. Please recall that "reformed nature" is everything. With this modern perspective of nature, we are now equipped to better understand our new concept. **Reformed natural selection is the comprehensive selection processes of all external and internal natural forces that directly or indirectly caused the evolution of individuals and populations.** This concept helps to provide a unified explanation of *all* evolutionary events that have occurred in life, particularly for both the evolution of an individual and the evolution of a population. It includes all aspects of nature including the organic and inorganic, the living and nonliving, and the external and internal forces. It also includes the fundamental units of organic nature—genes, for example—as well as the whole self that is expressed in the process of self-selection that we will discuss later.

Reformed natural selection also includes humans, which is in direct contrast to Darwin's view of traditional natural selection that generally includes nonhuman external forces only. Traditional natural selection still does have a role in the selection process but a less inclusive one. That is, it would become a part of the external reformed natural selection processes that helps to explain the evolution of a population. It is important to emphasize, however, that other selection processes also account for this type of evolution. This will be easier to understand through the Evolutionary Schematics for Life illustrated in Exhibit 36.2. As you can see, reformed natural selection is broken up into both external and internal selection processes for both individual and population evolution, which are then further divided as analyzed in this book.

Exhibit 36.2

The Evolutionary Schematics for Life

Individual Evolution

Reformed Natural Selection (Each process has a negative and a positive version.)

I.   External Reformed Natural Selection (It represents **luck**: the forces of nature that a living entity has no control over.)
   1. Evolutionary Intervention
     1) Traditional Evolutionary Intervention
     2) Monetary Selection
     3) Technological Selection
II. Internal Reformed Natural Selection (It represents **skill**: the forces of nature that a living entity has control over.)
   1. General Evolutionary Selection (An individual learns from others and self how to evolve into already existing forms. This is like reinventing the wheel.)
   2. Unique Evolutionary Selection
     1) Absolute Creativity Evolutionary Selection
     2) Hybrid Creativity Evolutionary Selection
   3. Monetary Selection
   4. Technological Selection

Population Evolution

Reformed Natural Selection (Each process has a negative and a positive version.)

I. External Reformed Natural Selection (It represents **luck**: the forces of nature that a living entity has no control over.)
    1. The Traditional Processes
        1) Traditional Natural Selection
        2) Traditional Artificial (or Human) Selection
        3) Traditional Sexual Selection
    2. The Upgraded Processes
        1) Reformed Artificial Selection
        2) Reformed Sexual Selection
    3. Other Processes
        1) Descendant Selection
        2) Miscellaneous External Reformed Natural Selection
    4. The Evolution of Evolution Processes
        1) Monetary Selection (It began with the evolution of money.)
        2) Technological Selection (It began with the evolution of technology.)
II. Internal Reformed Natural Selection (It represents **skill**: the forces of nature that a living entity has control over.)
    1. Self-Selection (An individual's choice to increase its population of one.)
    2. Monetary Selection
    3. Technological Selection

It is much easier to explain evolution with the new paradigm. Now, if maximum simplification is needed as an explanation, it could easily be said that reformed natural selection is the reason for all of organic evolution. It could include a selection by any natural force in the range of possibilities. The new comprehensive list of reformed nature that could be the selecting forces includes, but is not limited to, astronomical (e.g., meteors, stars, and/or the sun), geological (e.g., avalanches, earthquakes, and/or volcanic eruptions), meteorological (e.g., hurricanes, monsoons, tsunamis, and/or twisters), organic (e.g., animals (including humans), germs, and/or plants), the internal self (including genes), and so forth.

The reformed natural selection evolutionary formulas can be expressed in the format below (see also Exhibit 36.3). Note that two formulas account for all of the selection efforts of both the evolution of an individual and a population. Additionally, two consolidated formulas account for all of the evolutionary selection efforts throughout time. *To be clear, 100 percent of the evolutions of all living individuals in all living populations are due to reformed natural selection throughout time.* This is explained by the first consolidated reformed natural selection evolutionary formula below. *Further, 100 percent of the evolutions of all organic beings (both the living and the dead) are due to reformed natural selection throughout time.* This is explained by the second consolidated reformed natural selection evolutionary formula below. Please note that ">" signifies "selecting" and "=" signifies "the potential conclusion."

The reformed natural selection evolutionary formula for an individual:

Any part of reformed nature > A trait(s) of any individual = An evolved individual of any species

The reformed natural selection evolutionary formula for a population:
Any part of reformed nature > An individual(s) of any species = An evolved population of the species

IMPORTANT: The consolidated reformed natural selection evolutionary formulas:

1. The reformed natural selection processes of the evolutions of all living individuals + The reformed natural selection processes of the evolutions of all living populations = The complete reformed natural selection processes of the evolutions of all living individuals in all living populations

2. The reformed natural selection processes of the evolutions of all individuals throughout time + The reformed natural selection processes of the evolutions of all populations throughout time = The complete reformed natural selection processes of the evolutions of all organic beings (both the living and the dead) throughout time

Exhibit 36.3

The Reformed Natural Selection
Evolutionary Formulas

Please note that ">" signifies "selecting" and "=" signifies "the potential conclusion."

1. **The reformed natural selection evolutionary formula for an individual:**
   Any part of reformed nature > A trait(s) of any individual = An evolved individual of any species
2. **The reformed natural selection evolutionary formula for a population:**
   Any part of reformed nature > An individual(s) of any species = An evolved population of the species

The consolidated reformed natural selection evolutionary formulas (the most important simplified formulas for the evolution of life throughout time):

1. The reformed natural selection processes of the evolutions of all living individuals + The reformed natural selection processes of the evolutions of all living populations = The complete reformed natural selection processes of the evolutions of all living individuals in all living populations
2. The reformed natural selection processes of the evolutions of all individuals throughout time + The reformed natural selection processes of the evolutions of all populations throughout time = The complete reformed natural selection processes of the evolutions of all organic beings (both the living and the dead) throughout time

Reformed Artificial Selection

Armed with an understanding of reformed natural selection, we are now ready to understand the upgraded processes of the evolution of a population. Reformed natural selection, in addition to the processes that are derived from it, allows for a more organized explanation of the evolution of life. Some of the newer processes that have been added here also demonstrate that more unknown selection processes probably exist. Further, several selection processes may overlap with one another, for example, traditional natural selection and reformed artificial selection. Thus, multiple reformed natural selection processes probably account for any particular population evolution. In short, the upgraded processes that are being presented here should reaffirm to biologists that science should not be content with the explanation of our origins until we reach perfection. Even a really good, old explanation still may have room for improvement!

First, I will attempt to improve the traditional artificial selection process. In the original model, only human natural forces were the reason for a population evolution. Humans may be the dominant species that carries out this process. However, it is a reflection of our ignorance of nonhuman nature if we think that we are the only species that selects other species to potentially create an evolved population of that species. Other nonhuman life-forms also artificially select, whether consciously or unconsciously. For example, the leafcutter ants specifically select and cultivate fungus to feed their ant larvae. In essence, these highly evolved insects are farming like humans. That is, they are artificially selecting certain life-forms to make their desired outcome occur.

We need a more comprehensive explanation than Darwin's traditional artificial selection (which can also be called *human artificial selection*) as our understanding of various life-forms increases. Our new concept can help to explain other nonhuman artificial selection processes that exist, like that used by the farming ants. *Reformed artificial selection* will be a more comprehensive version of the older process, which includes humans as well as any other external living entity that can select another individual. ***Reformed artificial selection* is a process that occurs when an individual(s) of any species potentially evolve(s) a specific population by selecting another individual(s) of any species.**

Additionally, the traditional artificial selection process may become obsolete in the future as humans continue to evolve (we may one day become a different species). In that case, reformed artificial selection would still be applicable. This new concept is our insurance policy that artificial selection will always be able to help explain evolution. The reformed artificial selection evolutionary formula can be expressed in the format below. Please note that ">" signifies "selecting" and "=" signifies "the potential conclusion."

The reformed artificial selection evolutionary formula:
An individual(s) of any species > Another individual(s) of any species = An evolved population of the species

Reformed Sexual Selection
Darwin spent more than half of his famous book, *The Descent of Man*, elaborating on sexual selection. We do not have the time or

the space to tread that path in this book. Although imperfect and incomplete, the following section is my brief attempt to illustrate the possibilities of improving the traditional sexual selection process.

Several problems exist with the traditional sexual selection process. First, the process needs to be more clearly defined in order to avoid ambiguity. The analysis of this process in the previous related section hopefully resolved this issue. Second, this process is silent when it comes to homosexuality, which must have some effect, directly or indirectly, on evolution. Third, the process does not reflect the complex scenarios that modernity has added. Too many unique situations have been created by our medical technology since Darwin's theory was originally analyzed, for example, the creation of artificial insemination and transsexual surgeries. How do we incorporate these into an upgraded version of sexual selection? I think the best way to resolve these issues is to keep our definition open-ended to include all possibilities.

***Reformed sexual selection* is a process that occurs when an individual of any sexual species potentially evolves a specific population by selecting another individual(s) of either sex of the same species (as a consequence of the sexual process).** The key to understanding this process is to know that either the selector and/or the selectee can be the evolved individual. *Knowledge of how the selection occurred or the sexual orientation of the parties involved is trivial as long as the ultimate result can be an evolved population.*

For example, a homosexual woman may indirectly negatively select another evolved homosexual woman. Note that this may be considered indirect because this process was probably not intentionally activated by the selector. Contrast this with the direct negative selection by the Nazis in World War II of their targeted groups, which was certainly deliberate. The above homosexual example may be viewed as negative selection because the selectee may be excluded from being able to reproduce with another individual of the opposite sex (assuming that the couple is monogamous), which may eliminate her opportunity to evolve a large population (see the "Negative and Positive Selection" section above for more information). The above is true unless she is artificially inseminated. This new scenario gives us another example of why the concept of the traditional sexual selection process needs to be reformed.

Too many new complex reproductive scenarios of the sexual process are inadequately explained from the perspective of the distant past. With artificial insemination, the evolved homosexual individual, with the approval of her partner, may select an individual of the opposite sex to form an evolved population. However, she would have skipped the traditional sexual process that should have occurred. Instead, she positively selected a male, possibly one whom she had never met, based on information that was given to her by the sperm bank. She then used technology to complete the reproduction process. This increasingly common scenario incorporates at least two different selection processes in order to potentially evolve a population. In short, compared to the traditional sexual selection process, reformed sexual selection is more capable of explaining dynamic scenarios like this.

We can now apply reformed sexual selection to many different types of scenarios: two females fighting for a sexual partner, two males fighting for a sexual partner, a female and a male fighting for a sexual partner, a female sexually selecting a female, a male sexually selecting a male, a female and a male sexually selecting each other, and so forth. Whatever way, population evolution as a consequence of the sexual process now has a more comprehensive explanation.

Further, reformed sexual selection may be the closest that external nature can get in the external selection processes to help evolve an individual without actually intervening in its internal processes: the genetic material is directly flowing from two external forces into the new individual life. The sexual partners' descendant(s) may be directly responsible for any evolution that occurs to itself after this point. This event may be helpful in understanding the difference between the evolution of an individual and a population as presented in this book because it may be considered the bridge that links the two.

In retrospect, Darwin is justified for reflecting so much on this process. The other external selection processes of an individual, including traditional natural selection, can be in vain if two specific individuals cannot have sex and reproduce. Sexual selection is more powerful than we ever thought!

Please note that ">" signifies "selecting" and "=" signifies "the potential conclusion."

The reformed sexual selection evolutionary formula:
An individual of any sexual species > Another individual(s) of either sex of the same species (as a consequence of the sexual process) = An evolved population of the species

The Evolutionary Selection Processes: The Other Processes

Descendant Selection

Another important selecting process should be acknowledged in biology. It is generally accepted that individuals can select their mates. However, biologists are generally silent when it comes to people selecting their own children, which would surely have an effect on evolution worth acknowledging. **Descendant selection is a process that occurs when an individual(s) of any species potentially evolves a specific population by selecting its descendant(s).** This process can be applicable to any life-form that can reproduce, either sexually or asexually—unlike sexual selection, which is only applicable to sexual life-forms. In short, any life-form that can reproduce may have control over whether its offspring can continue to live and reproduce.

Self-selection (we will talk more about this in chapter 38), sexual selection, and descendant selection combined can result in an individual's total related population evolution. *That is, the full effect of the combination of an individual choosing itself, its mates, and its children can result in the control of the evolution of its future descendants (as opposed to the evolution of other individuals' future descendants).* Imagining the total effects of these processes on humans is much harder because we have a low average number of offspring relative to other life-forms. However, an extreme hypothetical example can help to illustrate these powers.

Imagine the effect that a male person with extreme powers (such as many male rulers of ancient empires) can have on evolving a population of his descendants if allowed complete control over his sexual partners. If he wants to live and re-produce under those circumstances, then he may select thou-sands of women to have his children. Next, he can then select any evolved descendants of their offspring that he wants and possibly kill or sterilize the rest. The evolved population that will directly descend from him can possibly grow (after thou-sands of years) into the billions or higher. The effects could be extraordinary if we applied this scenario to other species that have more offspring than humans. Clearly these processes de-serve biology's attention, both individually and in conjunction with one another.

Many variations of descendant selection can occur. For ex-ample, a parent can negatively select all genetically deformed children. The result would be that those children who are not deformed would be allowed to live. If those children have an evolved trait, then the population could evolve. This practice has been going on since antiquity and mainly occurs through infanti-cide or euthanasia. Various animals are also widely known to use descendant selection usually via negative selection of unwanted babies. Alternatively, the parents can also positively select chil-dren with desirable evolved traits and encourage, or even force, them to mate. For example, the human practice of arranged mar-riages can be considered descendant selection. Evolved grand-children can be born through the arrangement fully controlled by the grandparents.

Descendant selection is a concept that generally can be ap-plied to help create an evolved population. However, a variation of this process can be applied to stop one from being created. For example, the parents can stop evolution from occurring by negatively selecting any child that *has evolved* (as opposed to those that have not evolved). In this case, they may not want their descendants to be different. Finally, an ancient form of descendant selection called *sex selection* (not to be confused with *sexual selection*) still exists in which the parents negatively select one gender of their offspring, usually females. This can lead to an abundance of males, resulting in a situation like that which now exists in China. This must have some effect, even if negligible, on future population evolution.

The descendant selection evolutionary formula can be expressed in the format below. Please note that ">" signifies "selecting" and "=" signifies "the potential conclusion."

The descendant selection evolutionary formula:
An individual(s) of any species > Its descendant(s) = An evolved population of the species

Miscellaneous External Reformed Natural Selection
This very brief section was included here to acknowledge that other types of *miscellaneous external reformed natural selection* processes may exist. The various processes of selection mentioned in this book may represent the large majority of the explanations for population evolution. However, those explanations that are still undiscovered can temporarily have a home here. Either way, they must still fit within the new paradigm of reformed natural selection, which allows everything in nature to be a potential selector.

CHAPTER 37

The Evolution of Evolution

An Overview

One of the biggest mistakes biologists can make is to assume that we know all of the possibilities of evolution. This point is driven home almost yearly as newly discovered archaeological finds continuously demonstrate that we need to rethink what we think we already know. I am about to present to you a revised theory of evolution. It certainly may be shocking after your first reading. However, it may make more sense as you progress through this book and see how all of the pieces of the puzzle start to fit together. This theory is limited in that it is just a theory. But every giant leap, whether it is made on the moon or in our minds, must start with a first step. Even if it proves to be wrong, then at least a negative discovery will have been made.

What is the possibility that evolution will always follow the same patterns all of the time? How do we know for sure that natural laws as we know them always held true in the past and will always hold true in the future? Simply, we don't know. Principles were defined in *The Most Important Lessons in Economics and Finance* as "**natural laws that are indicative to have enduring, highly probable value**" (Criniti, 2014, 7). It is not accurate to state that natural laws will occur permanently everywhere. Those laws may have an extremely high chance of occurring, but that is not the same thing.

In recent times, we have realized the value of the above statements in our space-exploration efforts. We have found that the natural laws that we know on Earth are not always the same in other parts of space. For example, we have learned that different gravitational forces exist in deep space and on different planets. Specifically, water (or any earthly object for that matter) floats in space. The above knowledge may have only been the speculation of a few people with excellent imaginations before astronauts went into space. They never witnessed water floating in space as we can today! However, this demonstrates that scientists need to be open-minded about universal principles.

It appears highly probable from what we have learned over the past two hundred years or so in the natural sciences that evolution has been consistent starting from the first universal common ancestor(s) on this planet. However, even if this is true, how can we be certain that all of the reformed natural selection processes will stay the same forever? Can new processes of evolutionary selection be invented? Our present, like no other time in history, appears to offer clues.

I propose a theory called *the evolution of evolution* in which the natural laws of evolution itself may change. This theory is a consequence of the long-term success of the wealth-management efforts of a particular species and its ancestral line. In particular, the natural laws of evolution may follow a very strict format until a certain point. That point could occur for any species at any time but only when certain conditions are met, which may be highly correlated to survival and prosperity. When its tipping point is reached, the natural laws of evolution can then become more flexible.

It may be possible that the process of evolution has been waiting for the development of a species such as our own in order to take evolution to the next step. Humans, unlike any other species, provide the best combination of adaptability, cooperation, intelligence, mobility, and unity, among many other characteristics. These may be the right ingredients to manage the wealth of this planet to its fullest potential. Certainly other species are successful at wealth management too—for example, our great tiny rivals, ants. They are one of the most successful species other than humans when it comes to managing wealth. They can farm and even herd other life-forms. But as admirable as they are, let's face it—humans have them beat by a long shot!

Humanity's success at wealth management cannot be underestimated. We are not perfect, but we may be the *optimal* species that evolution needed in order to evolve. This process of the evolution of evolution may have been going on for some time, possibly thousands or even tens of thousands of years. This may seem very long, but it is just a tiny speck of time compared to the length of life on this planet. This unique state that we are now in can be attributed mainly to two new major reformed natural selection processes (see Exhibit 37.1), which are both related in some way to wealth management. These processes will be called *monetary selection* and *technological selection*. The former began with the evolution of money, and the latter began with the evolution of technology. We will now look at each one separately.

Exhibit 37.1

The Two Major Causes of the Evolution of Evolution

1. Monetary Selection
2. Technological Selection

The Evolution of Money: Monetary Selection

The biologist Edward Wilson asked an important question in a discussion of evolution: "This is the assembly of life that took a billion years to evolve. It has eaten the storms—folded them into its genes—and created the world that created us...All this seemed timeless, immutable, and its very strength posed the question: how much force does it take to break the crucible of evolution?" (Wilson, 2010, 15). How much force does it take? What a great question! The answer may be found in humanity's management of its wealth, particularly its money and its technology.

As stated earlier in this book, all of our innovations can be attributed to our achievements in survival and prosperity. Specific individuals must survive first before they can have the time to build families and, ultimately, successful populations. On a very basic level, other species follow a similar pattern. However, humanity invented a specific tool in its wealth-management process that no other known species use or even have a need for: money. Even beginner students in economics and finance know that money can be a powerful tool. However, when we study it from an evolutionary perspective, we find out that it is even more powerful than we ever thought. *Simply, money is a powerful force never before seen in evolution, injected into the evolutionary process several thousand years ago.* Its wonders have been recently revealed exclusively to us, considering that we are the only known living species that use it. The creation and evolution of money has led to the creation of a new powerful force that can accelerate the evolutionary processes of *all* species, and possibly of the process of evolution itself.

362

The complexity created by the evolutionary selection processes automatically leads to additional complexity. Spencer explained this phenomenon of "the multiplication of effects" when he wrote in volume 2 of *The Principles of Biology*, "And every increased multiplication of effects, further differentiating the organism and, by consequence, further integrating it, has prepared the way for still higher differentiations and integrations similarly caused" (Spencer, 2014, 384). Money helped facilitate the process of wealth management in many ways when it was created. People bartered by trading products and services before the use of standardized money. Bartering was certainly a major development in our evolution. However, bartering can be very time-consuming and many times unfair. Thus, only standardized money could be used most effectively in the most advanced human societies to exchange large quantities of products and services.

Could you imagine if modern civilization were to start permanently bartering instead of using money? That would lead to a disastrous regressive effect. If we reverted to a bartering system, too many people with too many specializations would not be able to trade their skills for basic survival essentials. For example, imagine the bartering transaction between a rocket scientist and a fruit huckster. Could the scientist get some fruit with his trained skill? Their conversation might go like this: "Excuse me. I would like to trade my rocket science formulas for a pound of your apples." The fruit huckster most likely would decline unless the scientist could find something more specifically useful to offer him. Obviously, this is not because rocket science is not useful; however, it just may not be directly useful to the seller in this situation. In contrast, simple transactions such as these can occur effortlessly and consistently with standardized money, regardless of someone's skill set.

Almost everything can be bought with money, up to the limits of the law and current technology. This has given humanity a distinct advantage over other species. Money allows us to adapt better to numerous environments generally regardless of what the situation physically requires. For example, if we need to reach tall trees like a giraffe, then we can buy a ladder or a helicopter. If we need to navigate in the ocean like a fish, then we can buy a ship or a submarine. If we need strength like a gorilla or a lion, then we can buy steel weaponry and heavy machinery. You name it, and we most likely can accomplish it—with money!

This is a unique situation in biology because for the first time, a living being can gain many mental and physical advantages based on one technological advance. With money, we can surpass the best-desired characteristics of almost all known species by buying a solution for whatever deficiency we have. Of course money, like any tool, is only as useful as its user makes it. You can give modern building supplies and tools to a dog, but he will not be able to build you a house. But for humans, our evolutionary process has made us able to use money.

Our accumulated wealth, represented by money, may essentially be like traditional natural selection insurance for humanity and other species that we desire to protect. For example, we may be able to guard ourselves against various struggles such as global warming, ice ages, meteorite attacks, and so forth, with resources bought by wealth. The optimistic conclusions of this work highlight that, for the first time, there is a highly probable method to managing the risk of the tyrant of traditional natural selection. Proper wealth management can provide various degrees of protection for multiple worst-case natural catastrophes.

Money is not necessary when there is only a small human population, for example, a small isolated tribe. Even a somewhat larger human population could survive, to a degree, with only advanced bartering methods. However, money is absolutely essential when populations and specialists significantly increase in quantity. **Accordingly, money has become an essential survival tool for everyone in our globalized civilization. Someone may not be able to live very long without it and, consequently, he or she may not be able to contribute to evolving a related population. Further, the survival and evolution of all life-forms may eventually only occur by money, which is the dominant method to manage all wealth by the dominant species on this planet (us).**

Monetary selection **is a process that occurs when an individual(s) of any species (in particular, humans) potentially evolve(s) a specific population by using money to select itself or another individual(s) of any species.** This advanced evolutionary process may only begin to gain full momentum after the optimal species creates and learns the proper use of money. Monetary selection affects every type of reformed natural selection process, both externally and internally. The formulas below apply only to the evolution of a population. However, two other formulas listed in Exhibit 36.1 can apply to the evolution of an individual. This further demonstrates the power that money can have over the entire evolutionary process.

Traditional natural-selecting forces probably explain a majority of living-population evolution since its origins (ignoring self-selection, which we will discuss in the next chapter).

However, monetary selection may eventually become the primary process of evolution, for both individual and population evolution, as money and its uses advance. Life was here for billions of years without money. But since the invention and use of money, an abnormal change in evolutionary events has occurred in a relatively short period of time. The lessons of economics and finance are starting to show that this was not a strange coincidence. **In short, the general evolutionary process has accelerated *its* evolution since the birth and the evolution of money.**

The monetary selection evolutionary formulas can be expressed in the format below, but other variations of these formulas may exist. Please note that ">" signifies "selecting" and "=" signifies "the potential conclusion."

The monetary selection evolutionary formula for a population: External reformed natural selection:
An individual(s) of any species (particularly humans) > Money as a tool > Another individual(s) of any species = An evolved population of the species

The monetary selection evolutionary formula for a population: Internal reformed natural selection:
An individual(s) of any species (particularly humans) > Money as a tool > Itself to live and to reproduce = An evolved population of the species

The Evolution of the Nonliving: Technological Selection

In volume 1 of *The Principles of Biology*, Herbert Spencer wrote, "Each further advance of knowledge, confirms the belief in the unity of Nature; and the discovery that evolution has gone on, or is going on, in so many departments of Nature, becomes a reason for believing that there is no department of Nature in which it does not go on" (Spencer, 2014, 348). This statement begs the question, "Are there any other departments of nature unaccounted for where evolution has also occurred, is occurring, or may occur?" Biologists have only been concerned with the evolution of living things since the beginning of the official science. This is certainly understandable as their job is to study life. However, as noted earlier, our new concept of reformed nature could be broken down into two major categories: living nature and nonliving nature. We have been focusing mostly on living nature, but it is time to determine if evolution occurs in nonliving nature and, if so, in what role. This interesting inquiry may help us to better understand the comprehensive evolutionary process.

Some nonliving things evolve on their own, for example, glaciers and mountains. However, as you will see below, this is not the same type of change that occurs for living things. To recall from chapter 4, life is defined as "a reproduced, energy- and water-requiring entity that has the ability and/or the potential capability of feeling, self-repairing, and thinking." Nonliving things may evolve individually, but they don't have evolved, related populations. Only life's unique reproduction process allows the evolution of a related population of more than one to occur.

Nonliving things that were not created by life will lack variety unless they can reproduce a related population, especially an evolved one. Without life on this planet, Earth might be just a tad more interesting than the moon or many other large, moving objects in space that we have discovered. We have been noticing a common theme on other planets with our telescopes and probes. Specifically, each planet may have some unique features compared to other planets, but each part of *the specific* planet is roughly the same. In contrast, almost any part on the surface of our planet may be completely different than the next. Certainly this has something to do with its geological history, but the large majority of it has to do with the varieties of life, both past and present, that have shaped it. Anthills, beavers' dams, beehives, birds' nests, coral reefs, pack rats' middens, and termite mounds are just some of the many examples of what nonhuman living nature can do with nonliving nature. All of life has left a mark on this planet in some way or another. Of course, there is also the human impact.

You can find examples of human products everywhere. For example, you will find humanity's footprints wherever you look from above any large modern city in the United States. You might see boats, bridges, cars, electric lines, helicopters, highways, houses, parks, planes, skyscrapers, smoky factories, stadiums, trains, and tunnels. That is just the big picture. Zoom in and you might see many smaller innovations, such as cell phones and fashionable clothing. Other life-forms have done a good job at customizing the nonliving to fit their lives. However, we must admit that their innovations can never compare to what humans have done.

All of the above nonliving creations that are made by the living, especially humans, can be considered wealth. Additionally, nonliving technology can be said to occur every time someone figures out a better use for a lifeless object. Unlike living nature, the nonliving does not highly evolve by itself: it needs a life-form to do it. In order to understand our new selection process, let's take a closer look at the basics of technology.

To be clear, *technology* is wealth. But specifically, *technology* is the last improved version of a specific type of wealth. The technology of the past is not considered technology *anymore* unless it was the *last* improved version until the present. Likewise, a new technology of the future is not considered technology *yet* until the current technology is officially improved again.

Certain existing technology could be one, five, ten, or even five hundred years old—there is no time limit. In modern times, we are used to technology advancing at a rapid pace. A new cell phone may become outdated the next year when something better has replaced it. In this example, a one-year-old cell phone would not be considered technology anymore—only the newer model would. But in the distant past, technology developed at a much slower pace. Something may have taken decades or even centuries to be improved.

Technology only happens with each new improvement. Thus, technology is a positive change, an evolution, to each specific type of wealth, whether it is living or nonliving nature. Life can be said to be chronologically organized by specific technological breakthroughs. The technology of the past, as primitive as it may be by our standards, developed every time some living thing improved its wealth since the universal common ancestor—for example, the creation of sexual organisms. Let's fast-forward to the birth of humanity!

Fire was possibly one of humanity's first major forms of nonliving technology. We discovered how to create a heat source from other nonliving objects, for example, sticks and stones. We also crafted technology with every dead part of the creatures that we killed for food. Recall that the nonliving consists of both dead objects (objects that came from living things) and other nonliving objects. Dead objects had plenty of things to offer early humans (and still do). A piece of sinew can be turned into a tough cord. A limb bone can be used to make a hammer or a spear. A fallen tree can result in a shelter. And so on. No other known life-forms had such a wide range of uses for these materials. This was just the beginning. Let's fast-forward again to modern times!

We now have technology of all sorts, from the living to the nonliving. For example, our food sources derived from the artificial selection process can be said to be living technology. Cows are not wild tasteless meat anymore. Instead, they may be supersized and full of tasty additives. Those who label this as an improvement to our wealth should also label it as technology. Some examples of nonliving technology were already given. However, if necessary, we can fill hundreds of volumes discussing the new products that were made in just the last century.

The vast majority, if not all, of our wealth has already been improved at least once. Thus, technology has been created in an extraordinary number of areas. Everything said so far should be easy to understand. But we need to discuss something else that could be happening simultaneously right in front of us, undetected. Nonliving nature is evolving because of us in a unique way never seen before in history. We may be that optimal species referred to earlier that is capable of taking the nonliving to another point in its evolution. Is it possible that the nonliving could be evolving into something else, perhaps a new life-form?

You may recall that robotics were a major part of the difficulties that I had with forming my original definition of life.

Humans have been inventing various types of machines for thousands of years. However, the evolution of the nonliving has been occurring exponentially in the past two hundred-plus years. The nonliving could not have highly evolved on its own. It needed a living species with the "right stuff"—and that would be us! Even ants, probably our biggest competitor on this topic, are no match for the task of evolving nonlife to its current state. Why are they not talking on cell phones or shooting satellites up into space?

You may be wondering how I jumped to such drastic conclusions. The strangeness of our era offers us clues like no other. Humans have been intrigued with robots for a long time. It was, and still is, a fantasy for many people to own a robot that does much of their daily work for them. TV shows throughout the ages demonstrate that our society has been fascinated with this subject, for example, *The Jetsons* and *Small Wonder*. Of course, *The Terminator* series mostly depicted the possible negative side of robots.

Among all our advancements in robotics, two forms appear to be converging: the *android* and the *cyborg*. An android is a robot with lifelike, usually human, features while a cyborg is a living organism with robotic parts. These terms were once pure science fiction, but every year they become more realistic.

At the time of this writing, cyborgs, once a fantasy, now have become a reality. Modern people are walking among us with robotic parts—robotic limbs, camera-like eyes, pacemakers, artificial hearts, and so on. New technology is continuously resurfacing, pushing us closer to becoming total cyborgs.

On the other hand, a movement is currently underway to make robots look and act more human. Primitive versions of androids now exist that are realistic enough to automatically convince any naysayer that this section has merit. Modern androids can walk and even appear to express human emotions. These are just the beginning stages. We may be able to produce a totally humanlike android in another twenty to fifty years (or less).

If this trend continues, as it probably will, then we can only conclude that this is another example of the evolution of evolution. The big question that still lingers is this: "What will happen if Club Life comes face-to-face with Club Nonlife?" In other words, who would end up in control: the android or the cyborg? As our brutal history of aggression against other top predators has demonstrated, only one leading species can exist. If we allow androids to surpass us in intelligence, then we may position ourselves to lose our supremacy on this planet. It is our decision to empower them enough to be capable of taking control of their masters.

Androids may one day be able to attain all of the characteristics of life, including emotions and reproduction. If our robots become alive, evolution will have undoubtedly transformed into something different. Two groups of life, each with its own tree, will then exist. The first group may have had a universal common ancestor created out of nonliving chemicals. The second group would then have a universal common ancestor created out of nonliving material by the first group of life. The evolutionary process could be following a strange but similar pattern: evolution alternating between the nonliving to the living and back to the nonliving again. If this is our future, it will certainly demonstrate the unity of all reformed nature.

The fate of evolution may occur in several ways if two groups of life are formed. First, the cyborg could possibly be united with the android: let's call it the *cydroid*. If that were to occur, then Club Life would be reproducing itself with its own lifelike invention.

Consequently, future life-forms would start to resemble the non-living. Life-forms might also transition into shapes never before possible, for example, a humanlike creature with detachable parts. It might have an arm that could be converted into various tools or legs that could be converted into wheels or a sled. **In this future scenario, we might not need to be stuck with the parts supplied to us at birth by the traditional evolutionary process. The cydroid may become anything we make it.**

The other possibilities that may occur if two groups of life are formed are less optimistic. Androids could become the top predator, and we could then be at their mercy. They could play nice and let us live together in peace. Alternatively, we probably could become their beasts of burden. Humans perhaps would have a hard time accepting that fate. Thus, unfortunately, the androids may attempt to just exterminate us.

It is time to connect our analysis with our selection processes. The transformation of the nonliving into the living is a slow process that has been occurring for a long time. Humans have been gradually selecting nonliving wealth to evolve it into better robotic technology. However, technology has also been used to evolve ourselves and other living forms. *Technological selection* **is a process that occurs when an individual(s) of any species (particularly humans) potentially evolve(s) a specific living population by using technology to select another living or nonliving individual(s) of any species or itself.** With this process, possibly for the first time, living nature truly may unite with nonliving nature. Alternatively, possibly for the first time, nonliving nature truly may replace living nature. **In short, the general evolutionary process has accelerated *its* evolution since the birth and evolution of human technology.**

The two major condensed technological selection evolutionary formulas can be expressed in the format below, but other variations of these formulas may exist. Please note that ">" signifies "selecting" and "=" signifies "the potential conclusion."

The technological selection evolutionary formula for the evolution of the living:
Any living individual(s) (particularly humans) > Technology = An evolved living population (of one or more individuals) of the species

And/or

The technological selection evolutionary formula for the evolution of the nonliving:
Any living individual(s) (particularly humans) > Technology = An evolved living individual(s) from a nonliving individual(s) and an evolved population of a new living group with its own tree of life

To conclude, technological selection combined with, but mostly implemented by, monetary selection are the driving forces behind what appears to be the evolution of evolution. Robotic forms and other technology are slowly filling this planet through the use of money. You need money to purchase the robotic parts for a cyborg, and you need money to make an android. If the nonliving come alive one day, then they may also need money to survive. The survival of the richest would then continue.

CHAPTER 38

Self-Selection

One more selection process for the evolution of a population still has not been discussed. You could say that I saved the best for last! **It is more important than Darwin's traditional natural selection. Frankly, self-selection is probably the most important evolutionary selection process for populations because the evolution of all populations larger than one may never occur without it!**

We have already discussed that an individual must evolve before a population of more than one can evolve. An individual can either learn how to evolve alone or an external force can intervene in the individual's evolutionary process. Next, various parts of reformed nature can negatively or positively select an evolved individual to influence the evolution of a larger related population. All of the processes discussed in chapter 36 are considered purely external processes that act on the individual. The monetary selection and technological selection processes discussed in chapter 37 are generally external processes, but they can also occur internally. Despite all of these different ways to explain the entire evolutionary process of life, we are still missing one key ingredient: the self. This time the individual will be revealed in another way.

Somehow the individual has again been forgotten. Are we to assume that its role is complete after it has been evolved? Does it have any say as to where its life can go? One of the most important steps still remains: the individual must select itself. ***Self-selection* is a process that occurs when an individual of any species potentially evolves a specific population by selecting itself to live and to reproduce.** This is not the same internal process as the evolution of an individual—this event occurs after that.

Self-selection is a mental process, taking place consciously or unconsciously, that occurs when an individual makes major life decisions about its *whole* self. This final stage of internal selection occurs after the individual variations were created. At this critical point, the individual must choose whether it wants to create an evolved related population of more than one.

The first major life choice that the individual must make is to decide whether it wants to live or die. If it positively selects itself, then it chooses to live. If it negatively selects itself, then it wants to die. Second, it also needs to decide whether or not it wants to reproduce. Positive selection means it chooses to reproduce. Negative selection means it chooses not to reproduce. Third, a combination of the above is also possible. By default, if an individual chooses to die, then it also chooses not to reproduce. However, it is possible for an individual to choose to live but not to reproduce. Many individuals exist who love life but don't want any children. **Ultimately, to reproduce a population, an individual must positively choose both options: to live and to reproduce.** Major roadblocks to population evolution emerge without these affirmatives.

After a double positive self-selection, the individual may still encounter other internal obstacles; for example, its reproductive system has to function properly. Many people want to live and to have children but cannot. Reproductive issues such as missing ovaries or a low sperm count can be an impediment to successful reproduction. Fortunately, you can buy modern technology that may correct many of these issues and allow reproduction to still occur. This is an example of the internal monetary and technological selection processes operating in unison with self-selection for the evolution of a population. The individual is using money to buy technology that can implement its positive self-selection decision to increase its evolved population of one. Specific necessary reproductive surgeries—for example, to correct endometriosis (a condition that makes it difficult for a woman to get pregnant)—may never occur without money and the right equipment. Thus, a potential evolved larger population may not be able to occur.

The effect of self-selection for asexual individuals is more severe because they can reproduce entirely by themselves. If an evolved asexual organism negatively self-selects, then an evolved larger population will not occur. In contrast, two sexual organisms from the opposite sex must positively self-select in order to potentially create an evolved larger population, even if only one of them is evolved. If only one sexual organism positively self-selects and the second sexual organism negatively self-selects, then another mate may still be found to potentially create an evolved larger population.

Many biological theories have been missing common sense for too long. Hopefully, the next few statements will convince anyone who still thinks that populations alone, and not individuals, evolve. **That is, generally, regardless of how powerful the external forces are that are doing the selecting, ultimately, they must answer to the evolved individual's will to live and to reproduce if a larger population evolution is to occur.** In other words, it is the individual who must ultimately determine its destiny.

For example, imagine if every member of a selected species suddenly decided to commit suicide. Would their population evolve? The strength of a random earthquake, hurricane, meteorite shower, or any other external force of nature wouldn't matter anymore. The answer still would remain unequivocally no. *This is the power of self-selecting over traditional natural selection. Traditional natural selecting forces can no longer select, positively or negatively, if everyone who was to be selected chose to die by negative self-selection—nobody would remain to be selected. Thus, if every member of Club Life participated in a mass suicide, then population evolution on Earth would be nonexistent.*

The above also applies for self-selection of reproduction. If an individual decides to live but not to reproduce, then the effect is still the same, although it may take longer to notice it. External natural selection can still try to positively select the individual, but if it stubbornly refuses to contribute to the reproduction process, then a larger evolved population generally cannot be created. The individual may simply not want to bear the responsibility and the stress of having children.

An individual could also have other reasons for not wanting to reproduce, sometimes very strange ones. I would like to offer an alternative hypothetical example of the *selfish-superman* to demonstrate this point. Imagine a human who was able to evolve great powers of intelligence, mobility, strength, and so forth. He may decide that he doesn't want anyone else on the planet to be able to compete with him, even his own offspring. Thus, he may decide to never have children to ensure that the evolved population always remains at one: just himself. This may seem like a silly reason for not reproducing, but it was a personal decision that the selfish-superman made. The evolution of a related population larger than one will never occur unless someone can force him to reproduce (or unless he changes his mind).

On very rare exceptions, an evolved individual's negative self-selection choices can still result in a larger, related population evolution. Generally, they occur in the presence of advanced living nature (particularly humans). For example, humans now have the capability, unlike other species, to force two sexual individuals of another species to live and mate, regardless of their self-selection considerations. For example, let's pretend that scientists wanted to chain a male and a female mouse down so that they could not commit suicide, thus forcing them to live. Next, they could take the male's sperm and artificially inseminate the female's eggs. Finally, the female mouse could be continuously monitored until birth to ensure that her offspring lived.

In this extreme hypothetical example, the self-selection process becomes almost irrelevant. The mice above were forced to live and to reproduce against their will. This example further demonstrates humanity's dominance over much of living nature.

Excluding rare exceptions such as the one noted above, self-selection is crucial for population evolution for the absolute majority of the time. It must not be forgotten that a population must always begin with one person. You can visit various places in the world with a welcome sign that states "Population of One." Statistically, these small towns, sometimes called ghost towns, are included as part of the national population. Similarly, we can pretend that every first evolved individual carries an imaginary sign that says the same thing. Its sign may reflect the next population increase when it finds its mate and reproduces.

To conclude, self-selection should not be too difficult to understand. As demonstrated in chapter 4, all living things can think at some level. If they can think, then they can make decisions, such as the ones necessary to self-select.

Humans make decisions every day, from the moment we wake to the moment we go to sleep (and debatably even in our sleep). For example, we may need to decide what we should eat for breakfast. The decisions keep coming: What clothes should we wear? How are we going to get to school or work? How do we get home? What friends should we have? How much money do we need? Even bacteria have to make simple choices. However, the most basic decision that every living organism has to make is to determine if it wants to survive. If it chooses not to survive, then generally we do not need to even wonder about what effects other natural selecting forces will have on it. The individual has thus already determined its fate and the fates of its potential descendants.

Biologists generally agree that individual choices may affect the population evolution of other living organisms. Even Charles Darwin also recognized that the individual's mind plays some kind of role in the traditional selection processes. In his *The Descent of Man*, he wrote, "He who admits the principle of sexual selection will be led to the remarkable conclusion that the cerebral system not only regulates most of the existing functions of the body, but has indirectly influenced the progressive development of various bodily structures and of certain mental qualities. Courage, pugnacity, perseverance, strength and size of body, weapons of all kinds, musical organs, both vocal and instrumental, bright colours, stripes and marks, and ornamental appendages, have all been indirectly gained by the one sex or the other, through the influence of love and jealousy, through the appreciation of the beautiful in sound, colour or form, and through the exertion of a choice; and these powers of the mind manifestly depend on the development of the cerebral system" (Darwin, 2006, 1246–1247).

You can infer from this quote that the mind of an individual must play a very important role throughout many selection processes. Biologists generally accept that an individual can choose to select, negatively or positively, its food, its mate, other living organisms, nonliving nature, and so forth. *If the individual has the power to select all of these other parts of reformed nature, then why shouldn't it be given the respect to say that it can also select its own natural self?*

The self-selection evolutionary formula can be expressed in the format below. Please note that ">" signifies "selecting" and "=" signifies "the potential conclusion."

The self-selection evolutionary formula:
An individual(s) of any species > Itself to live and to reproduce = An evolved population of the species

CHAPTER 39

Evolving to Survive and to Prosper

It is time to start bringing together everything that we have learned in this book. All of our analysis on evolution begs the question: "Why do individuals and populations evolve in the first place?" It is very hard to escape the overall conclusion that survival and prosperity are interconnected with both evolution and the answer to this question. In life, some people learn how to survive and to prosper while others don't. Similarly, some people learn how to evolve while others don't. Regardless of the reasons for evolving, evolution can be continuous during an individual's lifetime. But why does evolution need to occur? **Simply, the main reasons for evolving are to survive and to prosper.** If someone cannot change in order to adapt to adversity, then he or she might die quickly. This leads us back to the struggle!

Life is a constant battle with external nature: earthquakes; enemies; the tax collector; even family, friends, and lovers. They may all be a part of someone's struggle to stay alive. Various deadly struggles can force individuals to change their lives. Life has been busy working hard to survive by managing its wealth since the birth of the universal common ancestor. Our ancestors have always realized that if we don't have the right wealth, then we need to invent it. Life-forms have been steadily increasing their living technology through the evolution of the living and their nonliving technology through the evolution of the nonliving.

Individuals can maximize their wealth through proper wealth management, which will allow them to enter various Major Scientific Phases of Prosperity. Prosperity increases the chances that they can continue to survive both in the present and in the future while maintaining a quality existence. A large supply of the appropriate survival essentials can be very helpful over time. But that is not always enough. **To stay alive, individuals must be prepared to evolve to be able to manage the unique challenges of unknown future struggles.**

Our ancestors have had so many struggles with external nature since their beginning. The result of this is that life may now evolve not to confront a present hardship but *to anticipate* future ones. This is why evolution may continue to occur during prosperity. By now, life has got the point: as long as the struggle exists, then life must keep evolving to be at least one step ahead of adversity. The struggle of life has been going on for billions of years, and it does not seem like it will be ending anytime soon. Thus, evolution must continue…

We have learned from the processes of internal natural selection that an individual must want to evolve before it can actually evolve (unless, of course, an evolutionary intervention occurs). This desire to evolve must be present to increase one's chances for a change to occur. These facts are obvious in our society today for those who want to confirm it. Some people want to evolve into a species more advanced than human. Some examples include, but are not limited to, those who are involved in cyborg organizations; those who would like to permanently enhance their body with bionic parts; those who have strange plastic surgeries to make them appear less human, and those who want to be permanent Martians.

Undoubtedly, some humans would choose to become total cyborgs if the technology were present and available to them today. This may create pressure for other humans to follow their lead in order to survive the new struggles that may result from these changes. The result would be the strangest evolution yet, an evolution of evolution, which would occur from a combination of an internal version of monetary and technological selection. People would use money to select or deselect how they want to evolve. If it can be demonstrated that modern humans can choose to evolve, then it shouldn't be too difficult to extend this point to other life-forms throughout history.

Monetary selection is changing the evolutionary process of external reformed nature. Humans can buy other species that are for sale and the products and labor involved to evolve their population. They can also use money to help others to survive and to prosper. We will talk more about this shortly when we discuss survival by a third party applied to all nonhuman life.

Monetary selection is also changing the evolutionary process of internal reformed nature. It should be clear by now that humans need money to survive. However, to a degree, they can also use money to evolve themselves through the internal process of monetary selection. Humans can use money to pay for amazing medical technology that will help keep them alive longer. As technology increases, humans may one day be able to use money to evolve themselves into something else, such as a total cyborg or a cydroid. If this occurs, humans may be able to pay for increased levels of agility, communication, intelligence, mobility, speed, strength, time, unity, and so on. Money is certainly playing an ever-increasing role in survival, prosperity, and the evolutionary processes. In particular, monetary selection is increasingly becoming a part of every stage of evolution: from the birth of an evolved individual to the creation of the largest evolved population.

We can now incorporate evolution into a modified version of the Survival-Prosperity Sequence described in part 2 to get a rough idea of how individuals and populations evolve to survive and to prosper. Please look at the Modified Survival-Prosperity Sequence for Evolution in Exhibit 39.1. Please note that this sequence may vary, and it is limited because every life-form has unique survival needs. The steps may be slightly customized for each individual species since certain organisms have shorter lifespans and probably have little need for luxuries.

Exhibit 39.1

The Modified Survival-Prosperity Sequence for Evolution

These steps are listed in chronological order, but the order may vary in some circumstances. They occur in each Major Evolutionary Phase of Prosperity for each newly evolved united entity. Please note that evolution can occur in an individual at any time. To create an evolved offspring, the evolved individual must self-select and stay alive at least until the necessary timeframe in the reproduction process.

The Modified Survival-Prosperity Sequence for Evolution = The Survival Test + The Seven Steps of Prosperity
1. The Survival Test: The preliminary test before a new Major Evolutionary Phase of Prosperity begins. It is focused only on managing the present struggle to stay alive.
2. Prosperity Step 1: Accumulate a short-term emergency reserve of survival essentials. Each Major Evolutionary Phase of Prosperity begins here.
3. Prosperity Step 2: Accumulate a long-term emergency reserve of survival essentials and/ or luxury items.
4. Prosperity Step 3: Positive self-selection. The individual(s) must choose to live and to reproduce before going any further.
5. Prosperity Step 4: Sexual selection. (This step is for sexual organisms only.) The individual(s) must select the partner(s) that he or she (they) want(s) to reproduce with.
6. Prosperity Step 5: Reproduction.

7. Prosperity Step 6: Descendant selection. The individual(s) must choose to keep or kill her or his (their) offspring.
8. Prosperity Step 7: A larger, united evolved population is created. Each Major Evolutionary Phase of Prosperity ends after this step. However, the last step is omitted in the final Major Evolutionary Phase of Prosperity. This newly evolved united entity must survive before being promoted to the next Major Evolutionary Phase of Prosperity. The steps of prosperity would begin again, and the sequence would continue.

First, an individual chooses to evolve, directly or indirectly, in order to survive during the Survival Test of an individual. This pressure to evolve is coming from a struggle (usually via external reformed natural selection). If the individual succeeds in evolving, then the new internal technology is added to her or his wealth to be managed. The accumulative evolutions through one's genetic code, its inherited wealth, are retained in case they may need to be used again against future struggles. Second, if an individual makes it to Prosperity Steps 1 and 2, then it may choose to use its extra wealth for a variety of purposes: emergency reserves for future survival needs; reproductive purposes; and its own future evolutionary needs. Evolution can occur at any point in this process (and probably may occur the entire time).

Next, an individual may decide to positively self-select, find a mate, reproduce, and select its descendants in the later prosperity steps. All of this is occurring while the individual is still managing existing struggles and preparing for future ones. If this process is successful, then the first evolved offspring may be produced. The individual advances to the Survival Test of Phase 2 of the Five Major Evolutionary Phases of Prosperity: the Evolved United Family (see below). The Modified Survival-Prosperity Sequence for Evolution will be repeated for the evolved descendants until the largest evolved population is attained.

Population evolution can be loosely stated to occur for all species in a similar pattern as the Five Major Scientific Phases of Prosperity discussed for humans in part 2. The Five Major Evolutionary Phases of Prosperity for all of life are listed in Exhibit 39.2. Further, the Modified Survival-Prosperity Sequence for Evolution must repeat itself in every Major Evolutionary

Phase of Prosperity for each newly formed entity (see Exhibit 39.3). Let's discuss this a little more in detail! First, an individual evolves in order to survive and to prosper. The evolved individual may be prosperous enough to create an evolved united family, which is the beginning of a related small group. This advances the new family to the Survival Test before Phase 2.

Exhibit 39.2

The Five Major Evolutionary Phases of Prosperity

These phases are listed in chronological order, but the order may vary in some circumstances. Each respective evolved entity needs to advance through the Modified Survival-Prosperity Sequence for Evolution before being promoted to a higher phase. The entity begins each phase with Prosperity Step 1 after passing the Survival Test.

1. Phase 1: Evolved Individual
2. Phase 2: Evolved United Family (or a small to relatively large population)
3. Phase 3: Evolved United Nation (or a very large population)
4. Phase 4: Evolved United Planet
5. Phase 5: Evolved United Universe

Exhibit 39.3

The Modified Survival-Prosperity Sequence for Evolution Incorporated into the Five Major Evolutionary Phases of Prosperity

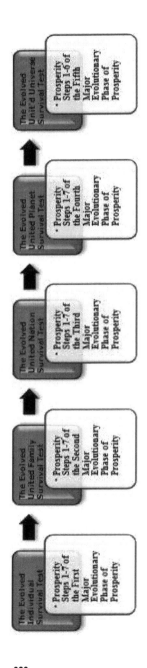

In Phase 2, the evolved group strives to reach the highest levels of prosperity. The evolved group may be prosperous enough to create an evolved united nation (loosely speaking). This advances them to the Survival Test before Phase 3. In Phase 3, the evolved united nation strives to reach the highest levels of prosperity. The evolved united nation may be prosperous enough to create an evolved united planet (loosely speaking). This advances them to the Survival Test before Phase 4. In Phase 4, the evolved united planet strives to reach the highest levels of prosperity. The evolved united planet may be prosperous enough to create an evolved united universe (loosely speaking). This advances them to the Survival Test before the final phase. In Phase 5, an evolved united universe strives to reach the highest levels of prosperity.

To conclude, if an evolved individual does not survive and prosper, then evolved populations of all sizes cannot occur. It is important to note that very few species have made it to Phase 3 to join the ranks of ants and humans. While we are not at Phase 4 yet, we are still the leader in this race!

Additionally, evolution can be continuously occurring in a species. An evolution generally gets absorbed into a sexual population when a newly evolved individual of a species mates with another member of the species. The eventual result may be a widespread evolutionary updated version of the existing population, regardless of which phase it is in. We will now move on to understand more about the effect of human wealth on nonhuman nature.

CHAPTER 40

The Wilderness Is Shrinking

As stated in chapter 9, civilization is different than the wild because it is a place where a human society resides, survives, and is the dominant life-form. However, the term *civilization* has been specifically applied to the top predator of this planet, which just so happens to be us. This title would not be ours though if we were a passive species or an inferior predator: it would belong to some other group. For example, if lions were the real chiefs of the planet, then our survival would depend on avoiding or appeasing them. This is obviously not the case though. We are the ones that make the rules of other species because we are in control. Thus, directly and indirectly, the fates of all living things are starting to rest entirely on the rules we make of the space that they dwell on.

As was noted in our discussion of the General Control Scale of Nature, humanity's control of other parts of reformed nature, living and nonliving, has been increasing. Consequently, civilization is also increasing as we become better masters of nature. Regrettably, this also means that its opposite, the wilderness, is shrinking at an alarming rate. Optimistically, one could argue that this is a reflection of the success of our species and should be considered a positive event. But this is not good long-term thinking because it demonstrates an incomplete understanding of the interconnectivity of life. Maximizing our control over nature can certainly be a positive event if we can exert that control as wisely as possible. Unfortunately, that does not appear to be the case, which is verified by the occurrence of massive extinctions of other species.

The human population has been dramatically increasing worldwide for a long time. However, the exponential effects of our population are becoming more visible. Less space is reserved for other life as more humans are put on this planet. Jack London's wild may one day call us all it wants, but we will not be able to answer. This planet is finite and has a maximum occupancy rate. Some other potentially useful species may have to become extinct for every piece of real estate that humans occupy. Simply, our population explosion has serious drawbacks for everyone, including us, if it is not kept in check.

Humanity's wealth is increasing in some ways but decreasing in others. For example, our current worldwide methods of managing the wild are reducing our total wealth. All life is connected and has some use, even if we don't know what it is yet. It is our job to find out this information, and that may take time. But if we make a species extinct, then that doesn't matter anymore.

Extinction is most likely permanent. An unknown species somewhere in the wild with a cure for our most deadly diseases—for example, cancer—can be just months away from being extinct because some company or government wants more parking space or fancy townhomes.

I agree with biologist Edward Wilson: "Wildlands and biological diversity are legally the properties of nations, but they are ethically part of the global commons. The loss of species anywhere diminishes wealth everywhere" (Wilson, 2010, 326). As the leaders of this world, all wealth can be ours to keep, but the price of this is more responsibility. If we can effectively manage it well, then it may be successfully argued that we have officially evolved as a species. This evolution will require massive education of our species on the value of nonhuman nature to the planet. If the loss of one species—for example, honeybees—may possibly bring humanity to its knees, imagine the result of the loss of so many other species. We are truly all in this together!

In addition, the massive ongoing deforestation is horrifying. Trees have helped humanity so much throughout time. They have provided us with various forms of survival essentials, including food, heat, and shelter. They have also played a huge role in the evolution of our hands, which are the major tools that make us who we are. In return, many of us pay our respects through a worldwide campaign of war against them. We need to protect our trees because they are very valuable to all of life, and especially to us. Fewer trees mean lower quality air, which is an attack on at least one of our immediate survival essentials.

All of humanity must understand that other species need some space to live too. A sufficient amount of land should be reserved for wild life-forms. This means enough space for them to stay alive and to continue reproducing a healthy population. We can still be in control of the wild and let other nature enjoy life too. Smarter long-term decisions will keep the wild special and protect our fellow members of Club Life.

Additionally, our failure to recognize the hidden wealth that may lay dormant in the wild now can cost us the respect of future humanity and its descendants. Our current decisions may one day deprive them of experiencing the beauty of the wild because it may then be all gone. They may never forgive us for that! Why should they?

CHAPTER 41

The Wealth Management of Other Living Things

This is a short chapter that demonstrates that the process of wealth management is common to all members of life. It builds a foundation to the next chapter, which shows the predicament that all nonhuman life-forms are now in: they are operating under the principle of the survival by a third party. We are the ones who have an impact on their survival, directly and/or indirectly, whether they like it or not. We must reflect on the survival process of various life-forms before we can understand this more clearly.

All life-forms need to learn about survival, regardless of how they do it. To recall from part 1, *human survivalism* is the science of survival for all living humans. *Comprehensive survivalism* is the science of survival for all living entities (including humans). We will now focus our attention on the latter concept, which is more general.

Other living things must also confront many hardships during their lifetimes. All life, from the microorganism to the tallest giraffe, is continuously trying to manage its struggles in order to stay alive. Each species may have a different approach to meeting its survival goals, but the general idea is the same. For example, the survival essentials for a fish are very different than those for a squirrel. Their bodies have different requirements for living. The fish needs to live in water, and the squirrel needs to live on land, preferably up in a tree. If the fish came out of the water for too long, then he would die. And if the squirrel went into the water for too long, then she might drown. This example illustrates that survival essentials rank differently for each species depending on its specific needs derived from its evolutionary process.

Despite the differences noted above, all life has some common ground. For starters, each species should meet the general requirements of life discussed in part 1. Second, it must be able to find a sufficient amount of survival essentials—whatever that unique life-form requires. If this does not occur, then it will die. This leads us to the same conclusions that were applied to humans in part 2 of this book. That is, if any individual life-form can amass an accumulation of emergency reserves, a concept that we can call *comprehensive prosperity*, then it can improve its chances of living longer and having a higher quality life. More accumulated wealth can translate to a larger increase in its chances of surviving better in the future. **This demonstrates that the connection of managing wealth during survival and prosperity is also present for all of life, both human and non-human. In other words, every living species must continuously manage wealth to stay alive.**

Let's recall the three major wealth-management possibilities for humans to see if it applies to other species as well. Another living organism that minimizes its wealth (this includes its survival essentials) also increases its risk of a quicker death. Let's use our squirrel again as an example. If she did not save enough nuts, then she may not have enough food for the upcoming winter. She will probably not survive until the springtime unless she finds food or someone who can help her get food.

Next, another living organism is living on the edge of survival if it only has enough wealth to survive. This is also not a good option because of the big risk of falling off the edge into the absolute poverty zone. Its chance of death will progressively increase if its struggles unexpectedly intensify and demand more wealth than what it has.

Finally, the ideal situation for any species is to maximize its wealth well beyond what is sufficient to survive, which may help to protect it from unanticipated events that could occur. Individual organisms should continuously maximize both their survival essentials and their technology. Eventually another species might arrive at a similar position as current humanity if it is as smart as humans have proven to be at managing its wealth (that is, assuming that it can also increase its evolutionary wealth).

If the above is true—at least to a certain degree—then the same Survival-Prosperity Sequence must also exist for every living entity, not just humanity. If they can survive and prosper to the highest step of the first Major Scientific Phase of Prosperity, then they may be able to advance through to the next phase (please review chapter 14). Thus, other living entities may arguably be said to study finance and economics (for example, ant economics) if they are able to advance to another major phase. Of course, they may not learn from reading science books like this one. However, somehow they must have found out how to manage their wealth successfully if they have achieved some version of prosperity. As usual, other living things are generally more intelligent than many people give them credit for!

This puts us in a good position to be equally compared to all of life. *We can determine the managerial success level of a species if we can determine what prosperity phase it is in.* Very few species make it to the higher levels of Phase 2, where the group's population level has increased. Even fewer species make it to Phase 3 where humanity currently stands with a tiny minority of other species including: ants, bees, beetles, and wasps. It is important to understand that just because a species is found all over the world doesn't mean that its members are functioning in unison—as with spiders, for example. It is unity at the end of every Major Scientific Phase of Prosperity that gives an entity of a species the right to be promoted to the Survival Test of the next phase.

Humans may dominate the world, but we are still not completely united. We are not alone in that regard. Ants also have the same problem. From cities to jungles, nations of ants exist all over the world. But if you pick up any one nation and place it next to another nation, then a war would probably occur. Optimistically though, humans are still in the lead. It appears that we have the highest chances of uniting than any other species in Phase 3. If we can overcome our current hurdles, we may be the first life-form to enter Phase 4 after uniting our entire planet's population. More on this later, in parts 4 and 5 of this book!

CHAPTER 42

The Survival by a Third Party Applied to All Nonhuman Life

I would like to pose a question: "What is the difference between a dog and a wolf?" Unfortunately, in modern times, the answer is mostly the difference between life and death. Wolves were a major top predator and a threat to humanity about ten thousand years ago, which was supposedly around the time that they were first domesticated to become dogs. Wolves began their descent in power as humans gained more control over living nature. Fortunately, unlike many other top predators that stood in the way of our ancestors' progress, they had many qualities that humans admired. For starters, wolves were loyal, and they knew how to live as social animals. They also were a great complement to us because of their excellent hearing, sense of smell, and intelligence. These combined traits put wolves in a unique position compared to all other life.

Dogs supported our ancestors' survival and prosperity in many ways including hunting, security, sheepherding, and even transportation. For their loyalty, they now rank as one of our top pets and have been granted the special title of "man's best friend." This special relationship between humans and dogs could only have been possible because of the initial human recognition of wolves' talents and our artificial selection of their most compatible offspring for our needs. But it also would not have been possible if some of the first dogs were not able to recognize the potential benefits of partnering with us. In exchange for their services, we have provided them with better and more consistent meals, fire, shelter, and so forth. The dogs' investment paid off big time. Dogs will most likely be taken good care of for as long as humanity is around. They probably will be right by our side wherever we may go, whether it is the seashore or another planet. The fates of the wolves, well, that's another story!

The problem with wolves is that most of them live in the wild and mostly don't care for the rules of our civilization. Wolf packs have their own rules, and this has led them into conflict with modern humans. Wolves still exist, but their world population levels are at an all-time low. If their trend continues, then they will eventually become extinct. Nevertheless, several strategies are being used to protect them, including special wolf reservations and sanctuaries. On the other hand, the population of dogs has exploded worldwide. They generally are at the top of the list for protection by animal cruelty laws. The negative fates of the wolves and the success of their dog descendants are a microcosm of what appears to be the fates of all living nonhuman entities.

As noted in chapter 41, all living things manage their wealth in order to survive, and hopefully, to prosper. This has not changed in recent times. The majority of life-forms are still trying to do their best during their many daily struggles. However, one of their biggest struggles is only multiplying: us. Other life-forms are being progressively caught in a predicament that grows more tangled with every increase in human control over nonhuman nature. **This leads to an interesting conclusion: species that can capture our attention by demonstrating their use to humanity have the highest chances of being saved from extinction.**

It is not enough for other species to manage their wealth using the techniques of the past. How can they compete with humanity at this point of evolution? Humanity may be on a potential path to control every aspect of every life-form on this planet at some near point in the future. We are slowly gaining total access to life's every move through increasing numbers of cameras, satellites, and scientists. In general, if humans like a species, then we keep them. And if we don't like them, then we kill them. This is nothing new! Humanity has probably contributed to the extinction of every major predator in our way since we left Africa, but now we can do it more easily and quickly. More on that later!

Simply, nonhuman life is faced with an option: manage its wealth under the rules of human civilization or under the rules of the wild. However, as noted in chapter 40, the wild is increasingly shrinking, and what remains is still under human control. Thus, if historical patterns continue, then it appears that the only real options for nonhuman life are to join us in civilization or perish. It can still manage its wealth but under the laws set by us. In other words, its freedom may be compromised in exchange for a little security. This exchange is not always even, however. Actually, it is usually very disproportionately in favor of humanity. For example, let's look at the life of a rooster.

The large majority of roosters are killed at birth to become human food. These extra male chickens are of little value because only a few of them are needed for reproduction. The result of living in civilization by our rules is that hundreds of millions of roosters live a very short life. A hen, on the other hand, usually gets to live as long as she can produce good quality eggs. Either way, any living hen or rooster is surviving by a third party whether he or she likes it or not.

If an animal is lucky, then it may get adopted as a pet by a good owner. This is becoming the best possible scenario for nonhumans. Well-favored pets like cats and dogs may live the most lavish lifestyles. Their owners may also love them very much. Actually, many humans care for their pets as much as (and sometime more than) their own children.

Farm animals manage the wealth that they have too; however, generally humans gave it to them. Further, they are always at the mercy of their masters. If the farmers love the animals, then they may be provided with a good life. If the farmers are indifferent to the animals' feelings, then they could lead a miserable existence.

It is a good time to briefly mention squirrels and pigeons, which both benefit from a unique relationship with humans. We allow them to manage their own wealth entirely within civilization, mostly without any interference from us. They have almost full roaming rights, as long as they don't cause a threat to someone's health. Imagine if a bear or a tiger tried to do the same thing. They would be tranquilized and relocated (and sometimes killed) immediately!

Another interesting group worth mentioning is pests—for example, rodents and cockroaches. They survive entirely on their own within our civilization and are generally unwanted. These creatures live a very risky existence though. They know if we catch them, then they are probably going to die. Yet they still take their chances coming into our homes to steal our food. They have caused us so many problems in the past. So why aren't they all dead yet? This is an old question resurfacing. Could we really kill all of our pests on this planet? Maybe we could, but not without any consequences.

The real question should be this: "Do we *all* want to kill all of our pests on this planet?" Despite their general repulsion, some humans value pests and want them to live. For example, biologists and other scientists love to study cockroaches, flies, fruit flies, and mice because they are very successful at surviving. Any living thing that is a master at survival automatically becomes a learning center for scientists. This may be one of the major reasons that many pests still exist today. Thus, pests may also be considered to be surviving by a third party.

This brings us full circle back to the beginning of the chapter. Humanity is increasingly becoming *the third party* that decides whose survival should be supported. The story of the protection of dogs and the destruction of wolves appears to contain a common pattern that can be applied to all nonhuman life. Living things that are useful to us increase their chances of becoming a candidate for survival by a third party.

It is necessary to understand that all life has potential value. Other living organisms may still have a useful purpose to us, even if we don't know what it is yet. If we are going to be the world's managers, then we must recognize that wealth exists in all life, and that it is our duty to discover it. Edward Wilson was correct in saying: "In all cultures, taxonomic classification means survival" (Wilson, 2010, 44). Those living things that are classified as enemies—for example, certain microscopic bacteria—become a target for extinction. Others who are classified as respected friends—for example, cats and dogs—get the best protection possible.

Money is the fuel that allows the operation of the survival by a third party. Humans use it for many biological tasks ranging from the payment of taxonomists' salaries to the purchase of laboratories and wildlife reserves. The human third party uses money to protect or extinguish all species that it encounters. With money, you can buy permits to hunt animals or pesticides to kill pests. With money, you can buy biological equipment to evolve species. With money, you can buy lawyers and various necessary specialists.

Some animals (for example, roosters and certain breeds of dogs) are captured and forced to fight by certain gambling organizations—*all in the name of money*! Illegal loggers continue to chop down trees worldwide, the homes of so many species—*all in the name of money*! Tens of thousands of elephants have been killed in Africa for their tusks in the past few years alone—*all in the name of money*! Exotic animals are captured and/or killed worldwide—*all in the name of money*! The list of bad things that can occur for nonhuman life because of money is endless.

On the other hand, with money, you can adopt stray animals and care for them. With money, you can create parks, pet-adoption programs, sanctuaries, wildlife reserves, and zoos run by the best specialists. With money, you can create worldwide educational programs to teach people the value of treating animals and plants with respect. With money, you can buy the best land and the best security to ensure wildlife's survival. Fortunately, the list of good things that can occur for nonhuman life because of money is also endless.

We have again ended a discussion at the crossroads of truth, where every sign still points in the direction of money. Biologists and conservationists have tried almost every method to protect-ing nonhuman nature, except the only one that will work. It should be obvious by now that almost all of nonhuman life is now surviving by its one and only third party: humanity. Further, we control all of this process with our money. **In short, without money, the goal of wildlife protection on our planet can never be fulfilled. The failure to realize the truth in this statement will lead to more unnecessary extinctions.**

CHAPTER 43

The Extinction of the Richest

Unconcerned readers may not be fazed by the following quote from the top biologist Edward Wilson: "The revelation of Centinela and a growing list of other such places is that the extinction of species has been much worse than even field biologists, myself included, previously understood. Any number of rare local species are disappearing just beyond the edge of our attention" (Wilson, 2010, 244). Their indifference may stem from the "out of sight, out of mind" mentality. But just because they cannot see extinctions happening, doesn't mean that they're not happening! It also doesn't mean that those extinctions are not affecting us.

The same unconcerned readers may have a totally different reaction when they read the next quote from Wilson: "So important are insects and other land-dwelling arthropods that if all were to disappear, humanity probably could not last more than a few months. Most of the amphibians, reptiles, birds, and mammals would crash to extinction about the same time" (Wilson, 2010, 133). We can easily conclude from both of the quotes above that we may be currently riding on a fast track to our mass extinction. Simply, if we are killing off many species that we all need to make the circle of life occur, then we are indirectly committing a massive suicide of our species.

To recall from earlier, the overall message of the title of this book is that being wealthier increases your probability of continuously surviving and prospering by providing you the greatest options to obtaining survival essentials. It does not mean that being rich will guarantee your survival. The survival of the richest concept can also apply to species. The richest species can also become extinct by not utilizing the option to survive better and by not taking care of the planet's wealth properly. Simply, if we do nothing about resolving the predicament of defenseless non-human life, then we may suffer.

If a rich man foolishly spends all of his money, then he will eventually pass the edge of survival and reach absolute poverty. It is a simple subtraction problem: any positive number that is continuously reduced will eventually get to zero. As demonstrated in part 2, the dangers of wealth minimization apply to a population of any size, including a whole planet.

Wealth is like a double-edged sword. If you can manage it properly, then the most amazing things can happen. But if you manage it poorly, then you can lose it all. It is not easy to replace wealth once it is gone, and in some cases, it may even be impossible. **No wealth can eventually result in no life. Managing wealth is not a game—it is very serious!**

Principle 193 in *The Most Important Lessons in Economics and Finance* is this: "*A fool and his wealth will eventually be separated*" (Criniti, 2014, 226). This principle can also be applied to the richest species: us. If we do not carefully manage our wealth, the greatest amount that any known species has ever accumulated, then we risk losing everything—including ourselves. We do not want to be labeled as an example of "the extinction of the richest."

Optimistically, this doesn't have to occur. We can fix these problems armed with the knowledge that we have gained so far. This will be the subject of part 4!

CHAPTER 44

Part 3 Summary

In part 3, we discovered that a significant underlying relationship exists between biology, economics, finance, and survivalism. Early biologists initially gained some of their strongest insights for their most important theories by studying wealth management, particularly economics. Recently, this pattern has been resurfacing as modern biologists are realizing that money is necessary to protect our planet.

In this part, we also analyzed the concept of nature and a new concept called reformed nature: a nature that includes everything in it. Moreover, we discovered that evolution means change, and that it can be applied to anything. However, biologists are mainly concerned with the evolution of life throughout time. We also discovered a fallacy in common biology: individuals do not evolve. Actually, individuals must evolve first before a larger related evolved population can occur.

We are better able to reevaluate the traditional evolutionary selection processes by understanding nature and evolution. Selection processes can be divided into external and internal selection and again into negative and positive selection. The traditional processes proposed by Charles Darwin include artificial, natural, and sexual selection. These processes are very helpful but need a modern upgrade. I proposed a modification of all three traditional processes with an improved, reformed version of each.

The concept of reformed nature led to the development of a new comprehensive selection process called reformed natural selection. This new process can be applied to the selection of both an individual and a population, and it incorporates every selection process known and unknown. Reformed natural selection can help to explain the whole evolutionary process of life throughout time.

In part 3, we learned the reasons *why evolution occurs*: to help life to survive and to prosper. I also introduced several other important processes of evolutionary selection in this book to help explain *how evolution occurs*. These processes are: absolute creativity evolutionary selection, descendant selection, evolutionary intervention, hybrid creativity evolutionary selection, miscellaneous external reformed natural selection, self-selection, and the two new selection processes of the evolution of evolution called monetary and technological selection. Living evolution has generally been viewed as a fixed process throughout time, which the archeological records indicate to be true. However, the analysis in this part revealed that the process of evolution itself might also be evolving, which is mainly occurring through money and technology.

Life may be evolving to a tipping point where money will be required throughout the whole process. Money is now necessary, both directly and indirectly, for almost all human artificial selection and a large part of traditional natural selection. A sign of its increased role in sexual selection is also slowly becoming apparent. For example, someone's monetary worth is becoming a large part of the human sexual selection process. In certain parts of the world, money has become almost the only criteria for finding lifelong partners. Without any money, someone will not get any honey! Further, in some places, money is also used to buy sexual toys to help avoid the need to find a mate.

Money can now buy lifelike robotic sexual mates, particularly in Japan, which may be a game changer for future human populations. The current forms of these robotic mates are extremely simplified; however, the potential market for them may make them more realistic one day. With more realistic, lifelike robots, it is possible that real relationships may be formed between robots and living nature, particularly humans. Money, and the technology that it can buy, can also lead to the creation of total androids and cyborgs. Further, the robotic technology that we are creating with money may eventually become life itself, a process called the evolution of the nonliving. At that critical junction, we may have two unrelated evolutionary systems of life occurring at the same time, which will mark the official change of the living evolutionary process.

All nonhuman life manages wealth to survive to some degree. Like humanity, it needs to follow the same Survival-Prosperity

Sequence in order to work its way up through the Five Major Scientific Phases of Prosperity. With this model, we are now able to compare ourselves to all other living things to see how successful we are at managing wealth. Interestingly, we are probably sharing Phase 3 with only a few other organisms—for example, ants and bees. However, humanity appears to be the closest to attaining the first planetary unity of a species, which may also promote us to Phase 4. Additionally, we are the only species in a position to potentially colonize other planets, as we almost have the technology to do so (ants and other similar species would need many great evolutionary leaps to catch up).

Finally, humans are gradually gaining control of all living and nonliving nature. Our use of money in our civilization has a spillover effect on other parts of nature. The use of our money is now the method in which almost all species can survive. Also, the use of our money is now slowly becoming the major method by which almost all species can evolve (via monetary selection). Certainly the role of money has not been given the credit it deserves in biology!

Considering that only humans control the major decisions of this planet with our money, nonhuman life-forms are in a difficult predicament. They are forced to survive by a third party: us. This leads me to a major conclusion that I will elaborate on in part 4. That is, it is our responsibility to protect our planet and all of its life-forms. If they die, then we may quickly follow. Our failure to realize the symbiotic relationship that all life has with one another may be catastrophic. To understand this point a little more clearly, we will now begin to close out the book by reviewing what we are capable of, what is at stake, and who we are!

PART 4
The Wake-Up Call

CHAPTER 45

An Overview: It's Time to Wake-Up

Doomsday preachers have probably existed since the birth of mankind. Many of them have been guilty of forecasting the exact day the world would end only to be left explaining why they were wrong for the rest of their lives. I thought carefully about how to conclude this book without becoming another doomsayer and sounding overly pessimistic about the future. However, with each new reflection on the topics in this book, the possibility of a catastrophic outcome occurring in our lifetime seems more likely.

I added Part 4 to demonstrate the severity of the human predicament. This analysis is not the result of some random conclusions made after a weekend marathon of watching Hollywood science fiction movies. The conclusions are drawn from scientific evidence provided by researchers from a variety of fields.

Anyone alive at the time of this writing only has to keep up with current events to at least acknowledge that something is very different about this time period relative to others. Modern doomsayers have a great argument in their favor compared to those of the past.

Despite all the progress of humanity, a quiet storm is currently brewing. First, deadly conflict is occurring all over the world in many places like Africa, Asia, Eastern Europe, and the Middle East. Terrorism has also found an open door into the most powerful nations. Second, many parts of the world are still in deep poverty, particularly in Africa. Many people in these places still live without even a good supply of food and water. How can this be when we have more millionaires and billionaires than ever before in history? Third, many more unstable nations with sinister leaders seem to be joining the ranks of the nuclear-capable nations. Finally, the most powerful nations appear to be not fully cooperating with one another, particularly China, Russia, and the United States. How can we fulfill our potential as a species if we do not learn from our mistakes? The World Wars are over, but our old habits seem to die hard. Unfortunately, now the stakes are even higher though as population levels have skyrocketed since the end of World War II. More people, especially leaders, need to relearn the crucial lessons of the value of less war and more peace and unity.

The theme of those crucial lessons is reflected in the words of Viktor Frankl, a Holocaust survivor and a famous psychologist. His quote is so important that it was placed on the cover of this book: "Since Auschwitz we know what man is capable of. And since Hiroshima we know what is at stake" (Frankl, 2006, 154).

Please now take a look at the cover of this book. You will see two pictures that I took many years ago. The first picture displays the ovens of the Crematorium I in Auschwitz, Poland that cremated the bodies of those who died in the concentration camp. The second picture displays a building in Hiroshima, Japan that survived the atomic bomb dropped by the United States in World War II. Those photographs cannot capture the horrors that must have occurred in each place. Much of humanity is still haunted today by the memories of all the death and destruction that transpired there. How could we let these events happen? How could we ensure that they never happen again?

We must dig deeper to better understand Frankl's quote and its relevance to our situation today. In order to do that, we need to investigate more closely what we really are capable of and what is really at stake. From that analysis, we may also emerge with a better understanding of who we are and what we need to do in order to answer what may be our last wake-up call.

CHAPTER 46

What Are We Capable Of?

We Are Capable of Doing Great Evil

The human species has demonstrated that it is capable of great things in two major categories: evil and good. In the spirit of optimism, let's get the bad part over with first! **Out of all living things, no other species has been able to compete with the intensity and quantity of human destruction.** We have been creating better ways to kill since the birth of our species including, but not limited to, automatic weapons, bows and arrows, cannons, dynamite, gas bombs, grenades, guns, knives, missiles, nuclear bombs, simple bombs, spears, swords, and the thermonuclear bomb. Our best weapons are capable of killing every single thing in its path instantaneously. Undoubtedly, we are capable of doing great evil, especially with an evil leader in control of those weapons!

The prehistory and history of humanity is plagued with examples of war. Many simple tribal wars worldwide have occurred in antiquity that we'll never know about because they were not recorded. War stories have become abundant though since the days of recordkeeping. Many wars with record-breaking death tolls occurred in the twentieth century alone. These wars include, but are not limited to, World War I, World War II, the Korean War, the Vietnam War, and the wars in the Middle East. As technology increased throughout history, the number of dead bodies also increased.

War demonstrates evil in itself, but the evil is magnified when it is mixed with genocide and other mass atrocities. As David Stannard, an expert on American genocide, wrote, "But even the worst wars end. Military defeat leads to political surrender, for it is politics that most wars are about. Genocide is different. The *purpose* of genocide is to do away with an entire people, or to indiscriminately consume them, either by outright mass murder or by creating conditions that lead to their oblivion" (Stannard, 1993, 254). Daniel Jonah Goldhagen, another genocide expert, has written a book with a title that sums up the horrors of genocide: *Worse Than War*. We will now take a walk down this wretched path in order to discover some sad truths about the evil capabilities of humanity. You may want to prepare yourself before you read any further.

The best place to start our understanding of genocide is in the Americas. According to Stannard, "The destruction of the Indians of the Americas was, far and away, the most massive act of genocide in the history of the world" (Stannard, 1993, x). In reference to the native population of 1769, Stannard wrote: "Nationwide by this time only about one-third of one percent of America's population—250,000 out of 76,000,000 people—were natives. The worst human holocaust the world had ever witnessed, roaring across two continents non-stop for four centuries and consuming the lives of countless tens of millions of people, finally had leveled off. There was, at last, almost no one left to kill" (Stannard, 1993, 146). Adam Jones, another genocide expert, generally agreed on this point: "The European holocaust of indigenous peoples in the Americas may have been the most extensive and destructive genocide ever" (Jones, 2011, 108).

The American genocide, as evil as it was, only gives a glimpse of what we are capable of. We need to go to the beginning of the twentieth century to have a more comprehensive understanding of humanity's worst side. Exhibit 46.1 includes two lists that I have created of various genocides. Although they are incomplete, they serve as an excellent simple illustration of the general message of this section. The first list includes examples of genocides that started before the twentieth century. The second list encompasses the major genocides that started after the twentieth century. This information was derived mainly from Adam Jones's comprehensive textbook on genocide.

Exhibit 46.1

Too Many Genocide Examples

The following two lists are in approximate chronological order. Although they are incomplete, they serve as an excellent simple illustration of the general message of this section. This information was derived mainly from the second edition of Adam Jones's comprehensive textbook on genocide: *Genocide: A Comprehensive Introduction*.

Some Genocide Examples That Started before the Twentieth Century

1. The Carthaginian genocide by the Romans (labeled by Ben Kiernan as "The First Genocide") at the close of the Third Punic War (149–46 BC): at least 150,000 Carthaginians died (Jones, 2011, 5).
2. The early Christian genocide by the Romans: death toll unknown.
3. The non-Christian genocide by the Christians: death toll unknown.
4. The genocide of various nations from Europe to Asia by the Vikings (around eighth to eleventh century): death toll unknown.
5. The genocide of various nations from East Asia to Western Europe by Genghis Khan of the Mongol Empire (around thirteenth century): death toll unknown.
6. The American Indian genocides by the Europeans and their descendants (1492 to present): possibly up to 100,000,000 American Indians dead (Stannard, 1993, 268).

7. The Vendean genocide by the French (1793–1796): about 150,000 Vendeans died (Jones, 2011, 7).

8. The various tribal genocides in South Africa and surrounding areas by Shaka Zulu of the Zulu kingdom (1810–1828): death toll unknown (Jones, 2011, 7).

9. The Atlantic slavery genocides by various nations (sixteenth to nineteenth centuries): about 15,000,000 to 20,000,000 African slaves died (Jones, 2011, 39).

10. The Australian genocide by the British (starting in 1788): about 719,000 Australian Aborigines died by 1911 (Jones, 2011, 119).

11. The Indian famine genocide by the British (1896–1902): about 19,000,000 Indians died (Jones, 2011, 68).

12. The Congo genocide mostly by the Belgium King Leopold (about 1885–1908): about 10,000,000 Congolese died (Jones, 2011, 70).

The Major Genocides That Started after the Twentieth Century

1. The Herero/Namas genocide in present day Namibia by Germany (1903–1906): more than 7,700 people died in Germany's first concentration camps (Jones, 2011, 122).

2. The Armenian genocide by Turkey (1914–1922): approximately 1,500,000 Armenians died (Jones, 2011, 150).

3. The Greek genocide by Turkey (1914–1922): approximately 750,000 Greeks of Asia Minor died (Jones, 2011, 151).

4. The Assyrian genocide by Turkey (1914–1922): approximately 250,000 Assyrians died (Jones, 2011, 151).

5. The Ukrainian famine genocide by Stalin's Soviet Union (about 1926–1937): about 3,900,000 people died (Jones, 2011, 194).

6. The controversial German genocide by the British and US air forces (by the end of World War II in 1945): about 300,000 to 600,000 German civilians died (Jones, 2011, 43).

7. The controversial Japanese genocide by the British and US air forces (by the end of World War II in 1945): about 900,000 Japanese civilians died (Jones, 2011, 43).

8. The Chinese genocide by the Japanese (1937–1945): about 2,600,000 Chinese civilians died plus 500,000 to 1,000,000 POWs (Jones, 2011, 72).

9. The Jewish genocide by Nazi Germany (also known as the Jewish Holocaust) (intensely from 1941–1945): about 6,000,000 people died (Jones, 2011, 233).

10. The genocide of disabled people by Nazi Germany (by the end of World War II in 1945): about 250,000 people died (Jones, 2011, 269).

11. The Polish genocide by Nazi Germany (by the end of World War II in 1945): about 6,028,000 Polish died (Jones, 2011, 271).

12. The Soviet POW genocide by Nazi Germany (by the end of World War II in 1945): about 3,300,000 people died (Jones, 2011, 273).

13. The Gypsy genocide by Nazi Germany (by the end of World War II in 1945): up to 1,500,000 Gypsies died (Jones, 2011, 275).

14. The Tibetan genocide by China (1950–present): about 1,200,000 Tibetans died since 1950 (Jones, 2011, 211).

15. The Chinese famine genocide by the Chinese dictator Mao Zedong during the Great Leap Forward (about 1958–1961): about 40,000,000 Chinese died (Jones, 2011, 212).
16. The Bangladesh genocide by Pakistan (1971): about 3,000,000 Bengalis died (Jones, 2011, 340).
17. The controversial Indochina genocide by the Unites States and its allies (by the end of the Vietnam War in 1975): about 2,000,000 to 5,000,000 Indochinese died (Jones, 2011, 76).
18. The Cambodian genocide by the Khmer Rouge government (1975–1979): about 1,900,000 Cambodians died, which is about one-quarter of the original Cambodian population (Jones, 2011, 293).
19. The East Timor genocide by Indonesia (1975–1999): about 170,000 East Timorese died, which is about one-quarter of the original East Timor population (Jones, 2011, 312).
20. The political genocide by the Argentinean government (1976–1983): up to 30,000 people died (Jones, 2011, 512).
21. The Mayan genocide by the Guatemalan army and its security forces (1978–1983): as many as 250,000 Mayans died (Jones, 2011, 142–143).
22. The Afghanistan genocide by the Soviets (1979–1989): about 2,000,000 Afghans died (Jones, 2011, 78).
23. The genocide of the Iraqi Kurds under Saddam Hussein in Iraq (1987–1988): as many as 180,000 Kurds died (Jones, 2011, 178).
24. The controversial economic genocide on Iraq by the United Nations (about 1990–2003): about 500,000 Iraqi children alone died (Jones, 2011, 45).

25. The Bosnian-Muslim genocide by the Bosnian-Serbs in Srebrenica (about 1992–1995): more than 7,000 Bosnian Muslims died (Jones, 2011, 327).
26. The Tutsi genocide by the Hutu in Rwanda (1994): about 1,000,000 people died, mostly Tutsis (Jones, 2011, 346).
27. The Kosovar Albanian genocide by the Serbs in Kosovo (1998–1999): several hundred civilians died (Jones, 2011, 329).
28. The controversial US genocide by al-Qaeda (September 11, 2001): about 3,000 civilians died in one day (Jones, 2011, 46).
29. The Darfur genocide by the Sudanese government (mainly 2003–2004): about 200,000 people died (Jones, 2011, 374).
30. The genocide of political prisoners by North Korea (ongoing): possibly over 1,000,000 people have died in the past several decades (Jones, 2011, 216).

R. J. Rummel provides an interesting perspective of genocide. According to Jones, "Rummel's book *Death by Government* (1997) coined the term "democide" to describe "government mass murder" – including but not limited to genocide as defined in the UN Convention. Examining the death-toll from twentieth-century democide, Rummel was the first to place it almost beyond the bounds of imaginability. According to his study, somewhere in the range of *170 million* "men, women, and children have been shot, beaten, tortured, knifed, burned, starved, frozen, crushed, or worked to death; buried alive, drowned, hung, bombed, or killed in any other of the myriad ways governments have inflicted death on unarmed, helpless citizens and foreigners." If combat casualties in war are added to the picture, "Power has killed over 203 million people in [the twentieth] century"" (Jones, 2011, 447). The footnote to the above is this: "He considers this a fairly conservative estimate: "The dead could conceivably be nearly 360 million people"" (Jones, 2011, 460). You can add these numbers to the sum of those killed in the American genocides over a span of five centuries to reach incomprehensible figures. This doesn't even count all the other genocides that may have occurred in history—for example, the Carthaginian genocide by the Romans and various religious genocides throughout the ages.

Wealth, particularly money, was used to carry out this evil. Without wealth, armies and weapons could not have been bought. Without wealth, the evildoers could not have been provided their necessary survival essentials that allowed them to carry out their destruction. Further, wealth also has been a chief motivator of crimes against humanity. According to Jones, "Few factors seem so influential in genocidal violence as economic upheaval and catastrophe. When the material base of people's lives is thrown into question, they are prone to seek scapegoats among minorities (or majorities); to heed an extremist political message; and to be lured by opportunities to loot, pillage, and supervene" (Jones, 2011, 569).

The many roles wealth played in genocide and other mass atrocities seemed to resurface numerous times throughout my research on this topic. For example, Stannard describes the role of wealth in the American genocides: "But the extermination of entire communities and cultures, though commonplace, was rarely the Spaniards' declared end goal, since to do so meant a large expenditure of energy with no financial return. As with Hispaniola, Tenochtitlan, Cuzco, and elsewhere, the Spaniards' mammoth destruction of whole societies generally was a by-product of conquest and native enslavement, a genocidal means to an economic end, not an end in itself. And therein lies the central difference between the genocide committed by the Spanish and that of the Anglo-Americans: in British America extermination *was* the primary goal, and it was so precisely because it made economic sense" (Stannard, 1993, 221). In other words, economics and finance played a crucial role, directly or indirectly, in the various genocides that occurred in the Americas.

In short, genocide is seriously evil. This subject has caused me the most stress in all of my research for this book. The few words written here can never do justice to its evils. It is disturbing to look at photographs of genocides that happened all over the world throughout various points in history. The same upsetting feeling recurs for every picture viewed, regardless of the place or time that it occurred. It is hard not to feel connected to the victims. Just like us, they were once living people trying to survive day by day on this crazy but beautiful planet. It is hard not to wonder how many of these victims could have become great leaders and scientists, people that this world so desperately needs.

Genocide has occurred in all races and on every continent (excluding Antarctica). The killings were enacted by many different methods, from the machetes of Rwanda to the gas chambers of Germany. The people who committed these crimes ranged from top military officers to ordinary civilians, both male and female. Many people even committed crimes against their best friends. **If we are capable of committing these atrocities against our own species, then it is hardly necessary to detail what we are capable of doing to the rest of living nature.**

We Are Capable of Doing Great Good

It is quite possible that you may be in a state of depression after reading and reflecting on the first part of this chapter. Don't worry—this part will hopefully balance that feeling out! You see, humanity is also very capable of doing great good for this world. Realistically, the human species has the best chance of creating the correct technology that can help protect the planet and every species. The following is a list of some of the most important inventions and/or discoveries made almost exclusively by humans. This obviously incomplete list, placed in alphabetical order, is included here as a quick demonstration of our talent as a collective whole: agriculture, air conditioners, airplanes, the alphabet, art, the assembly line, batteries, bicycles, books, bridges, calculators, cameras, cars, ceiling fans, cell phones, central heaters, clocks, cloning, clothing, combustion engines, compasses, computers, concrete, contraceptives, credit cards, democracy, dishwashers, dryers, dynamite, electricity, elevators, the evolution of life, fire, flushing toilets, freezers, furniture, genetics, glass, glasses, GPS, gunpowder, helicopters, indoor plumbing, instruments, the Internet, languages, light bulbs, maps, matches, mathematics, medicine, microscopes, microwaves, mirrors, money, motorcycles, movies, music, pasteurization, penicillin, plastic, the printing press, radar, radios, refrigerators, roads, robotics, rockets, rubber, satellites, science, search engines, sewing machines, shelters, ships, skyscrapers, soap, space probes, space shuttles, space stations, stairs, steamboats, steam engines, steel, stoves, submarines, surgeries, tanks, telegraphs, telephones, telescopes, televisions, tools, trains, vaccinations, washing machines, weaponry, wheels, windmills, writing, and X-rays.

In addition to creating great technology, humanity is also capable of demonstrating some of the greatest examples of altruism ever displayed by a species. Currently, in the United States alone, thousands of different charities are dedicated to helping specific groups, including, but not limited to, aging, animal cruelty, animal rights, antipollution, archaeological conservation, bird conservation, child protection, clean-water protection, climate change, the disabled, disaster relief, educational support, ending world poverty, fighting cancer, forest conservation, human rights, international medical assistance, military families, ocean conservation, population control, sick children, tribal protection, eradication of various diseases, and wildlife conservation. This small sample of formal charities does not account for the daily acts of altruism that occur everywhere but go unnoticed.

Several more examples demonstrate what good we are capable of. First, the green revolution that is underway clearly demonstrates people's desire to clean up the planet and keep it safe. Many people are changing their daily habits for no other reason but to do good deeds. Various energy efficient products ranging from energy efficient cars to solar panels are being produced more. Additionally, recycling is now becoming popular on a massive level. Ironically, the increase in recycling may be due to the recent discovery that money could be made from converting recyclables into good products—for example, creating polyester from plastic soda bottles. This positive trend should be embraced regardless of its real motivation.

Second, certain groups love animals so much that they refuse to eat them. For example, the strictest vegans only eat food from plants, such as fruits and vegetables. The vegan lifestyle may be considered a positive step toward protecting our planet's life-forms. However, those people who are more omnivorous still can do their share by not wasting food. As most survivalists already know, all food should be respected, as it came from other life. *Generally speaking, when food is wasted, some life-form was killed for no reason.*

Next, good pet owners are a perfect example of humanity's capability of giving love to other life-forms. In many cases, they treat their pets like members of their family. It can be argued that pets should be left outside to roam free as wild animals. However, as part 3 demonstrated, the wilderness is shrinking. Adopting pets may be a great tool to saving animals that have lost their homes or would not have a home if they were forced to live on the streets.

Finally, everyday a hero gives her or his life for another person for no reason other than pure altruism—for example, firefighters and law enforcement. Further, some of our greatest leaders have risked their lives for the greater good of the entire human species including: Mahatma Gandhi, Dr. Martin Luther King Jr., Mother Theresa, and Nelson Mandela. These people have set the example for how we can live together and love one another.

In 1961, President John F. Kennedy set a goal for the United States to land *a man* on the moon by the end of the decade. Some people thought he was crazy. However, although he did not survive to see it, Kennedy's goal was achieved in 1969. In about eight and a half years, the NASA space program achieved much more than the unthinkable: they put *two men* on the moon. Humans had gazed and wondered in amazement at that big object in the sky for thousands of years, only wishing to visit. In less than a decade, the United States met that challenge as a united group. It begs the question: *How much more can we do as a united peaceful world—a place without war?*

In short, it should be apparent by now that we are not a bad species, although at times it appears that way. We are capable of great good including creating better technology designed to protect our planet. We are also capable of doing good deeds, and in many cases, unconditionally. However, we are not good enough yet at realizing how much more greatness we are still capable of. **Despite our many discoveries, collective humanity has yet to make its greatest discoveries: who we are as a species and our potential capabilities to better serve this planet, and possibly, our universe.**

CHAPTER 47

What Is at Stake?

Time Is Running Out

Considering humanity's massive destructive capabilities, a dead end is approaching if we do not make some major changes to our worldly wealth management approach soon. Further, death is almost inevitable without the correct changes implemented on *a united scale*. With our current solutions, the real questions are the following: "How much longer do we have?" and "Who else are we bringing down with us?"

Most agree that we are capable of wiping out our whole species and some others. However, many disagree that we will ever be able to kill all of them, including the cockroaches and mice. They say that these species have been here long before humans, and they will be here long after. This may be true on some levels but not in its entirety. The full argument must include the true realization of what we are capable of. These naysayers may not fully comprehend how powerful we are.

Frankly, I am convinced that humans can achieve anything they want to if they commit to that goal, no matter how constructive or destructive it is. We cannot deny our potential to destroy this planet in the absolute sense if we wanted to. If we can get to the moon within eight and a half years using only a small fraction of the entire human population, then there should be no doubt that we can eliminate this whole planet somehow if we desired. The only question would be: "How long will it take?"

To the naysayers, please reflect on the following: If we detonate the strongest hydrogen bombs (or create even stronger bombs) in strategic places either here or on the moon, then could it be possible to essentially knock Earth out of its orbit and purposely drive ourselves into the sun? In other words, if we found a way to drive Earth into the sun and made it our unwavering goal, then the whole party would be over for both Club Life and Club Nonlife on this planet! This may be a laughable thought at first but so was every major human undertaking before it was accomplished. Honestly, the human potential is never a laughing matter.

From our perspective, the answer to the "What is at stake?" question is that everything that means anything to us is at stake. I am not alone in my conclusions. Many great minds from different specialties over the past century seem to agree. For example, while he was analyzing the human predicament, the great psychologist Sigmund Freud stated: "The fateful question for the human species seems to me to be whether and to what extent their cultural development will succeed in mastering the disturbance of their communal life by the human instinct of aggression and self-destruction. It may be that in this respect precisely the present time deserves a special interest. Men have gained control over the forces of nature to such an extent that with their help they would have no difficulty in exterminating one another to the last man. They know this, and hence comes a large part of their current unrest, their unhappiness and their mood of anxiety" (Freud, 2010, 149). It is worthy to note that the above statements were made in the early 1930s in Europe as the Nazi movement was gaining momentum.

Let's fast forward to the 1960s after the tolls of destruction during World War II were well known! Arthur Koestler derives a similar conclusion that time is running out: "Nature has let us down, God seems to have left the receiver off the hook, and time is running out" (Koestler, 1989, 339). Fast forward again to modernity and the great biologist Edward Wilson also reaches the same conclusion: "Eventually idealism and high purpose may prevail around the world. Eventually an economically secure populace will treasure their native biodiversity for its own sake. But at this moment they are not secure and they, and we, have run out of time. The rescue of biological diversity can only be achieved by a skillful blend of science, capital investment, and government: science to blaze the path by research and development; capital investment to create sustainable markets; and government to promote the marriage of economic growth and conservation" (Wilson, 2010, 336). Please note that Wilson also acknowledges the role of money as a part of the solution to our problem (capital investment), which presents more evidence for the earlier arguments in this book.

From these three different great scientists who have been quoted from three well-separated points over a century, we can conclude that the human problem is escalating. But what can we do about it? Many problems need very quick resolutions. In addition to the increased risk of nuclear war, many other difficulties are occurring as a by-product of our prosperity. Our success as a species has resulted in new struggles that were probably never encountered before by nonhuman living nature including, but not limited to: extreme poverty, global warming, instability of Earth's movement around the sun, pollution, unique climate change, unique mass extinctions, a waste disposal crisis, a worldwide population crisis, and, as this book demonstrates, the evolution of evolution. On top of all this, similar to a teenager confronting the hardships of puberty, our species is facing an identity crisis brought about by scientific self-discovery, particularly the biological conclusions discussed in this book. Considering this huge list of serious issues that must be confronted in such a short time, we can't be blamed for feeling unhappy, full of unrest, and anxious as diagnosed by Freud above. These feelings should be accepted as normal. However, this should not be an excuse to cowardly retreat from our struggles.

Besides, we can't turn back now nor can we put the brakes on civilization. Famous psychologist B. F. Skinner agrees with this point: "Unfortunately we cannot stand still: to bring scientific research to an end now would mean a return to famine and pestilence and the exhausting labors of a slave culture" (Skinner, 1965, 5). **This point highlights the paradox of prosperity: The more prosperity that is achieved, the more that it is desired when it is taken away.**

Our species is approaching one of the highest Major Scientific Phases of Prosperity. Humanity's perspective on life will never be the same again even if war destroyed all of our wealth and only a handful of human survivors remained. Those remaining humans would be permanently scarred with the remnants of the intellectual wealth of our species. They would always know what we are truly capable of, and they would relentlessly pursue recreating a prosperous life as they knew it. As Arthur Koestler wrote, "There is no turning back on housing, clothing, artificial heating, cooked food; nor on spectacles, hearing aids, forceps, artificial limbs, anaesthetics, antiseptics, prophylactics, vaccines, and so forth" (Koestler, 1989, 328). Most importantly, money is surely the one invention they wouldn't forget about. The monetary system would begin again when their population grows to a size where money would be necessary, and the evolution of evolution could get one more chance to realize its purpose.

Our role in global wealth management includes a high responsibility. As long as humans exist, it appears that our best and worst inventions will exist too. To quote Koestler once more: "An invention, once made, cannot be dis-invented; the bomb has come to stay. Mankind has to live with it forever: not merely through the next crisis and the next one, but forever; not through the next twenty or two hundred or two thousand years, but forever. It has become part of the human condition" (Koestler, 1989, 324). Since Koestler wrote these words decades ago, numerous other wars have occurred worldwide while the nuclear threat has been increasing exponentially. *When will we learn?*

In short, we can never forget about our prosperity knowing what we now know. From money to nuclear warheads, we are stuck with all of our inventions. These godlike powers that we have earned add to the evidence of who we are and what we need to do. The faster we learn this as a species, the brighter and safer our future may be!

The Sixth Mass Extinction

According to Wilson, five major extinction periods occurred: Ordovician (440 million years ago); Devonian (365 million years ago); Permian (245 million years ago); Triassic (210 million years ago); and Cretaceous (65 million years ago) (Wilson, 2010, 29). After each of these periods, life came back stronger with more diversity and with a higher population. This fact has resulted in our present supply of species on this planet.

According to Wilson, another mass extinction is still un-accounted for: the current extinction created by humanity. He says, "Clearly we are in the midst of one of the great extinction spasms of geological history" (Wilson, 2010, 280). This *sixth mass extinction* is not a theory, but it is something that is actually occurring right under our noses. This mass extinction becomes increasingly more noticeable every time a new tree is cut down or a new oil spill occurs.

The sixth mass extinction has a different element to it though. The other extinctions probably occurred because of the activities of nonliving nature, such as climate changes, geological changes, and/or even a crashed meteorite. In this unique case, the extinc-tions are occurring exclusively because of the direct and indirect effects of only one living species: humans.

At this point, we can't reverse the damage that has already been done: millions of species are already extinct because of humanity. However, we can reduce or eliminate the risk of losing any more. We lose the option of learning from a species when it disappears. We also lose another part of the human story. We also may have lost a species that may have been invaluable to our future technology. We are learning so much from living things today that helps us to create all types of products, especially medicinal. The cures for all our current diseases may be species that are quietly awaiting death in a forest marked for immediate removal.

This mass extinction can have many possible endings. For starters, nuclear wars may put an end to all humanity and many other species. Second, we may not go to war but may kill ourselves by the destruction of the life necessary to sustain our food supply. For example, we automatically affect a large part of our produce just by killing all bees. If we were to kill *all* insects, then the whole chain of life unravels, and humanity will not survive long. In both of these scenarios, some life-forms will probably still survive and continue evolving.

Third, as noted before, humanity's destructive impulses may lead to the most devastating technological advances. We may just find a way to blast this planet right into the sun! Consider that in 1961, the Soviet Union dropped a hydrogen bomb called the *Tsar Bomba*, which was supposedly the strongest bomb ever detonated. This bomb would have created exponentially more devastation than that caused by the two nuclear bombs dropped on the Japanese cities of Hiroshima and Nagasaki combined. In less than twenty years, humanity went from creating a nuclear bomb to its super equivalent—and this was over fifty years ago!

As stated before, imagine the destruction that we could unleash if we wanted to. In this possibility, the sixth major extinction would also be the final one for all of Club Life (including the cockroaches and the mice): a true Earthly apocalypse.

Next, another alternative is to be reactive, which requires us to wait complacently to arrive at the dead end that we are heading for. This ending is also unacceptable! Fortunately, there is one more possibility.

Finally, this sixth mass extinction can end another way... quietly. Humanity can realize the truths of our predicament and proactively do something about it. We can take care of our planet better while striving for unity and peace. **We must use the same determination and energy level to resolve the current human predicament that we have used to create it. That is, we must exert as much control over our destiny as we have done over the rest of reformed nature. Self-control is a major part of our solution!**

CHAPTER 48

Who Are We?

The Ultimate Universal Survivors

There is an old saying in the martial sciences: "A black belt is a white belt who never quit." A white belt represents the lowest level student, and the black belt is generally the highest. Statistically, many white belts quit before they even get a fraction of the way to achieving a black belt. Only the toughest survivors make it to the finish line after facing an almost endless number of struggles. We can apply a variation of the above saying to humanity: *Homo sapiens are a microscopic species who never quit.*

Our humble origins are never to be forgotten. Our ancestral line started from the beginning of life, and it has survived the entire way to the present. Our ancestors have survived conditions that we aren't even fully aware of. Further, any currently living species had to be reproduced from a continuous chain of survivors. If even one of our ancestors was to die approximately before its offspring was conceived (but not necessarily born), then the whole chain of its descendants from that point to the present would have been disrupted, and consequently, never born.

Actually, any currently living species can also claim that they have been born from the oldest chain of survivors (assuming that we all came from a universal common ancestor). The human species is no exception. So what makes us so different than other present species? As you will see, we are not only bred from a tradition of survivors, but we are indeed the most versatile survivors. We may even be considered the ultimate universal survivors!

Like our ancestors, all living humans can be considered survivors too. Supposedly the average ejaculation contains about one hundred million sperm. (Some experts agree that this number is as high as several hundred million sperm per ejaculation.) Pregnancy only requires one sperm from one ejaculation to make it to the finish line and fertilize an egg. Many individuals were born after many (possibly thousands of) unproductive ejaculations had already occurred. Thus, every living human is automatically a survivor from the very beginning of her or his life. Each one of us has survived the struggle *just to be conceived* over millions (and possibly trillions) of other competitors.

Considering the above facts, the chances of being born (both in general and as a human) are slim. Every one of us, against all odds, has survived the pre-birth process and emerged into this world in what appears to be almost a miracle. Despite this, another Survival Test awaits after each human is born. Can this person survive after birth? If so, what step could he or she eventually reach on his or her Survival-Prosperity Sequence? We must analyze humanity's essential characteristics in order to understand our ability to survive during our lifetime.

Ironically, humans may appear to be an inferior species based on various physical attributes. First, we are significantly weaker than some other animals—for example, the elephant or the hippopotamus. But as noted earlier, the concept of the survival of the fittest does not always mean that the strongest survives. If that were true, dinosaurs would still be here. Second, we are significantly shorter and smaller than some other animals—for example, the giraffe and the whale. Third, we are significantly slower than some other animals—for example, the cheetah or the greyhound dog.

Fourth, we are highly unlikely to survive long in arctic conditions without clothing, unlike some other animals—for example, the penguin or the polar bear. We are tropical animals by nature. The skin we are born with is not built for the cold.

The next example may come as a surprise to many. We have significantly smaller brains than some other animals—for example, the dolphin, the elephant, and the whale. In addition, unlike certain other animals, humans cannot permanently climb, fly, or swim—that is, without the aid of our technology. And that is where our strengths begin to shine!

It is amazing that humanity has reached its superior standing considering all of its deficiencies relative to other animals. What makes us so special? I'm glad you asked! The combination of all our qualities is what makes humans the best predators this planet has ever seen. Our arsenal of attributes include binocular vision; high levels of flexibility; high levels of mobility; large, efficient brains; opposable thumbs; optimal bipedal structure; and a host of other physiological advantages. In addition, we are social animals who are excellent at communicating, cooperating, organizing, planning, problem solving, and, of course, managing reformed nature.

These and many other qualities have allowed us to become possibly the greatest survivors that evolution has ever produced. We don't need to have any of the specific strengths of the various animals mentioned above. *We are the quintessential role models for the survival of the fittest: we are able to adapt to the maximum number of survival scenarios in the maximum number of survival environments.* Our species has maximized it survival ability through the maximization of its wealth. We have learned how to use technology to help us surpass the best qualities of every other living thing that has ever existed. This may win us the award for the ultimate universal survivors and possibly the ultimate universal managers. We must now shift to discussing what may be our single best quality in order to more clearly understand who we are. Actually, it may be the sole reason for our success as a species: excellent wealth management.

The Ultimate Universal Managers

As we learned above, the human species is not the biggest, the fastest, the most insulated, the strongest, the tallest, and possibly even the smartest living species. We also cannot camouflage our skin like a chameleon, climb like a monkey, fly like a bird, hear or smell like a wolf, swim like a fish, turn our heads like an owl, spin webs like a spider, or do many other advantageous specialized things that other uniquely evolved species can do. We should not worry though because we can do something better. As you will see, we don't need to be born with all those special traits to still enjoy the use of them.

Of all our greatest attributes, probably the single most important trait is our ability to manage reformed nature. Humans are able to control living and nonliving reformed nature in order to use their greatest qualities for our own benefit. In other words, we are able to use the wealth of non-human reformed nature and manage it in a way that helps us to achieve our survival and prosperity goals. *Thus, our wealth becomes an extension of us in the same way that the sword becomes an extension of the samurai.*

If we can properly control the best qualities of everything, especially everything that we are not, then we can become the best at anything. Our technology allows us to live almost anywhere and to be almost anything. We don't need to be as strong as whales or elephants if we can make a moving steel version of them with a hydrogen bomb inside. We don't need to be as tall as giraffes if we can make exponentially higher scaffolds and ladders. We don't need to be as fast as cheetahs, or even falcons, if we can make cars, planes, and rockets that can transport us much faster. We don't need to be as winter-proof as polar bears if we can build the best shelters around. Actually, if necessary, we can even use polar-bear skin for warmth. We also don't need the largest brains if we have super computers to help us.

Humans can do almost anything other species can do to an extreme degree with our wealth. We can use artificial lighting, camouflage clothing, microscopes and telescopes, spider web-like material, and ultrasound to make up for our physical deficiencies. We also can live anywhere on land from pole to pole. We also can live underwater—consider the various aquanauts from NEEMO (NASA Extreme Environment Mission Operations) who were sent to live in Aquarius, the world's only undersea research station. We can even live in space as do the astronauts living in the International Space Station.

Our diverse population throughout Earth demonstrates our success as a species, and it increases the probability that we will continue to survive unknown struggles. All of this evidence illustrates that humanity represents an accumulation of the most successful ways to survive. We also may be considered to represent the best collection of internal wealth that ever existed.

These examples, and many others not mentioned, reflect the qualities of the ultimate survivor species. *The best survivors, by the definitions established in this book, must be the ones who are the best managers of the highest quantity of diverse deadly struggles to stay alive (especially under the most diverse environments).* We have been very successful survivors because we are excellent at managing wealth. This talent, combined with money, our great unique survival tool, may also help us to become the ultimate universal survivors and the ultimate universal managers.

When reflecting on a quote by Louis Pasteur, Koestler once wrote, "'Fortune favors the prepared mind', wrote Pasteur, and we may add: fortunate mutations favour the prepared animal"

(Koestler, 1989, 156). It is our fortunate mutations that can help us—that is, if we want help. If we can manage our way through our current predicament, then we may be able to advance to the next Major Scientific Phase of Prosperity and, ultimately, to Phase 5.

We are currently trying to squeeze through a tight bottle-neck. Our prosperity has forced us to quickly solve too many serious problems. If we can emerge through these tough times though—our future may be brighter than the brightest stars in the sky. *We may find out one day that these times were just the ideal training grounds necessary to unlock our fullest potential of who we were supposed to be: the ultimate universal managers.*

CHAPTER 49

Part 4 Summary

Part 4 demonstrated that the current human predicament is affecting this entire planet. The situation is serious, and the countdown to its conclusion has begun. We are heading into a dead end on our current path of complacency. Our history has demonstrated our amazing capabilities of doing both great evil and good. We must use our talents to resolve our situation with the same intensity that put us in this predicament.

The sixth mass extinction has already begun on our watch, and it has several ways of ending. On one extreme scenario, we may be able to kill everything on this planet. On the other extreme, we may be able to quietly end this extinction and come out of the bottleneck stronger. Thus, our lack of alternatives requires us to do something if we want to survive.

Our species is physically inferior to many others in various ways, for example, in speed and in strength. However, the combination of our attributes has led to our rise as the superior predator on this planet. But our excellent ability to manage reformed nature is our best characteristic, which allows us to compensate for any possible deficiencies. **Simply, our wealth is an extension of us. We are able to survive almost anywhere on this planet, and possibly beyond, through the powers of our wealth.**

We have become a picture-perfect role model species for the survival of the fittest: we are a physically inferior species that is capable of using other parts of nature to help us adapt to anything! **Further, our species has demonstrated that the survival of the richest is a more accurate concept than the survival of the fittest.** We have proved that you don't always need to be biologically the most aggressive, deadliest, fastest, longest, most peaceful, most poisonous, shortest, smallest, smartest, strongest, tallest, and most warm-blooded, and so forth, to be the best adapted survivor in an environment. *Actually, a species does not need any biological adaptation to an environment if it has created manageable technology that can adapt for it.* Make no mistake—this conclusion is revolutionary in biology!

Humans have shown that wealth management should be the new measuring stick for adaptation and survival. We have learned to control the various strengths of reformed nonhuman nature to be used for our purposes. Thus, our wealth may represent the best qualities of all the reformed nature that we manage. **The management of our wealth might also help us correct our predicament, save the world and everything in it, and position us to become both the ultimate universal survivors and the ultimate universal managers.**

PART 5
Final Summary and Conclusions

CHAPTER 50

Final Summary

Let's now briefly summarize what we have learned in this book! First, part 1 was important because we had to understand what survival was before we were able to see its direct relationship to prosperity and biology. We went over many aspects of survival including defining related terms, such as *life* and *death*. **Survival is the management of the present struggle to stay alive for a living entity. In the context of survival, a struggle can only be a confrontation with a potentially deadly hardship.**

We also went over a variety of survival literature as well as various examples of survival scenarios. Survival was also categorized as occurring in civilization, the wilderness, or a combination of the two. Survival can also occur in many different types of environments. The analysis of our survival essentials was the crucial link to understanding our analysis of prosperity in part 2. These essentials represent our most important forms of wealth because we will die quickly without them.

Part 2 made the link between survivalism and what is titled "the sciences of prosperity" by demonstrating that wealth was managed in all cases in order to stay alive. The Five Major Scientific Phases of Prosperity listed in chronological order are: personal finance, group finance, economics, planetonomics (pertains to the planet but in our case it is called Earthonomics), and universonomics. A new entity must progress through the Survival-Prosperity Sequence in each phase, which includes a Survival Test that an entity must pass before it can move on to that phase's prosperity steps. From this analysis, we also learned that survivalism is the root of prosperity and that finance is the parent of economics (unlike what is commonly taught).

The three major possibilities in wealth management illustrate the relationship between survival and prosperity. First, you can minimize your wealth below the level of your bare minimum survival essentials necessary to survive (this is referred to as the edge of survival). Minimizing wealth, especially in a survival situation where every asset counts, may be considered equivalent to suicide—death will surely be close by. Second, you can live on the edge of survival and have just enough wealth to survive. Finally, you can maximize your wealth above the level of your bare minimum survival essentials necessary to survive. By maximizing your wealth, you can reach into the realms of prosperity and gradually increase your chances of surviving better now and in the future. This option reflects the goals of the sciences of prosperity.

Learning about survival and prosperity is necessary for all of life. **To recall from earlier, the overall message of the title of this book is that being wealthier increases your probability of continuously surviving and prospering by providing you the greatest options to obtaining survival essentials. It does not mean that being rich will guarantee your survival.** This concept can also be applied to helping others survive and prosper as in the concepts called the survival and the prosperity by a third party. An entity can use its wealth to provide support for another entity's existence, including other nonhuman life-forms. You cannot live today without wealth or the supporting wealth of another. The proper management of wealth can help you to conquer your struggles. Thus, it can help you, and others whom you love, to survive and to prosper.

Part 3 began to integrate all of the sciences mentioned in this book. If the sciences of prosperity are truly interrelated with survivalism, then they must have something to do with biology, the science of life. Our analysis revealed that they always had various connections, which ranged from the borrowing of economic ideas to the many interpretations of biological theories from an economic perspective.

Darwin's theories of evolution are still very useful to biology today. However, they need to be upgraded to improve our modern understanding of evolution. To start, *nature* was redefined to include everything in nature including humans, which is represented by a new concept called "reformed nature." *Evolution* was also clarified to mean "change" in its simplest form.

Contrary to what is taught in modern biology, two major types of evolution, not just one, occur by external and/or internal forces: the evolution of an individual and the evolution of a population. Simply, the evolution of an individual automatically starts the evolution of a population. However, the evolution of an individual must occur *before* the evolution of a population larger than one. In the simple beginnings of life, if our original ancestors were exactly the same, then we would have stayed the same unless someone evolved. *Just like the modern academic disciplines of economics and finance, biology too has forgotten about the role of the individual!*

We also went over various selection processes for both major types of evolution. In particular, I introduced the concept of *reformed natural selection*, which aggregates all known and unknown evolutionary selection processes under one umbrella. **Reformed natural selection is the comprehensive selection processes of all external and internal natural forces that directly or indirectly caused the evolution of individuals and populations. It is much easier to explain evolution now by stating that reformed natural selection is the reason for *all* of organic evolution.**

In part 3, we learned the reasons *why evolution occurs*: to help life to survive and to prosper. We also analyzed the traditional processes of evolutionary selection that help to explain *how evolution occurs*—which include artificial, natural, and sexual selection—along with their upgraded versions. I also introduced several other important processes of evolutionary selection in this book to help explain *how evolution occurs*. These processes are: absolute creativity evolutionary selection, descendant selection, evolutionary intervention, hybrid creativity evolutionary selection, miscellaneous external reformed natural selection, self-selection, and the two new selection processes of the evolution of evolution called monetary and technological selection. Our analysis led to the conclusion that the evolutionary process itself may be in the process of change. The future of life may be evolving to a tipping point where money is required throughout the whole process.

Money is now necessary, both directly and indirectly, for almost all human artificial selection and for a large part of traditional natural selection. A sign of its increased role in sexual selection is also slowly becoming apparent. Money, and the technology that it can buy, can also lead to the creation of total androids and cyborgs. Further, the robotic technology that we are creating with money may eventually become life itself, a process called the evolution of the nonliving. At that critical junction, we may have two unrelated evolutionary systems of life occurring at the same time, which will mark the official change of the living evolutionary process.

Evolution can be continuous during an individual's lifetime. But why does evolution need to occur? The main reasons for evolving are to survive and to prosper. Additionally, in each Major Evolutionary Phase of Prosperity, the evolved population can increase more if the species is successful at surviving and prospering.

All nonhuman living organisms manage wealth to survive to some degree. They need to follow a similar Survival-Prosperity Sequence as humanity in order to work their way up through the Major Scientific Phases of Prosperity. With this model, we are now able to compare ourselves to all other living things to determine how successful we are at managing wealth. Interestingly, we are probably sharing Phase 3 with only a few other organisms—for example, ants and bees. However, humanity appears to be the closest to attaining the first planetary unity of a species, which may also promote us to Phase 4. Additionally, we are the only species in a position to potentially colonize other planets, as we almost have the technology to do so (ants and other similar species would need many great evolutionary leaps to catch up).

In part 4, we realized what a mess we have made of our world. We are currently experiencing the sixth major extinction phase of life, which was created by humanity. Part 4 was certainly a wake-up call. From various examples, I demonstrated that our species is capable of doing great evil and great good.

We have many great attributes that have led to our rise as a top predator on this planet. However, our sole defining attribute is our ability to manage wealth. This quality has quickly led to our immense prosperity, and it has caused the side effect of our great time-sensitive crisis. However, this same quality that has led us to this difficult position can be what is needed to lead us out of it and beyond!

CHAPTER 51

Conclusions

I share Darwin's sentiments that he expressed in his last chapter of *On the Origin of Species* because I realize that this book is definitely also "one long argument." Nevertheless, such a situation was required because the original goals could only be fulfilled with the right balance of analysis. I have crossed the borders of my true specialty as a financialist, and I have entered the realms of biology and beyond as a matter of necessity. The world is slowly dying, and the ones who are trying to help it out the most have been approaching it from the wrong angle. I am tired of watching many good-hearted biologists, conservationists, peace advocates, and similar groups struggle to meet their goals when, from the perspective of my specialty, the answer is blatantly obvious. *Simply, in modern civilization, you need money to do good things right.*

Our world problems can never be resolved without first understanding the crucial role of the sciences of survivalism and prosperity, particularly economics and finance. The knowledge presented here can be used to help humanity to create a better plan of attack to combat our most important struggles. We should be better prepared to determine what we need to do now that we know what we are capable of, what is at stake, and who we are as a species.

Prosperity, particularly finance and finance's child, economics, and prosperity's parent, survivalism, were as absolutely necessary to stay alive in the past, as they are in the present, and as they certainly will be in the future. Civilization will continue heading down a dead end for as long as we understate the significance of their roles. John Maynard Keynes, one of the most famous economists of the twentieth century, recognized the necessity of economics: "…the ideas of economists and political philosophers, both when they are right and when they are wrong, are more powerful than is commonly understood. Indeed the world is ruled by little else. Practical men, who believe themselves to be quite exempt from any intellectual influences, are usually the slaves of some defunct economist. Madmen in authority, who hear voices in the air, are distilling their frenzy from some academic scribbler of a few years back" (Keynes, 2009, 258). The fact is that all of the sciences of prosperity, including economics, are more powerful than is commonly understood. **An entity without wealth *and* the ability to acquire it is always an entity that is quickly approaching death.**

We need to understand some more numbers before we fully conclude. Earth is about four and a half billion years old, and the first forms of life started less than four billion years ago. There are many ways that life on our planet will come to an end without human intervention. Even if humans unite and break out of our current predicament safely, our sun will age and supposedly destroy us through its expansion between roughly one and seven and a half billion years from now. It is much safer to focus on the conservative number here, which will also add evidence to our earlier conclusion. *In other words, conservatively, life has a maximum of one billion years remaining to leave this planet if it wants to continue to stay alive.*

This time remaining to emigrate is only about 20 percent of the approximate total life expectancy of Club Life on this planet. The calculation for this is the following: one billion years remaining divided by about five billion years of total life expectancy (which is the original approximate four billion years plus the one billion years remaining). Simply, life may not have time for another mass extinction to occur and to possibly create further, more advanced life-forms. The countdown for evacuation of all life has begun! If this current mass extinction isn't dealt with properly, then there may not be enough time to create a species similar to humanity (or better) that will help the living emigrate before our planet dries up or is swallowed up by the sun. Consequently, all life *from* Earth may be gone forever!

Combined with our earlier conclusions, the point above helps to illustrate more that humanity may possibly be *the chosen ones*. We are the best wealth managers that ever existed on this planet and can help to create the technology to continue life indefinitely. But we must start somewhere. The first place to start is to admit the significance of wealth management. Second, we must admit both our capabilities and the seriousness of our predicament. Third, we must start to treat everything on this planet as our wealth to be managed properly, and hence, protect it. The bleeding needs to stop before it is irreversible. Fourth, we need unity of nations to help us to rise to Phase 4 of prosperity. I could go on further, but the steps listed above are enough for the purposes of this book.

Unity is easier than it looks with the right leadership. The bitterest national enemies have become great friends. Some examples include Italy and Greece, Portugal and Spain, France and Great Britain, France and Germany, Great Britain and the United States, the North and the South of the United States (after the Civil War), and Japan and the United States. These examples demonstrate that peace and unity for all nations is possible and within our reach *if* we want it. *But time no longer can wait for what we want! Our unity is now a matter of necessity in order to manage our shared struggles to stay alive on this planet.*

To conclude, the biggest illusion that a youth is born with is not that life is beautiful but that life can be without any struggles. Life is certainly magnificent and precious everywhere, from the smallest insects to the tallest trees. But the struggle probably will be with us until the end of time. However, money and other wealth can help us to reduce or potentially eliminate the large majority of our struggles. Our acceptance of this fact is progress that allows us to see our bigger purpose more clearly. We are the ultimate managers of Earth's wealth—a huge responsibility. No other living species comes close to filling our role. We also may be the ultimate managers of the universe's wealth, but that will be up to us. This may depend on whether we can evolve enough as a collective whole to reconcile these truths. This may also depend on whether we can learn how to survive as the richest species!

Bibliography

This bibliography mainly lists works whose authors were specifically quoted in this book. Please see the "Additional Survival Literature" section and/or the index for all other authors and works not listed here.

Aviation Training Division. 1943. *How to Survive on Land and Sea*. Original edition. Annapolis, MD: US Naval Institute.

Bergreen, Laurence. 2003. *Over the Edge of the World: Magellan's Terrifying Circumnavigation of the Globe*. New York: William Morrow.

Brown, Tom, Jr., and Brandt Morgan. 1983. *Tom Brown's Field Guide to Wilderness Survival*. New York: The Penguin Group.

Campbell, Neil A., Jane B. Reece, et al. 2011. *Campbell Biology*. Ninth edition. Boston: Benjamin Cummings.

Columbus, Christopher. 1969. *The Four Voyages of Christopher Columbus*. Edited and translated by J. M. Cohen. London: The Penguin Group.

Cook, James. 2003. *James Cook: The Journals*. Edited by Philip Edwards. London: The Penguin Group.

Corry, Stephen. 2011. *Tribal Peoples for Tomorrow's World*. Freeman Press.

Craighead, Frank C., Jr., and John J. Craighead. [1943] 1984. *How to Survive on Land and Sea*. Fourth edition. Annapolis, MD: US Naval Institute Press.

Criniti, Anthony M., IV. 2013. *The Necessity of Finance: An Overview of the Science of Management of Wealth for an Individual, a Group, or an Organization*. Philadelphia: Criniti Publishing.

Criniti, Anthony M., IV. 2014. *The Most Important Lessons in Economics and Finance: A Comprehensive Collection of Time-Tested Principles of Wealth Management*. Philadelphia: Criniti Publishing.

Darwin, Charles. [1859] 2003. *The Origin of Species*. 150th anniversary edition. Introduced by Sir Julian Huxley. New York, NY: Signet Classics.

Darwin, Charles. 2006. *From So Simple a Beginning: The Four Great Books of Charles Darwin*. Edited and introduced by Edward O. Wilson. New York: W. W. Norton & Company.

Defoe, Daniel. [1719] 2008. *Robinson Crusoe*. New York: Oxford University Press Inc.

Diamond, Jared. 1999. *Guns, Germs, and Steel: The Fates of Human Societies*. New York: W. W. Norton & Company.

Dual Survival. 2013. Season 2. Discovery Communications. DVD.

Frankl, Viktor E. [1946] 2006. *Man's Search for Meaning*. Boston: Beacon Press.

Freud, Sigmund. 2010. *Civilization and Its Discontents*. Translated and edited by James Strachey and introduced by Christopher Hitchens. New York: W. W. Norton & Company.

Geronimo. 1996. *Geronimo: His Own Story: The Autobiography of a Great Patriot Warrior.* As told to S. M. Barrett and introduced by Frederick Turner. Meridian.

Grylls, Bear. 2012. *A Survival Guide for Life: How to Achieve Your Goals, Thrive in Adversity, and Grow in Character*. New York: William Morrow.

Hitler, Adolf. [1943] 1999. *Mein Kampf.* Translated by Ralph Manheim. Boston: Houghton Mifflin Company.

Hogan, C. Michael. 2014. "Bacteria." *The Encyclopedia of Earth*. http://www.eoearth.org/view/article/150368.

Johns Hopkins Medicine. 2008. *Mendel Didn't Have the Whole Picture: Our Genome Changes Over Lifetime, Johns Hopkins Experts Say*. News release. June 24, 2008. http://www.hopkinsmedicine.org/news/media/releases/mendel_didnt_have_the_whole_picture_our_genome_changes_over_lifetime_johns_hopkins_experts_say.

Jones, Adam. 2011. *Genocide: A Comprehensive Introduction*. Second edition. New York: Routledge.

Kahn, David. 2004. *Krav Maga: The Contact Combat System of the Israel Defense Forces*. New York: St. Martin's Griffin.

Keynes, John Maynard. [1936] 2009. *The General Theory of Employment, Interest and Money*. Edited by John McClure. Orlando, FL: Signalman Publishing.

Kochanski, Mors. 1987. *Bushcraft: Outdoor Skills and Wilderness Survival.* Canada: Lone Pine Publishing.

Koestler, Arthur. [1967] 1989. *The Ghost in the Machine*. Arkana Books.

Kummerfeldt, Peter. 2006. *Surviving a Wilderness Emergency: Practical Advice on What to Do When You Find Yourself in Trouble in the Backcountry*. Colorado Springs, CO: OutdoorSafe Press.

Kyle, Chris, Jim DeFelice, and Scott McEwen. 2013. *American Sniper: The Autobiography of the Most Lethal Sniper in U. S. Military History*. Memorial edition. New York: William Morrow.

Lewis, Meriwether, and William Clark. 1997. *The Journals of Lewis and Clark*. Edited by Bernard DeVoto. New York: Houghton Mifflin Company.

London, Jack. 1998. *The Call of the Wild, White Fang & To Build a Fire*. Introduced by E. L. Doctorow. New York: Modern Library.

Lundin, Cody. 2007. *When All Hell Breaks Loose: Stuff You Need to Survive When Disaster Strikes*. Layton, UT: Gibbs Smith.

Mandela, Nelson. [1990] 2013. *The Struggle Is My Life*. Second edition. Pathfinder Press.

McPherson, John, and Geri McPherson. [1993] 2013. *Primitive Wilderness Living & Survival Skills: Naked into the Wilderness*. Randolph, KS: Prairie Wolf.

Mears, Ray. 2003. *Essential Bushcraft: A Handbook of Survival Skills from around the World*. Great Britain: Hodder & Stoughton.

Olsen, Larry Dean. [1967] 1997. *Outdoor Survival Skills*. Sixth edition. Chicago, IL: Chicago Review Press.

Ong, Thuy, and Michael O'Boyle. 2014. *El Salvador Fisherman Washes Up in Marshall Islands after Year Adrift*. Reuters.

February 3rd, 2014. http://www.reuters.com/article/us-pacific-castaway-idUSBREA121KY20140203.

Pigafetta, Antonio. 1994. *Magellan's Voyage: A Narrative Account of the First Circumnavigation*. Translated and edited by R. A. Skelton. New York: Dover Publications, Inc.

Polo, Marco. 2012. *The Travels of Marco Polo*. Illustrated edition. Edited by Morris Rossabi. New York: Sterling Signature.

Read, Piers Paul. [1974] 2005. *Alive: Sixteen Men, Seventy-Two Days, and Insurmountable Odds—The Classic Adventure of Survival in the Andes*. New York: HarperCollins Publishers.

Rocky Balboa. 2007. Directed by Sylvester Stallone. United States: MGM. DVD.

Seal. "Crazy," in *Seal*. 1991. Sire/Warner/Zoo. CD.

Severin, Tim. [1978] 2000. *The Brendan Voyage*. New York: Modern Library.

Skinner, B. F. [1953] 1965. *Science and Human Behavior*. New York: The Free Press.

Spencer, Herbert. [1864–1867] 2014. *The Principles of Biology*. Two volumes. Cornell University Library Digital Collections.

Stannard, David E. 1993. *American Holocaust: The Conquest of the New World*. New York: Oxford University Press.

Stewart, George R. [1936] 1992. *Ordeal by Hunger: The Story of the Donner Party*. New York: Houghton Mifflin Company.

Stroud, Les. 2010. *Will to Live: Dispatches from the Edge of Survival*. Canada: Collins.

Strunk, William, Jr., and E. B. White. 2000. *The Elements of Style*. Fourth edition. Needham Heights, MA: Allyn & Bacon.

Survival Basics I & II: The Adventure. 2004. Written by Dr. Ron Hood. Stoney-Wolf Productions, Inc. DVD.

University of California Museum of Paleontology, Berkeley. "Misconceptions about Evolution." 2016. *Understanding Evolution*. Retrieved May 7, 2016 from http://www.evolution.berkeley.edu/evolibrary/misconceptions_faq.php#a3.

US Department of the Army. 1970. *FM 21-76 US Department of the Army Field Manual: Survival*. Washington, DC: US Government Printing Office.

Wilson, Edward O. [1992] 2010. *The Diversity of Life*. Cambridge, MA: The Belknap Press of Harvard University Press.

Wiseman, John 'Lofty.' [1986] 2009. *SAS Survival Handbook: For Any Climate in Any Situation*. Revised edition. New York: Collins.

Additional Survival Literature

This section contains additional literature on the topic of survival and its science of survivalism. To my knowledge, although it is far from exhaustive, it is the most comprehensive list that exists. This list does not contain authors who were specifically quoted in this book. That information can be found in the bibliography. Additionally, many of these publications were derived from the excellent survival bibliographies of Peter Kummerfeldt's *Surviving a Wilderness Emergency* and the US Naval Institute's *How to Survive on Land and Sea* (from both the first and fourth editions).

Acerrano, Anthony J. 1976. *The Outdoorsman's Emergency Manual*. New York: Winchester Press.

Aitken, Jim. 1990. *Take the Survival Challenge*. Arms and Armour.

Alloway, David. 2000. *Desert Survival Skills*. University of Texas Press.

American Red Cross. 1974. *Basic Rescue and Water Safety*. Washington, DC: American Red Cross.

American Red Cross. 1974. *Lifesaving: Rescue and Water Safety*. Garden City, NJ: Doubleday.

Angier, Bradford. 1956. *Living Off the Country*. Harrisburg, PA: Stackpole Books.

Angier, Bradford. 1972. *Feasting Free on Wild Edibles*. Harrisburg, PA: Stackpole Books.

Angier, Bradford. 1972. *Survival with Style*. Harrisburg, PA: Stackpole Books.

Angier, Bradford. 1976. *On Your Own in the Wilderness*. New York: Hart.

Angier, Bradford. 1983. *Bradford Angier's Backcountry Basics*. Harrisburg, PA: Stackpole Books.

Angier, Bradford. 1998. *How to Stay Alive in the Woods: A Complete Guide to Food, Shelter, and Self-Preservation That Makes Starvation in the Wilderness Next to Impossible*. Fireside.

Ashcroft, Frances. 2002. *Life at the Extremes: The Science of Survival*. University of California Press.

Assiniwi, Bernard. 1972. *Survival in the Bush*. Toronto: Copp Clark Pub. Co.

Bailey, Maurice, and Maralyn Bailey. 1974. *Staying Alive! 117 Days Adrift*. Lymington, UK: Nautical Publishing Co.

Baird, Patrick D. 1964. *The Polar World*. New York: John Wiley & Sons.

Beattie, John. 1980. *Lifeboats to the Rescue*. North Pomfret, VT: David & Charles.

Berglund, Berndt. 1972. *Wilderness Survival*. New York: Scribner.

Bezruchka, Stephen. 1994. *Altitude Illness: Prevention and Treatment*. Mountaineers Books.

Boswell, John, ed. 1980. *The U. S. Armed Forces Survival Manual*. New York: Rawson, Wade.

Bowman, Warren D. 1998. *Outdoor Emergency Care: Comprehensive Prehospital Care for Nonurban Settings*. Third edition. National Ski Patrol System.

Boy Scouts of America Staff, editors. 1979. *Official Boy Scout Fieldbook*. Boy Scouts of America.

Boy Scouts of America Staff, editors. 1980. *Lifesaving*. Boy Scouts of America.

Boy Scouts of America Staff, editors. 1997. *Okpik: Cold Weather Camping*. Boy Scouts of America.

Brandner, Gary. 1974. *Living Off the Land*. New York: Galahad Books.

Brooks, Maurice. 1967. *The Life of the Mountains*. New York: The World Book Encyclopedia/ McGraw Hill.

Brown, G. W., Jr., ed. 1968. *Desert Biology*. New York: Academic Press.

Brown, Tom, Jr. 1979. *The Tracker*. Berkley edition. As told to William Jon Watkins. New York: The Penguin Group.

Brown, Walter R. 1983. *Rescue!* New York: Walker.

Brown, William H., and Elmer D. Merrill. 1919. *Philippine Palms and Palm Products*. Bulletin No. 18. Manila Bureau of Printing.

Brown, William H. 1921. *Minor Products of Philippine Forests*. Manila Bureau of Printing.

Brown, William H. 1921. *Wild Food Plants of the Philippines*. Manila Bureau of Printing.

Bruemmer, Fred. 1973. *The Arctic*. New York: Quadrangle/New York Times Book Co.

Burch, Monte. 1973. *The Good Earth Almanac: Survival Handbook*. New York: Sheed & Ward.

Burns, Bob, and Mike Burns. 1999. *Wilderness Navigation: Finding Your Way Using Map, Compass, Altimeter and GPS*. Mountaineers Books.

Chartres, John. 1980. *Helicopter Rescue*. London: Ian Allan.

Cheff, Bud, Sr. 1997. *The Woodsman and His Hatchet: Eighty Years on Back Country Survival*. Stoneydale Press Publishing Company.

Churchill, James E. 1989. *The Basic Essentials of Survival*. ICS Books.

Clark, Champ. 1982. *Planet Earth: Flood*. Alexandria, VA: Time-Life Books.

Cochran, Doris M. 1943. *Poisonous Reptiles of the World: A Wartime Handbook*. Smithsonian War Background Series, No. 10. Washington, DC: Smithsonian Institution.

Cornett, James W. 1995. *Indian Uses of Desert Plants*. Palm Springs, CA: Palm Springs Desert Museum.

Costello, David F. 1980. *The Seashore World*. New York: Thomas Y. Crowell.

Dalrymple, Byron W. 1972. *Survival in the Outdoors*. New York: Outdoor Life.

Deleo, Peter. 2005. *Survive: My Fight for Life in the High Sierras*. Simon & Schuster.

Dickey, Esther. 1978. *Skills for Survival: How Families Can Prepare*. Bountiful, UT: Horizon.

Doran, Jeffry. 1980. *Search on Mount St. Helens*. Bellevue, WA: Imagesmith.

Dubas, Frederic, and Jacques Vallotton, editors. 1991. *Colour Atlas of Mountain Medicine*. Elsevier Science, Health Science Division.

Dunlevy, Maurice. 1978. *Stay Alive*. Canberra: Australian Government Publication Service.

Edholm, O. G., and A. L. Bacharach. 1965. *Physiology of Human Survival*. London, New York: Academic Press.

Edible Wild Plants: Video Field Guide to 100 Useful Wild Herbs. 1998. Directed by Jim Duke and Jim Meuninck. Edwardsburg, MI: Media Methods. VHS.

Fear, Gene. 1975. *Surviving the Unexpected Wilderness Emergency*. Tacoma, WA: Survival Education Association.

Findley, Rowe. 1972. *Great American Deserts*. Washington, DC: National Geographic Society.

Fleming, June. 2001. *Staying Found: The Complete Map and Compass Handbook*. Third edition. Seattle, WA: Mountaineers Books.

Fletcher, Colin. 1984. *The Complete Walker III*. Third revised edition. New York: Alfred A. Knopf.

Forgey, William W. 1985. *Hypothermia: Death by Exposure*. ICS Books.

Forgey, William W. 1991. *The Basic Essentials of Hypothermia*. ICS Books.

Forgey, William W. 1999. *Wilderness Medicine: Beyond First Aid*. Fifth edition. Globe Pequot Pr.

Forgey, William W., ed. 2000. *Wilderness Medical Society Practice Guidelines for Wilderness Emergency Care*. Second edition. Globe Pequot.

Frazier, Kendrick. 1979. *The Violent Face of Nature*. New York: William Morrow.

Fry, Alan. 1996. *Wilderness Survival Handbook: A Practical All-Season Guide to Short-Trip Preparation and Survival Techniques for Hikers, Skiers, Backpackers, Canoeists, Snowmobilers, Travelers in Light Aircraft—and Anyone Stranded in the Outdoors*. St. Martin's Griffin.

Fuchs, Sir Vivian, ed. 1977. *Forces of Nature*. New York: Holt, Rinehart and Winston.

Ganci, Dave. 1979. *Hiking the Desert*. Chicago: Contemporary Books.

Ganci, Dave. 1991. *The Basic Essentials of Desert Survival*. ICS Books.

Gatty, Harold. 1943. *The Raft Book: Lore of the Sea and Sky*. New York: G. Grady Press.

Gearing, Catherine. 1973. *A Field Guide to Wilderness Living*. Nashville, TN: Southern Pub. Association.

George, Uwe. 1977. *In the Deserts of This Earth*. New York: Harcourt Brace Jovanovich.

Gibbons, Euell. 1971. *Stalking the Good Life: My Love Affair with Nature*. New York: D. McKay Co.

Godshall, Ammon B. 1942. *Edible, Poisonous and Medicinal Fruits of Central America*. The Panama Canal Zone.

Gonzales, Laurence. 2004. *Deep Survival: Who Lives, Who Dies, and Why*. W. W. Norton & Company.

Gonzalez, Ellice B. 1982. *Storms, Ships, & Surfmen*. Patchogue, NY: Eastern National Park and Monument Association.

Gould, Laurence McKinley. 1931. *Cold*. New York: Brewer Warren and Co.

Graham, Samuel A., and Earl C. O'Roke. 1943. *On Your Own*. Minneapolis: The University of Minnesota Press.

Graves, Richard. 1972. *Bushcraft: A Serious Guide to Surviving and Camping*. New York: Schocken Books.

Graves, Richard. 1986. *Bushcraft: A Serious Guide to Surviving and Camping*. Warner Books, Inc.

Grubbs, Bruce. 2004. *Desert Sense: Camping, Hiking & Biking in Hot, Dry Climates*. Seattle, WA: Mountaineers Books.

Harding, A. R. 1970. *Deadfalls and Snares*. Fur Fish Game.

Hare, Trevor. 1995. *Poisonous Dwellers of the Desert: Description, Habitat, Prevention, Treatment*. Western National Parks Association.

Harlow, William Morehouse. 1979. *Ways of the Woods*. Washington, DC: American Forestry Association.

Harvey, Mark. [1983] 1999. *The National Outdoor Leadership School's Wilderness Guide*. Simon & Schuster.

Hedrick, U. P., ed. 1919. *Sturtevant's Notes on Edible Plants*. Albany, NY: J. B. Lyon Company.

Henderson, A. Kenneth. 1942. *Handbook of American Mountaineering*. Boston: Houghton Mifflin Co.

Henderson, M. A., ed. 1980. *The Survival Resource Book*. New York: St. Martin's Press.

Henderson, Richard, Bartlett S. Dunbar, and William E. Brooks, III. 1979. *Sail and Power*. Third edition. Annapolis, MD: Naval Institute Press.

Hildreth, Brian. 1970. *How to Survive in the Bush, on the Coast, in the Mountains of New Zealand*. Wellington: Government Printing.

Hobbs, Richard R. 1981. *Marine Navigation*. Two volumes. Annapolis, MD: Naval Institute Press.

Hodgson, Michael. 1999. *Weather Forecasting. Basic Essentials* series. Second edition. Globe Pequot.

Hose, Charles, and William McDougall. 1912. *The Pagan Tribes of Borneo*. Two volumes. London: Macmillan & Co., Ltd.

Houston, Charles. 1998. *High Altitude: Illness & Wellness*. Globe Pequot.

How to Survive in the Wilderness. 1975. New York: Drake Publishers.

Howarth, Patrick. 1974. *Life-boats and Life-boat People*. New York: White Lion Publishers.

IMCO Search and Rescue Manual. 1980. London: Intergovernmental Maritime Consultative Organization.

International Maritime Organization. 1981. *A Pocket Guide to Cold Water Survival*. London.

Jacobson, Cliff. 1992. *The Basic Essentials of Trailside Shelters and Emergency Shelters. Basic Essentials* series. ICS Books.

Jacobson, Cliff. 1999. *Knots for the Outdoors. Basic Essentials* series. Second edition. Globe Pequot.

Jacobson, Cliff. 2005. *Map and Compass. Basic Essentials* series. Globe Pequot.

Jaeger, Edmund C. 1957. *The North American Deserts*. Stanford, CA: Stanford University Press.

Jamison, Richard L. 1985. *Primitive Outdoor Skills: More Wilderness Techniques from Woodsmoke Journal*. Horizon Publisher & Distributors.

Janowsky, Chris, and Gretchen Janowsky. 1989. *Survival: A Manual That Could Save Your Life*. Paladin Press.

Johnson, Mark. 2003. *The Ultimate Desert Handbook: A Manual for Desert Hikers, Campers, and Travelers*. International Marine/ Ragged Mountain Press.

Kals, W. S. 2005. *Land Navigation Handbook: The Sierra Club Guide to Map, Compass & GPS*. San Francisco, CA: Sierra Club Books.

Kephart, Horace. [1906] 1936. *Camping and Woodcraft*. New York: The Macmillan Co.

Kimble, G. H. T., and Dorothy Good. 1955. *Geography of the Northlands*. New York: John Wiley & Sons.

Kirk, Donald R. 1975. *Wild Edible Plants of Western North America*. Headlsburg, CA: Naturegraph Publishers.

Kjellstrom, Bjorn. 2010. *Be Expert with Map and Compass*. Third edition. Hoboken, NJ: Wiley.

Knap, Jerome J. 1974. *The Complete Outdoorsman's Handbook*. Toronto: Pagurian Press.

Kotsch, William J. 1977. *Weather for the Mariner*. Annapolis, MD: Naval Institute Press.

Kraus, Joe. 1978. *Alive in the Desert*. Boulder, CO: Paladin Press.

Krutch, Joseph Wood. 1951. *The Desert Year*. New York: William Sloane Associates.

Lacefield, Eric M. 1975. *Survival in the Marsh*. New Orleans: Louisiana Wildlife & Fisheries Commission.

Leach, John. 1994. *Survival Psychology*. New York University Press.

Lehman, Charles A. 1979. *Emergency Survival*. Los Angeles, CA: Technical Book Co.

Lehman, Charles A. 1988. *Desert Survival Handbook*. Phoenix: Primer Publishers.

Letham, Lawrence. 2003. *GPS Made Easy: Using Global Positioning Systems in the Outdoors*. Fourth revised edition. Seattle, WA: Mountaineers Books.

Lewis, Thomas R. 1979. *Organization, Training, Search, and Recovery Procedures for the Underwater Unit*. Marquette, MI: Northern Michigan University Press.

Ley, Willy. 1962. *The Poles*. Part of *Life Nature Library* series. New York: Time Inc.

MacInnes, Hamish. 1973. *International Mountain Rescue Handbook*. New York: Scribner.

Maloney, Elbert S. 1978. *Dutton's Navigation & Piloting*. Third edition. Annapolis, MD: Naval Institute Press.

Manhoff, David. 1996. *Mosby's Outdoor Emergency Medical Guide: What to Do in an Outdoor Emergency When Help May Take Some Time to Arrive*. Edited by Stephen N. Vogel. St. Louis, MO: Mosby Year Book.

Maniguet, Xavier. 1994. *Survival: How to Prevail in Hostile Environments*. New York: Facts on File.

Manual of U. S. Cave Rescue Techniques. 1981. Huntsville, AL: National Cave Rescue Commission of the National Speleological Society.

Mason, Rosalie. 1977. *Beginners Guide to Family Preparedness*. Bountiful, UT: Horizon.

Matheson, Robert. 1932. *Medical Entomology*. Springfield, IL and Baltimore, MD: Charles C. Thomas.

McDougall, Len. 1993. *Practical Outdoor Survival: A Modern Approach*. The Lyons Press.

Mears, Raymond. 1993. *The Outdoor Survival Handbook: A Guide to the Resources and Materials Available in the Wild and How to Use Them for Food, Shelter, Warmth, and Navigation*. St. Martin's Griffin.

Medsger, Oliver Perry. 1939. *Edible Wild Plants*. New York: Macmillan Co.

Merchant Ship Search and Rescue Manual. MERSAR. 1980. London: Intergovernmental Maritime Consultative Organization.

Merril, E. D. 1943. *Emergency Food Plants and Poisonous Plants of the Islands of the Pacific.* Washington, DC.

Merrill, W. K. 1972. *The Survival Handbook.* New York: Winchester Press.

Moir, John. 1980. *Just in Case.* San Francisco, CA: Chronicle Books.

Mooers, Robert L., Jr. 1984. *Finding Your Way in the Outdoors.* New York: Outdoor Life Books.

Morton, Julia Frances. 1982. *Wild Plants for Survival in South Florida.* Fifth edition. Miami, FL: Fairchild Tropical Gardens.

Muston, John. 1987. *Survival: Training and Techniques.* London: Arms and Armour Press.

NASA. 1983. *SARSAT: Search and Rescue Satellite Aided Tracking: Space-Age Technology for Rescue with Minimal Search.* Greenbelt, MD: Goddard Space Flight Center.

National Lifeguard Manual. 1974. New York: Association Press.

National Science Foundation, Division of Polar Programs. 1979. *Survival in Antarctica.* Washington, DC: US Government Printing Office.

Nault, Andy. 1980. *Staying Alive in Alaska's Wild.* Washington, DC: Tee Loftin Publishers.

Naval Arctic Operations Handbook. 1950. Revised edition. Washington, DC: US Department of the Navy.

Neider, Charles. 1954. *Man Against Nature.* New York: Harper & Brothers.

Neimark, Paul G. 1981. *Survival.* Chicago: Children's Press.

Nelson, Dick, and Sharon Nelson. 1977. *Desert Survival.* Glenwood, NM: Tecolote Press.

Nessmuk, George W. Sears. 1963. *Woodcraft and Camping*. Dover Publications.

Nester, Tony. 2003. *Desert Survival: Tips, Tricks, & Skills*. Diamond Creek Press.

Nuttle, David A. 1979. *The Universal Survival Handbook*. Latham, KS: David A. Nuttle Survival Association.

Oliver, Douglas L. 1951. *The Pacific Islands*. Cambridge: Harvard University Press.

Olsen, Larry Dean. 1974. *Wilderness Survival*. North Brunswick, NJ: Boy Scouts of America.

Owen, Peter. 1993. *The Book of Outdoor Knots*. New York: Lyons & Burford.

Patterson, Craig E. 1979. *Mountain Wilderness Survival*. Berkeley, CA: And/Or Press.

Paulcke, Wilhelm, and Helmut Dumler. 1973. *Hazards in Mountaineering*. Translated by E. Noel Bowman. New York: Oxford University Press.

Perry, Richard. 1973. *The Polar Worlds*. New York: Taplinger.

Peterson, Lee Allen. 1999. *Field Guide to Edible Wild Plants*. Peterson Field Guides. Illustrated by Roger Torry Peterson. Houghton Mifflin.

Petzoldt, Paul K. 1974. *The Wilderness Handbook*. New York: Norton.

Plate, M. W. 1971. *Australian Bushcraft*. Melbourne: Lansdowne Press.

Platt, Charles. 1976. *Outdoor Survival*. New York: Watts.

Platten, David. 1979. *The Outdoor Survival Handbook*. North Pomfret, VT: David & Charles.

Pond, Alonzo William. 1974. *Afoot in the Desert*. Maxwell Airforce Base, AL: Air Training Command, 3636th Combat Crew Training Wing Environmental Information Division.

Porsild, A. E. 1937. *Edible Roots and Berries of Northern Canada*. Ottawa, Canada: J. O. Patenaude, I. S. O.

Poynter, Margaret. 1980. *Search & Rescue*. New York: Atheneum.

Price, Larry W. 1981. *Mountains & Man*. Los Angeles: University of California Press.

Randall, Glenn. 1987. *Cold Comfort: Keeping Warm in the Outdoors*. Lyons and Burford Publishers.

Richards, Paul W. 1970. *The Life of the Jungle*. New York: The World Book Encyclopedia/ McGraw Hill.

Richards, Phil, and John J. Banigan. 1942. *How to Abandon Ship*. New York: Cornell Maritime Press.

Richardson, Joan. 1981. *Wild Edible Plants of New England: A Field Guide*. Yarmouth, ME: Delorme Publishing Co.

Ricketts, F. Edward, and Jack Calvin. 1939. *Between Pacific Tides*. Stanford University Press.

Rile, Michael J. 1977. *Don't Get Snowed*. Matteson, IL: Greatlakes Living Press.

Risk, Paul H. 1983. *Outdoor Safety and Survival*. John Wiley & Sons, Inc.

Robertson, Dougal. 1973. *Survive the Savage Sea*. New York: Praeger.

Robertson, Dougal. 1975. *Sea Survival: A Manual*. New York: Praeger.

Roughley, T. C. 1936. *Wonders of the Great Barrier Reef*. Sydney: Angus and Robertson, Ltd.

Salsbury, Barbara G. 1975. *Just in Case: A Manual of Home Preparedness*. Salt Lake City: Bookcraft.

Saunders, Charles Francis. 1976. *Edible and Useful Wild Plants of the United States and Canada*. Dover Publications.

Schimelpfenig, Tod, and Linda Lindsey. 2000. *Wilderness First Aid*. Third edition. National Outdoor Leadership School.

Schneider, Bill. 1996. *Bear Aware: Hiking and Camping in Bear Country*. Helena, MT: Falcon Press.

Schuh, Dwight R. 1983. *Modern Outdoor Survival*. New York: Arco.

Scott, David. 1997. *Survivalist's Little Book of Wisdom*. ICS Books.

Self, William L. 1975. *Survival Kit for the Stranded*. Nashville, TN: Broadman Press.

Setnicka, Tim J. 1980. *Wilderness Search and Rescue*. Boston: Appalachian Mountain Club.

Shanks, Bernard. 1987. *Wilderness Survival*. New York: Universe Books.

Simer, Peter. 1983. *The National Outdoor Leadership School's Wilderness Guide*. New York: Simon and Schuster.

Siple, A. Paul. 1941. *General Principles Governing Selection of Clothing for Cold Climates*. US Antarctic Service.

Smith, David. 1997. *Backcountry Bear Basics: The Definitive Guide to Avoiding Unpleasant Encounters*. Mountaineer Books.

Southward, A. J. 1967. *Life on the Sea-Shore*. Cambridge, MA: Harvard University Press.

Staender, Vivian. 1983. *Our Arctic Year*. Anchorage, AL: Northwest Pub. Co.

Stark, Peter. 2001. *Last Breath: Cautionary Tales from the Limits of Human Endurance*. Ballantine Books.

Stefansson, Vilhjalmur. 1913. *My Life with the Eskimo*. New York: The Macmillan Co.

Stefansson, Vilhjalmur. 1943. *The Friendly Arctic*. Last edition. New York: The Macmillan Co.

Stefansson, Vilhjalmur. 1945. *Arctic Manual*. New York: Macmillan.

Stewart, Charles E. 1990. *Environmental Emergencies*. Baltimore: Williams & Wilkins.

Stoffel, Robert, and Patrick LaValla. 1980. *Survival Sense for Pilots*. Emergency Response Institute.

Sundt, Captain Wilbur A. 1978–1981. *Naval Science*. Volumes two and three. Annapolis, MD: Naval Institute Press.

Survival at Sea: Instruction Manual. 1978. Canberra: Australian Government Publishing Service.

Sutton, Ann, and Myron Sutton. 1966. *The Life of the Desert*. New York: The World Book Encyclopedia/McGraw Hill.

Sweeney, James B. 1981. *Disaster!* New York: McKay, Co.

Szczelkun, Stefan A. 1973. *Survival Scrapbook*. New York: Schocken Books.

Temple, Ernest. 1978. *Survival*. Aldergrove, British Columbia: Frontier Pub.

The NSPS Ski Mountaineering Manual. 1982. Denver, CO: National Ski Patrol System.

The Outdoors Survival Manual. 1978. New York: Drake Publishers.

Thygerson, Alton L. 1979. *Disaster Survival Handbook*. Provo, UT: Brigham Young University Press.

Tilton, Buck. 2002. *Back Country First Aid and Extended Care*. Fourth edition. Falcon.

Tobin, Wallace E., III. 1974. *The Mariner's Pocket Companion.* Annapolis, MD: Naval Institute Press.

Torney, John A. 1981. *Teaching Aquatics.* Minneapolis, MN: Burgess Pub Co.

Torres, Steven. 1997. *Mountain Lion Alert.* Falcon.

Tucker, John. 1970. *A Jungle Handbook.* Singapore: Donald Moore for Asia Pacific Press.

Uman, Martin A. 1986. *All About Lightning.* Dover Publications, Inc.

US Coast Guard. 1978. *Air Search and Rescue.* Washington, DC: Department of Transportation, Coast Guard.

US Coast Guard. 1980. *A Pocket Guide to Cold Water Survival.* US Coast Guard Commandant Instruction M3131.5.

US Department of the Air Force. 1969. *Search and Rescue: Survival.* Washington, DC: US Government Printing Office.

US Department of the Army Field Manual. 1969. *Survival, Evasion, and Escape.* Washington, DC: US Government Printing Office.

US Lifesaving Association. 1981. *Lifesaving and Marine Safety.* Piscataway, NJ: Association Press, New Century Publishers.

US War Department. 1941. *Operations in Snow and Extreme Cold.* Basic Field Manual, FM31-15. Washington, DC: US Government Printing Office.

Vignes, Jacques. 1976. *The Rage to Survive.* Translated by Mihailo Voukitchevitch. New York: William Morrow.

Walker, Bryce. 1982. *Earthquake. Planet Earth* series. Alexandria, VA: Time-Life Books.

Waltham, Tony. 1978. *Catastrophe: The Violent Earth*. New York: Crown.

Watson, Warren N. 1939. *Early Fire-Making Methods and Devices*. Washington, DC: Gibson Bros., Ind.

Weir, Ben, Carol Weir, and Dennis Benson. 1987. *Hostage Bound Hostage Free*. Westminster Press.

Weiss, Hal. 1999. *Secrets of Warmth: For Comfort or Survival*. Mountaineers Books.

Welch, Mary Scott. 1973. *The Family Wilderness Handbook*. New York: Ballantine Books.

White, Gilbert F., ed. 1974. *Natural Hazards: Local, National, Global*. New York: Oxford University Press.

Whitley, G. P. 1943. *Poisonous and Harmful Fishes*. Melbourne, Australia: Council for Scientific and Industrial Research, H. E. Daw, Gov. Printer.

Whittow, John. 1979. *Disasters: The Anatomy of Environmental Hazards*. Athens, GA: University of Georgia Press.

Wilkerson, James A. 1993. *Medicine for Mountaineering & Other Wilderness Activities.* Fourth edition. Mountaineers Books.

Wilkerson, James A., Cameron C. Bangs, and John S. Hayward. 1986. *Hypothermia, Frostbite, and Other Cold Injuries*. Mountaineers Books.

Wilkinson, Ernest. 1992. *Snow Caves for Fun and Survival*. Johnson Books.

Williams, Jerome, John J. Higginson, and John D. Rohrbough. 1973. *Sea & Air: The Marine Environment*. Annapolis, MD: Naval Institute Press.

Wilson, Jack. 1979. *Australian Surfing and Surf Life Saving*. Adelaide, Rigby.

Winkelman, Jack L. 1981. *Essentials of Basic Life Support.* Minneapolis, MN: Burgess Pub. Co.

Zwinger, A. H., and B. E. Willard. 1972. *Land above the Trees: A Guide to American Alpine Tundra.* New York: Harper & Row.

Index

Absolute creativity evolution-
    ary selection, 318–324,
    343, 416, 462
Afghanistan, 91, 431
Age of Discovery, 221–222
Agency problem, 175
Albarengo, Jose Salvador, 71
Aliens, 28, 69, 221–222, 234
Alive: defined, 22
American genocide, 426–428,
    433–434
American Indians, 73, 91,
    426–428
Andaman Islands, 82–83

Androids, 69, 222, 234, 371–
    374, 417, 463; defined, 371
Antarctica, 67, 94, 435
Arctic, 49, 66, 88, 108, 220,
    449
Auschwitz, cover page, ii, 58,
    72, 97, 422–423
Autotrophs, 30

Baden-Powell, Robert
    (*Scouting for Boys*), 50
Bartering, 363–365
Beard, Daniel (*Camp-Lore
    and Woodcraft*), 50

Bergreen, Laurence, 43, 94

Biodiversity, 253–254, 441

Biology: defined, 249

Bombs: atomic, ii, 422–423, 425, 443; hydrogen, 425, 440, 445, 451; *Tsar Bomba*, 445

Boy Scouts of America, 50

Brown, Tom, Jr., 11, 107, 114, 272–273; (*The Tracker*), 52; (*Tom Brown's Field Guide to Wilderness Survival*), 52, 83

Bushcraft, 52–53, 110, 267

Cambodia, 96, 431

Campbell Biology, 282

Canada, 45, 52, 118

Cancer, 144, 182, 397, 436

Canessa, Roberto, 65

Cannibalism, 49–50, 63

Canterbury, Dave, 90

China, 4, 41, 213, 355, 422, 430–431; Great Leap Forward, 4, 431

Civilization: defined, 80, 86

Civilization survival, 79–86

Clark, William, 45–47

Club Life, 31, 34–35, 126, 279, 372, 378, 398, 440, 446, 467

Colon, Hernando, 42

Columbus, Christopher, 40–42, 45, 70

Comprehensive prosperity, 400

Comprehensive survivalism: defined, 19, 399

Cook, James, 44–45, 70, 94

Copernicus, Nicolaus, 154

Corry, Stephen, 23–24, 109, 116

Cost of living, 241

Criniti, Anthony M., IV (*The Most Important Lessons in Economics and Finance*), xviii, 137, 155, 171, 174, 202, 216, 358, 413; (*The Necessity of Finance*), xv, xviii, xx, 125, 129, 150, 170, 239, 241

Cruzatte, Pierre, 46

Cyborgs, 371–374, 385–386, 417, 463; defined, 371

Cydroids, 372–373, 386

Da Vinci, Leonardo, 155, 278

Darwin, Charles, xvi, 154, 250–251, 253, 255, 257, 259–260, 263, 265–266, 272–273, 279–281, 292, 307–308, 325, 334, 338–342, 349–350, 352, 375, 416, 461; (*On the Origin of Species*), 250, 256–257, 264, 283, 285, 332, 334, 465; (*The Descent of Man*), 256, 258, 271, 332–333, 349, 381; (*The Expression of the Emotions in Man and Animals*), 256; (*The Voyage of the Beagle*), 250–251

Death: defined, 35–36

Defoe, Daniel (*Robinson Crusoe*), 10, 22, 47–48, 82, 107, 149, 266

Del Verrocchio, Andrea, 278

Descendant selection, xviii, 336, 344, 353–355, 388, 416, 462; defined, 353; formula, 336, 355

Descent with modification, 280, 293, 321

Diamond, Jared: artificial and natural selection, 334; (*Guns, Germs, and Steel: The Fates of Human Societies*), 207–213

Dinosaurs, 259–260, 449

Diversification, 251, 253

Division of labor, 251–252

Donner Party, 48–49, 62–66, 130

Earth, 15, 29, 36, 51, 57, 64, 145, 219–223, 226, 285, 358, 368, 378, 440, 442, 446, 452, 466–468

Earthonomics, 135–137, 145, 147, 460; defined, 137

Economic entities: defined, xv

Economics: defined, 129, 137; extended definition, 141; extended major goal, 147

Economists, 128, 130, 211, 250–251, 466

Edge of survival, 131, 152, 157–167, 200, 205, 223, 242, 246, 401, 412, 460

Edison, Thomas, 319, 325

Egypt, 39, 155, 211

Einstein, Albert, 154

Emergency reserves, 134, 146, 216

Encyclopedia of Earth website, 29–30

Eugenics, xvi, 331

Evolution: defined, 280; major reasons why evolution occurs, 383–393, 462–463; major types, 283, 461–462; major ways how evolution occurs, 343–344, 462–463

Evolution of a population, 259, 283, 285, 325–355, 365, 375, 377, 462; total related population evolution, 353–355

Evolution of an individual, 283, 285, 290, 311–325, 331, 341, 345, 352, 365, 376, 462; two general ways an individual can evolve (or General Evolutionary Selection), 311–312, 343

Evolution of evolution, xviii, xxi, 344, 357–374, 385, 416, 442–443, 463; defined, 359; two major causes, 359–361

Evolution of money, 344, 360, 362–366

Evolution of the nonliving, 337, 367–374, 384, 417, 463

Evolutionary Control Scale of Nature, 297, 299–305, 310

Evolutionary intervention, 304, 314–315, 318–324, 343, 385, 416, 462

Evolutionary Schematics for Life, 342–344

Existential frustration, 59

External natural selection, 296–297, 315–318, 343–344, 352, 355, 365, 376, 378, 384–385, 389, 416, 461–462; defined, 315

External nature: explained, 316–317

Extinction, viii, 200, 280, 300, 395–398, 403–409, 411–413, 442, 444–446,

455, 464, 467; five major
extinction periods, 444;
sixth mass extinction,
xviii, 444–446, 455, 464
Extremophiles, 29–30

Family tree, 285, 322
Fertile Crescent, 208–210
Fight: defined, 229
Finance: defined, 129, 137;
extended definition, 141;
extended major goal, 145;
parent of economics, 148–
151, 460
Financial entities: defined, xv
Financialist, 128, 465
Food: defined, 30
France, 91, 468
Frankl, Viktor, 55–59, 72,
113, 115–117, 119, 422–
423; (*Man's Search for
Meaning*), 55–59
Freud, Sigmund, 56, 440–442

Galilei, Galileo, 154
Gandhi, Mahatma, 438
Gates, Bill, 211

General Control Scale of
Nature, 274–277, 299,
301, 310, 396
Genocide, iii, v, xvi, 70, 84,
96–97, 236, 329, 426–
435; list of, 428–432
Germany, 71, 429–430, 435,
468
Geronimo, 49, 73–74, 91,
95–96
Ghinsberg, Yossi, 66
Girl Scouts, 50
Goldhagen, Daniel Jonah
(*Worse Than War*), 426
Great Britain, 50, 52–53, 91,
211, 213, 250–251, 429–
430, 434, 468
Great Northwest Passage, 45
Greece, 468
Grylls, Bear, 114; (*Man vs.
Wild*), 53

Hiroshima, cover page, ii,
422–423, 445
Hitler, Adolf, 230–233, 273;
(*Mein Kampf*), 230
Holocaust, 56–59, 422, 430
Hood, Ron (*Survival Basics I
& II: The Adventure*), 110

Human altruism: examples of, 436–438

Human identity crisis, 442

Human nature, 266, 272–278, 299–305; best trait, 451; chosen ones, 467; what human nature is capable of, 425–438; what is at stake for human nature (and Earth), 439–446; who is human nature, 447–453

Human survivalism: defined, 19, 399

Hybrid creativity evolutionary selection, 318–324, 343, 416, 462

Internal natural selection, 267, 292, 296–297, 304, 309, 311–318, 341–344, 365–366, 376, 416, 461–462; defined, 315

Internal nature: explained, 316–317

International Space Station, 225, 452

Inuit, 88

Inventions and discoveries: cannot be disinvented, 442–444; list of, 435–436

Italy, 41, 468

Jackson, Michael, 155

Japan, ii, 212, 417, 423, 430, 445, 468

Jefferson, Thomas, 45

Jetsons, 371

Johns Hopkins Medicine, 292–293

Jones, Adam, 97, 112; (*Genocide: A Comprehensive Introduction*), 427–434

Kahn, David, 75–76

Karluk ship, 66

Kennedy, John F., 438

Kephart, Horace (*Camping and Woodcraft*), 50

Kepler, Johannes, 154

Keynes, John Maynard, 466

King, Martin Luther, Jr., 438

Kochanski, Mors (*Bushcraft: Outdoor Skills and Wilderness Survival*), 52, 118

Koestler, Arthur, 23, 261, 292, 341, 441, 443, 452–453

Kreps, Elmer Harry (*Woodcraft*), 50

Kummerfeldt, Peter, 10–18, 66, 79, 84, 108, 111; (*Surviving a Wilderness Emergency: Practical Advice on What to Do When You Find Yourself in Trouble in the Backcountry*), 54, 475

Kyle, Chris, 24–25, 72–74, 96, 114

Lamarck, Jean Baptiste, 279–280

Lewis, Meriwether, 45–47, 71, 95

Life: defined, 29

Living nature, 81, 272, 275, 299, 304, 329, 367–368, 370, 373, 379–380, 403, 417, 435, 442

Living versus nonliving, 36

Logotherapy, 56–58

London, Jack, 22–23, 50, 266–267, 396; (*The Call of the Wild*), 8, 48, 83; (*To Build a Fire*), 48; (*White Fang*), 48

Low, Juliette Gordon, 50

Luck, 18, 110, 152, 165–166, 307–310, 343–344, 406; defined, 309

Lundin, Cody, 11–12, 23, 30, 90, 108, 111, 114; (*98.6 Degrees: The Art of Keeping Your Ass Alive*), 54, 108, 111; (*Dual Survival*), 54, 89–90, 273; (*When All Hell Breaks Loose: Stuff You Need to Survive When Disaster Strikes*), 54

Luxury items, 132, 134–135

Magellan, Ferdinand, 42–44, 70, 94–95

Major Evolutionary Phases of Prosperity, 387–393, 463

Major Scientific Phases of Prosperity, xix, 132–133, 135–151, 153, 169–172, 176–177, 197, 200, 202, 209, 245, 250, 384, 389,

401–402, 418, 443, 453, 460, 463

Malthus, Thomas Robert, 250–251; (*An Essay on the Principle of Population*), 250

Mandela, Nelson, 201–202, 229–233, 438; (*The Struggle Is My Life*), 201, 230

Mangino, Alvaro, 65, 72

Marine mammals, 62, 320–321

Markowitz, Harry, 150

Martial science, 5, 74–75, 447

Mawson, Douglas, 66–67

McCandless, Chris (*Into the Wild*), 66

McPherson, John, 11; (*Primitive Wilderness Living & Survival Skills: Naked into the Wilderness*), 53, 84

Mears, Ray, 52–53, 110, 118, 267

Mendel, Gregor, 280, 292–293, 322

Michelangelo, 155

Miscellaneous external reformed natural selection, 344, 355, 416, 462

Miscellaneous-location survival, 79–86

Modified Survival-Prosperity Sequence for Evolution, 386–393

Monet, Claude, 155

Monetary Selection, 343–344, 360–366, 374, 376, 385–386, 418; defined, 365; formulas, 336–337, 366

Money, xxi, 4, 42, 58–59, 103, 118, 130, 144, 155, 165, 174–176, 178–195, 198–199, 204, 210–211, 216, 232–233, 235–236, 239–242, 253–254, 336–337, 344, 360–366, 374, 377, 380, 385–386, 412, 415–418, 433, 436–437, 441, 443, 452, 463; necessity of, 365; our great unique survival tool, 103, 365, 452; the power of money, 408–409, 465–468

Mongolia, 81

Mother Theresa, 438

Mozart, 155
Multiplication of effects, 363

Nagasaki, 445
NASA, 438, 452
Natural laws, 358–359
NEEMO (NASA Extreme
    Environment Mission
    Operations), 452
Negative selection, 300–301,
    318, 328–331, 338, 351,
    354, 376; defined, 328,
    331
New York City, 76, 85
Newton, Isaac, 154
Ngor, Haing, 96–97
Nobel Prize, 150
Nonhuman nature, 272–278,
    299–305, 335, 338, 348,
    393, 397, 405, 409, 456
Nonliving nature, 272, 304,
    329, 367–374, 381, 418,
    444

Olsen, Larry Dean, 11, 51–52,
    91; (*Outdoor Survival
    Skills*), 51–52
One and two of circles, 288–
    291, 319

Optimal species, 359, 365,
    370, 450, 456
Organic versus inorganic, 36

Parrado, Fernando, 57, 65–66
Pasteur, Louis, 280, 436,
    452–453
Philadelphia, 76–77, 85, 90–
    91, 228
Picasso, Pablo, 155
Pigafetta, Antonio, 43–44
Planetonomics, 135–137, 145,
    147, 245, 460; defined,
    136–137; extended defini-
    tion, 145; extended major
    goal, 147–148
Polo, Marco, 41–42
Population: defined, 284
Population of one, 284–285,
    326, 344, 377, 380
Portugal, 468
Positive selection, 300, 318,
    328–331, 338, 351, 376,
    416; defined, 328, 331
Poverty, 165–166, 231, 401,
    412, 422, 436, 442
Prosperity: defined, 19, 130–
    131; side effect of too
    much prosperity at once,

464; significance of prosperity, 151–156

Prosperity by a third party, xvii, xx, 239–243, 246, 403–409, 461; defined, 242; partial prosperity by a third party, 243; total prosperity by a third party, 242–243

Prosperity tipping point, 166–167

Pure selection, 308

Purpose to live, 102, 106, 113, 115, 120, 128, 237

Random selection, 308–309

Read, Piers Paul (*Alive*), 49–50, 57, 64–65, 112, 117

Reformed artificial selection, 328, 344, 348–349; defined, 349; formula, 336, 349

Reformed natural selection, 318, 328, 335, 340–348, 355, 358, 360, 365–366, 389, 416, 462; defined, 341, 462; formulas, 335–337, 345–347

Reformed nature, xviii, 270–272, 341, 345–347, 367, 372, 375, 381, 385–386, 396, 415–416, 446, 450–451, 456, 461; categories of, 271–272; defined, 270

Reformed sexual selection, 344, 349–352, 387, 416–417; defined, 350; formula, 336, 352

Robertson family, 66

Robots, 28, 31, 35, 341, 370–374, 417, 436, 463

Rome, 211

Rossabi, Morris, 41

Rummel, R. J. (*Death by Government*), 433

Russia, 94, 422

Rusticello, 41

Rwanda, 432, 435

Sacajawea, 47

Saint Brendan, 40–41

Scurvy, 43–45, 62, 94

Seal, 227

Selection, 308–310; defined, 308

Self-control, 446

Self-defense, 74–77, 84

Selfish-superman, 379
Self-selection, xviii, 330, 337, 342, 344, 353, 365, 375–382, 387, 389, 416, 462; defined, 376; formula, 337, 382; the power of, 375, 378
Severin, Tim, 40–41
Sex selection, 355
Skill, 3–4, 7, 11, 13, 40, 47, 53, 90, 95, 108–109, 112, 114, 199, 204, 236, 238, 309–310, 343–344, 363–364, 441; defined, 309
Skinner, B. F., 442
Small Wonder, 371
Smith, Adam (*The Wealth of Nations*), 150, 251
Social Darwinism, xvi
South Africa, 201–202, 230, 429
Soviet Union, 4, 91, 97, 112, 430–431, 445; Ukrainian famine, 4, 430
Spain, 42, 212–213, 434, 468
Spencer, Herbert, xvi, 28–29, 35, 253, 255–256, 260, 266, 292, 333, 341; (*The Principles of Biology*), 25–28, 252, 257–259, 264–265, 267–268, 291, 363, 367
Spontaneous generation, 279–280, 283, 286
Stallone, Sylvester (*Rambo*), 96; (*Rocky*), 76, 228
Stannard, David, 426–428, 434
Stefansson, Vilhjalmur (*My Life with the Eskimo*), 49
Stewart, George, 48–49, 63–64
Stolpa family, 66
Stroud, Les, 62, 112–113; (*Survivorman*), 53–54; (*Will to Live*), 66–67, 109–110
Struggle: defined, 14–15, 459; inseparable role of the struggle in survival, 227–228; list of struggles, 69–70; various examples of struggles that can be conquered with wealth, 229–238
Strunk and White (*The Elements of Style*), 267
Suicidalism: defined, 18

Survival: defined, 13, 459; major goal of survival, 16; major reasons to survive, 59; major survival categories, 79–86; significance of survival, 125–127, 151–156; survival environments, 87–92, 269; survival essentials list, 101–104

Survival by a second party, 240–242

Survival by a third party, xvii, xx, 239–243, 246, 385, 399, 403–409, 418, 461; applied to nonhuman life, 403–409; defined, 240; partial survival by a third party, 243; total survival by a third party, 242–243

Survival of the fittest, xvi–xvii, xxi, 25, 255–261, 307, 332–333, 449–450, 456; ideal example of, 450

Survival of the richest, xvii, xx, xxi, 211, 374, 412, 461, 468; groups, 197–200; individuals, 177–196; more accurate concept than the survival of the fittest, xxi, 456; nations, 201–205; planets, 219–223; species, 411–413, 468; universe, 225–226

Survival-Prosperity Sequence, 131–133, 136, 138, 140, 164, 169–171, 194, 198, 209, 246, 386, 401, 449, 460, 463

Survivalism: defined, 13; extended definition, 141; major goal, 16; root of prosperity, 138–148, 460

Survivalist: defined, 18

Survivor: defined, 18

Survivor (TV series), 8, 53

Technological Selection, 343–344, 360–361, 367–374, 376–377, 385, 416, 463; defined, 373; formulas, 337, 374

Technology: defined, 369

Terminator, 371

Traditional artificial (human) selection, 331–340, 344, 348–349; defined,

339; examples, 300–301, 327–328; formula, 335, 339

Traditional natural selection, 328, 331–340, 342, 344, 348, 352, 364–365, 375, 378, 417, 463; defined, 338; formula, 335, 338

Traditional sexual selection, 331–340, 344, 349–352; defined, 339–340; formulas, 335, 340

United States, 45, 49–52, 73, 91, 213, 293, 368, 422–423, 436, 438, 468; Civil War, 468

Unity, iii, 170, 217, 221–222, 267, 359, 367, 372, 386, 402, 418, 422, 446, 464, 468

Universal common ancestor, 31, 284–285, 288–291, 296, 313, 319–323, 358, 369, 372, 384, 448

Universal managers, xviii, 226, 450–453, 456

Universal survivors, xviii, 46, 447–450, 452, 456

University of California Museum of Paleontology, Berkeley, 282

Universonomics, 135–137, 145, 148, 245, 460; defined, 136–137; extended definition, 145; extended major goal, 148

Uruguayan rugby team (plane crash survivors), 49, 57, 62, 64–66, 72, 112–113, 117, 130

US Air Force (*Search and Rescue Survival Training: AF Regulation 64-4*), 51

US Army (*Survival* field manual), 11, 51, 109, 114–115, 274

US Navy, 24, 72, 96, 114; (*How to Survive on Land and Sea*), 10–11, 51, 54, 71, 109, 119, 267, 475

Vietnam, 91–92, 426, 431

Vikings, 40, 428

Waddington, C. H., 261

Wallace, Alfred Russel, 256

Wallenberg, Raoul, 97

Wealth: defined, 127; extension of the manager, 451, 456; role of, 127–130, 229–238; significance of, 412–413, 466; survival essentials as the most basic forms of wealth, 99

Wealth management: new measuring stick for adaptation and survival, 456; nonhuman wealth management, 399–402; significance of, 456; three major wealth management possibilities, xvii, 161–167, 246, 401, 460

Welles, Orson, 48

Wilderness: defined, 82–83; shrinking, 395–398

Wilderness survival, xv, 7, 48, 51–54, 64, 70–71, 79–86, 184, 234, 266

Will to live, 12, 17–18, 55, 64–67, 73–74, 91–92, 102, 106, 110, 114–116, 120, 126, 153, 159, 195, 229, 237, 278

Wilson, Edward O., 24–25, 35, 83, 253–254, 263–265, 281, 286, 333–334, 362, 397, 408, 411–412, 441, 444

Wiseman, John 'Lofty', 10, 12, 52, 87, 89, 91, 108, 114, 118, 273–274; (*SAS Survival Handbook*), 52

Wyss, Johann (*The Swiss Family Robinson*), 48

65184682R00289

Made in the USA
Charleston, SC
13 December 2016